FROM PLATONISM TO NEOPLATONISM

IAMBLICHUS (?)
See H. P. L'Orange, *Studien zur Geschichte des spätantiken Porträts* (Oslo 1933) p. 43

PHILIP MERLAN

DR. IUR., DR. PHIL. (VIENNA)
PROFESSOR OF PHILOSOPHY
SCRIPPS COLLEGE AND CLAREMONT GRADUATE SCHOOL

FROM PLATONISM TO NEOPLATONISM

Third edition, revised

THE HAGUE
MARTINUS NIJHOFF
1968

PRINTED IN THE NETHERLANDS

UXORI

PREFACE TO THE THIRD EDITION

The first edition of this book appeared in 1953; the second, revised and enlarged, in 1960. The present, third edition is essentially a reprint of the second, except for the correction of a few misprints and the following remarks, which refer to some recent publications* and replace the brief preface to the second edition.

Neither Eudemus nor Theophrastus, so I said (p. 208f.) knew a branch of theoretical philosophy the object of which would be something called ὂν ᾗ ὄν and which branch would be distinct from theology. And there is no sign that they found such a branch (corresponding to what was later called *metaphysica generalis*) in Aristotle.

To the names of Eudemus and Theophrastus we now can add that of Nicholas of Damascus. In 1965 H. J. Drossaart Lulofs published: *Nicolaus Damascenus On the Philosophy of Aristotle* (Leiden: Brill), i.e. fragments of his περὶ τῆς Ἀριστοτέλους φιλοσοφίας preserved in Syriac together with an English translation. In these fragments we find a competent presentation of Aristotle's theoretical philosophy, in systematic form. Nicholas subdivides Aristotle's theoretical philosophy into theology, physics, and mathematics and seems to be completely unaware of any additional branch of philosophy the object of which would be ὂν ᾗ ὄν distinct from theology with its object (the divine). Drossaart Lulofs is puzzled by this, as should indeed be everybody who attributes to Aristotle a distinction between theology (or what was later called *metaphysica specialis*) and a science of ὂν ᾗ ὄν. To solve the puzzle, Drossaart Lulofs avails himself of a theory of Aubenque **. According to Aubenque, when Aristotle introduced the science of ὂν ᾗ ὄν, he made an entirely original contribution to philosophy, a science *sans*

---

* Some theses of the present book are referred to in the context of the current reinterpretation of Plato, the originators of which are H. J. Krämer (*Arete bei Platon und Aristoteles* [1959]; *Der Ursprung der Geistmetaphysik* [1964]) and K. Gaiser (*Platons ungeschriebene Lehre* [1963]), sometimes critically, more often approvingly. In this place, this brief notice must suffice.

Part of my reply to Strycker's review of the first edition of my book (below, p. 85–7) is now beside the point, as in his review of the second edition (*L'Antiquité Classique* 33 [1964] 166f. Strycker modified one of his criticisms.

** P. Aubenque, *Le problème de l'être chez Aristote* (1962).

ancêtres et sans tradition. But precisely for this reason he was misunderstood by his successors. They (particularly the author of Arist. *Met.* K which Aubenque considers to be spurious) named the science of being-qua-being metaphysics; a name designating at the same time theology. They were blind to the radical difference between the two.

It seems to me that prospects to understand Aristotle better than he was understood by his immediate pupils and as we see now, also by Nicholas of Damascus, who must have had access to works by Aristotle which we no longer possess, are rather dim.

The traditional interpretation of Aristotle with the dichotomy theology — science of being-qua-being has most recently been upheld by Duering *. He objects especially to my interpretation of Aristotle's *Met.* E 1, 1026a27–32, where I, erroneously, says Duering, found Aristotle professing that the subject matter of 'first philosophy' is πρώτη οὐσία.

But I think a simple juxtaposition of two keypassages justifies my interpretation.

<table>
<tr><td>

Γ 3, 1005a33-1005b1

ἐπεὶ δ᾽ἔστιν ἔτι τοῦ φυσικοῦ τις ἀνωτέρω (ἓν γὰρ τι γένος τοῦ ὄντος ἡ φύσις), **τοῦ καθόλου** καὶ τοῦ περὶ τὴν **πρώτην οὐσίαν θεωρητικοῦ** καὶ ἡ περὶ τούτων (scil. περὶ τῶν ἐν τοῖς μαθήμασι καλουμένων ἀξιωμάτων καὶ περὶ τῆς οὐσίας) ἂν εἴη σκέψις·ἔστι δὲ σοφία τις καὶ ἡ φυσική, ἀλλ᾽ **οὐ πρώτη**.

</td><td>

E 1, 1026a27-32

εἰ μὲν οὖν μὴ ἔστι τις ἑτέρα οὐσία παρὰ τὰς φύσει συνεστη κυίας, ἡ φυσικὴ ἂν εἴη **πρώτη ἐπιστήμη**; εἰ δ᾽ἔστι τις **οὐσία ἀκίνητος**, αὕτη (scil. φιλοσοφία περὶ οὐσίαν ἀκίνητον, προτέραν τῆς φυσικῆς οὐσίας) προτέρα καὶ **θιλοσοφία πρώτη**, καὶ **καθόλου** οὕτως ὅτι **πρώτη**· καὶ περὶ τοῦ ὄντος ᾗ ὂν ταύτης ἂν εἴη **θεωρῆσαι** καὶ τί ἔστι καὶ τὰ ὑπάρχοντα ᾗ ὄν.

</td></tr>
</table>

Verbal differences notwithstanding both passages express one and the same idea: physics has no claim to be declared first philosophy, because there exists an οὐσία higher than the οὐσία

---

* I. Duering, *Aristoteles* (1966), passim, esp. 598f. Duering is of the opinion that the two definitions of First Philosophy in Aristotle (viz. as theology and as science of being-qua-being) are incompatible. This is the 'classic' position of Jaeger.

PREFACE TO THE THIRD EDITION

of physics and this higher οὐσία can also be designated as πρώτη οὐσία. Because it is first οὐσία, the branch of 'theory' dealing with it can be called first philosophy. The 'theorist' of this first οὐσία can also be designated as 'catholicist'; and first philosophy as 'catholic' – in the sense of firstness. *This* first philosophy deals with ὂν ᾗ ὄν. When juxtaposed, the two passages leave no room for two first philosophies or for one first philosophy with two different subject matters *.

---

* In his *Aristotle's Protrepticus* (1961), esp. p. 123; 158; 209, Duering also objects to my assertion (below, p. 151) that ch. XXIII of Iamblichus, *De communi mathematica scientia* essentially consists of excerpts from Aristotle's *Protrepticus*. Unfortunately, Duering expresses himself very briefly and somewhat dogmatically (the language of the chapter is chatty and inflated and many of its ideas are un-Aristotelian, he says) so that it is very difficult for me to reply. But it seems to me that some of these objections have been met in advance by A.-J. Festugière in "Un fragment nouveau du Protreptique d'Aristote", *Revue philosophique* 81 (1956) 117–27, a paper never mentioned by Duering. Even so, Duering is ready to admit that p. 72, 1–6 Festa could have been written by Aristotle, that some Aristotelian ideas "shimmer through" and that Iamblichus is spinning them out.

ACKNOWLEDGMENTS

My colleagues, Dr. Richard Armour of Scripps College and the Claremont Graduate School and Dr. Benjamin F. Bart, formerly of Pomona College, now at the University of Michigan, corrected the English of the original draft of the present book. However, in view of numerous changes in and additions to that draft, I must assume full responsibility for the style of the whole.

Criticisms from several anonymous readers helped me very greatly with the manuscript.

The Claremont Graduate School, the American Philosophical Association, and the Pacific Coast Committee for the Humanities contributed to the expenses connected with the writing and publication of this book.

The library staff of the Claremont Graduate School was extremely cooperative, especially the head librarian, Dr. David W. Davies, who assisted me in many ways.

One set of proofs was read by my colleague Dr. William T. Jones of Pomona College and the Claremont Graduate School.

To all these persons and institutions I want to express my most sincere gratitude.

Claremont, Calif.

TABLE OF CONTENTS

Four reasons for deriving *De communi mathematica
scientia* ch. XXIII from Aristotle, particularly from
his *Protrepticus* (141–144).

The general content of this chapter: mathematics
praised by Aristotle as a branch of theoretical knowledge

The problem: Does the term being-as-such, when used by Aristotle to designate the subject matter of metaphysics (theology, first philosophy) mean that which is most abstract, making, thus, Aristotle's metaphysics a *metaphysica generalis*? If this question is answered in the affirmative, how can we explain that Aristotle described his metaphysics as knowledge of just one (the uppermost) sphere of being and, thus, as *metaphysica specialis*? In other words: is the entity described by the term being-as-such comparable to a mathematical interpreted non-realistically (a mere, not subsistent abstraction) or rather to a mathematical interpreted realistically (as subsistent) and not merely an object of abstraction (160–161)?

Analysis of the pertinent passages in *Met. Γ*. It becomes obvious that in all relevant passages the complete equivalence of the terms "being-as-such" and "supreme sphere of being" is assumed by Aristotle; it becomes, further, obvious that metaphysics is for Aristotle an inquiry into the opposite elements, ultimately being and non-being, of which the supreme

Divisions of being from Plato, as interpreted by Aristotle, to Posidonius and hence to Iamblichus and Proclus, with mathematicals interpreted realistically, as a sphere of being intermediate between metaphysicals and physicals; survival of this tripartition to the 18th century. The problem concerning the identification of (intermediate) mathematicals with the (intermediate) soul and of the causality of mathematicals. The difficulties resulting from detaching certain doctrines (tripartition of theoretical knowledge; the

INTRODUCTION

How close are Platonism and Neoplatonism? * There had been ages when the two were considered virtually identical. The 19th century saw the victory of the opposite point of view. The claim of Plotinus to be nothing else but an interpreter of Plato was rejected and the complete difference between the two systems stressed. The last decades have again seen a change taking place. This change is characterized by four main factors.

First, we concentrate our attention on what Aristotle presented and criticized as Plato's philosophic system. This leads to three main problems. The first is to ascertain with precision the meaning of this presentation of Plato; the second to determine the sources from which Aristotle derived his knowledge of that system; the third to evaluate the correctness and fairness of Aristotle's report and critique. Only the first of these three problems is relevant to the present investigation, because what-

---

* The following assumptions seem to be among those characteristic of what is called Neoplatonism.

1. A plurality of spheres of being strictly subordinated to one another, so that we have a series the single terms of which represent higher and lower degrees of being — with the last, most unreal sphere of being comprising what is usually called perceptible being, i.e. being in time and space.

2. The derivation of each inferior sphere of being from its superior, this derivation not being a process in time or space and therefore comparable to a mental (logical) implication rather than to a causal (spatio-temporal) relation, thus the "causality" of all spheres with regard to each other not being of the type of efficient causality.

3. The derivation of the supreme sphere of being from a principle which as the source of all being cannot be described as being — it is above being and therefore fully indeterminate, this indeterminateness being not the indeterminateness of a most universal concept, but an ontic indeterminateness, i.e. fullest "being" precisely because it is not limited to being this or that.

4. The description of this ontic indeterminateness also by saying that the supreme principle is One, this oneness expressing not only its uniqueness but also its complete simplicity, i.e. the lack of *any* determination, "One" designating not some kind of adjectival description, but being rather the comparatively positive expression of the supreme principle being neither this nor that.

5. The increasing multiplicity in each subsequent sphere of being, greater multiplicity designating not only the greater number of entities in each subsequent sphere, but also increasing determination (limitation) of each entity, until we arrive at spatio-temporal determination and therefore at the minimum of oneness.

6. The knowledge appropriate to the supreme principle as being radically different from the knowledge of any other object in that the former in view of the strictly indeterminate character of the supreme principle cannot be predicative knowledge, which knowledge is appropriate only to beings exhibiting some determination.

And the most fundamental difficulty characteristic of what is called Neoplatonism is the explanation and justification of the why and how of the passage from the One to the multitude, with the principle of matter playing an important role in this process.

ever the sources and whatever the correctness or fairness of Aristotle, the system of Plato as set forth by him, exhibits unmistakable similarities to a neoplatonic system.

Second, we prefer to compare Neoplatonism to the systems of Plato's first generation pupils, Xenocrates, Speusippus, Heracleides, Hermodorus, rather than to Plato himself. Again, the thoughts of these members of the Old Academy resemble neoplatonic doctrines. To describe this similarity, many scholars speak of the Pythagorism of the Old Academy (or even of the late Plato), admitting at the same time that what is called Neopythagorism is obviously a forerunner of Neoplatonism. And even the specifically magico-religious coloring of Neoplatonism seems to have originated in the Old Academy, including a demonology and an interest in occult phenomena.

Thirdly, the study of some lesser writers like Agatharchides, Moderatus, Eudorus reveals in their doctrines some elements anticipating Neoplatonism. But none of these writers gives the impression of originality; each seems to transmit ideas which could stem from the Old Academy. Here again the term Neopythagorism is applied to them and again we are reminded that Neopythagorism might very well be Pythagorism as assimilated by the Old Academy. In addition to these lesser men one more can be claimed as a link between the Old Academy and Neoplatonism. It is Posidonius. Few would deny that in some sense of the word he prepared the way for Neoplatonism, yet the fact that he commented on Plato's *Timaeus* proves that he himself was inspired by the Old Academy.

Fourthly, Plotinus, once considered to be the founder of Neoplatonism, is now being interpreted as its greatest member — important but not all important in the history of Neoplatonism. The soil out of which he grew, sometimes referred to as pre-Neoplatonism, sometimes as Middle Platonism, exhibits qualities precisely mediating between the Academy and Neoplatonism. Many Neoplatonists, either Plotinus' contemporaries or belonging to a later period, are not exactly Plotinists. This can particularly be said of Iamblichus, at least of some of his writings. And it would not be surprising to discover that the connection between these un-Plotinian Neoplatonists and the Old Academy is more obvious than the one between Plotinus and Plato.

To these four factors, characteristic mainly of modern scholarship, we should add another. Of all dialogues by Plato none proved a more obstinate obstacle to all denials of essential similarity between Platonism and Neoplatonism than did the *Parmenides*. Time and again the "neoplatonic" interpretation of that dialogue found its champions, regardless of the general trend of viewing all such attempts with suspicion.

In short, the present tendency is towards bridging rather than widening the gap separating Platonism from Neoplatonism.

This book wants to contribute to this tendency by strengthening some of the factors indicated above. It will pay very little attention to the problem of Aristotle's fairness or correctness in presenting Plato's system or to the sources from which Aristotle drew; and the knowledge of that presentation in its main, hardly controversial features it will take for granted *. It will devote much more space to Speusippus and Iamblichus than to Plato and Plotinus and it will elucidate Posidonius' interpretation of Plato as mediating between the Academy and Neoplatonism. But it will also add another factor to those mentioned above. It will do so by establishing the neoplatonic character of some fundamental doctrines of Aristotle.

There should not be anything particularly suprising about this. The presence of strictly Platonic elements in some of Aristotle's writings has been proved beyond any reasonable doubt by recent scholarship, whatever the explanation of this presence. Now, if it is true that Plato's philosophy as presented by Aristotle is similar to Neoplatonism, it would only be natural to expect Aristotle's Platonism to be Neoplatonism at the same time. Aristotle's presentation of Plato can be assumed to be correct or erroneous; his sources can be considered to be either exclusively Plato's published writings, or exclusively Plato's

---

* The main features of Plato's system as presented by Aristotle will be assumed to be the derivation of the supreme sphere of being, i.e. ideas, from two principles, mostly called by Aristotle One and indeterminate dyad, and the existence of another sphere of being, i.e. mathematicals, mediating between ideas and the third and last sphere of being, i.e. sensibles, the two principles in some way being related to the Aristotelian concepts of form and matter and also to the principles of good and evil and in some way by being the principles (causes) of ideas being at the same time principles (causes) of all that exists. The vexed problem concerning the relation of ideal numbers to ideas and of the very concept of ideal numbers (or perhaps rather ideal mathematicals) will remain outside of the scope of the present book.

oral doctrines, or a combination of both. Whichever we accept —
if Aristotle ever was a Platonist, it is unlikely that he never
professed some of the "neoplatonic" doctrines which he imputed
to Plato. The notion of a platonizing Aristotle implies a neoplatonizing Aristotle, if Plato, the way Aristotle understood —
or misunderstood — him, was a neoplatonizing Plato himself.

There is nothing new about a neoplatonizing Aristotle either.
The Arabic commentators interpreted him in this manner. To
the extent to which their interpretation was based on neoplatonic
writings erroneously ascribed to Aristotle, such as the *Theologia
Aristotelica* or the *Liber de causis*, they were mistaken. But it
is not unreasonable to hold that this mistake should not have
been the only basis of their construction. Without explicitly
investigating the relation of the present interpretation of Aristotle
to that of the Arabs, the present book reopens the case for an
Aristoteles Arabus.

Much of the material of this book is well known. But some of
it is not so. This is mainly the result of utilizing a work which
hardly received full attention from scholars of Greek philosophy.
It is Iamblichus' little book *De communi mathematica scientia*.
It is part of his larger work on Pythagorism, portions of which
(*De vita Pythagorica, Protrepticus, In Nicomachi arithmeticam
introductionem, Theologoumena arithmeticae*) are preserved, while
others are lost. The most obvious justification for the interest
paid to it in the present book lies precisely in the fact of its
being neglected, in strong contrast to his Pythagorasvita for
example, on which an ample literature exists. But the results
seem to justify it even more. Among its sources we shall find
Aristotle, represented by a new fragment, Posidonius, and
most gratifying of all, Speusippus. The latter find will make
possible a re-evaluation of his system.

At the same time, this work of Iamblichus will provide us
with a new perspective in which to see two old problems, that
of the classification of sciences and the idea of the quadrivium.

Finally, his treatise will remind us of the importance of a way
of thinking often designated as that of excessive or conceptual
realism * and permit us to uncover some of its more obliterated

---

* Excessive realism or, to use N. Hartmann's term, *Universalienrealismus*, is
not very fashionable among contemporary historians of philosophy. Moderate

stretches, connecting classical antiquity with the middle ages,
and even with modern times *.

realists and nominalists alike, empiricists of all denominations, see in it hardly
anything but a mistaken hypostasizing of concepts. And most historians of philosophy
seem to agree on that. We still remember the controversies regarding Plato. Philologists had difficulties defending their interpretation of Plato as an excessive
realist (in his idea theory) against the onslaughts of philosophers who felt that they
had to "save" Plato from being "accused" of conceptual realism. A great philosopher simply could not have professed a doctrine so palpably wrong. The philologists,
generally, confined themselves to proving once more that the principle *dasz nicht
sein kann was nicht sein darf* is a poor guide — also when one interprets Plato. But,
on the other hand, they were not particularly interested in proving that excessive
realism is a good philosophic doctrine.

   This book is written with full sympathy for, though without approval of, excessive
realism. To explain this sympathy, the following thesis could be suggested. The only
relation which we can understand is the relation of implication and explication (in the
sense in which Nicholaus of Cusa used the latter term). A causal explanation, i.e. an
action of one thing on another in space and time is no explanation at all — an attempt
to explain at best. To replace even causal explanation in neo-positivist fashion by
description is simply the giving up of even such an attempt. If there are things "in
reality" which cannot be explained by implication and explication ("logical" deduction or derivation, *Ableitung*) or if reality in its totality cannot be explained by
implication and explication, they cannot be understood at all. Excessive realism,
rather than to be characterized by hypostasizing concepts, should be referred to as
the doctrine assuming only "the reasonable" (mind, spirit) to be real. Understanding
(knowledge) is not the only form of significant mental activity of man. We may
enjoy something esthetically; we may be in empathy with an animal or our fellow-
man; any mood is some kind of mental engagement. But none of these activities
is of the order of understanding — they are attitudes, reactions, modes of being. All
philosophies which insist on the non-intelligible character of being terminate in being
not explanations of reality, but appeals to a certain mode of being. But it may be
not true that it is the exclusive business of philosophy to appeal. Excessive realism
is the insistence that philosophy should neither be an appeal nor surrender its rights
to understand to positive sciences, which profess not to understand; the insistence
that it is up to philosophy to understand and that only what we can put in terms of
"logical" implication and explication is understood.

   Of course, when we speak of logical implication and explication or derivation, we
do not mean necessarily or exclusively the traditional syllogistic logic (and even
less so modern formal logic). Hegel's logic is the most outstanding example of a
non-traditional, non-formal logic. Another seems to be the diairesis method of the
Academy. In general, every philosophy which assumes that reality can be understood,
will also assume that the structure of reality is mind-like, that its parts possess some
kind of mind-like coherence; and whatever logic is used, its validity is in the last
resort justified by the fact that is exhibits this coherence.

   * A word should be devoted to the fact that the present work refers sometimes to
modern philosophy and philosophy of science. Many historians of philosophy find
this objectionable, as it may introduce ideas that from the historic point of view are
foreign to the matter on hand.

   It should therefore be stressed that all such references in this book serve one
purpose only. It is to prevent common sense from objecting to an interpretation on
the ground that it would make a philosopher hold an opinion contradicting common
sense. The attempt to prevent this is based on the conviction that much of what
common sense assumes is simply the residuum of some philosophy or scientific
theory which is actually obsolete or if not obsolete, no longer goes uncontested.
Thus reference to modern philosophic or scientific theories is the invocation of a
theory conscious of its nature as an alternative to another which, in the disguise of

Appendix

AD INTRODUCTION

1. It was the merit of Jaeger to have established the platonic
character of some of Aristotle's lost writings, this Platonism
including even the doctrine of ideas. But it seems that the
assertion that Aristotle for some time did profess the very
doctrine which he later made one of his main targets of criticism
is about to become a center of controversy.

It is particularly Duering * who denies that Aristotle ever
professed the idea theory. Now, there is one particular passage
in Proclus (fr. 42 Rose) which Jaeger considered a clear proof of
his thesis, whereas Duering denies its conclusiveness. The passage
reads:

Λέγει δὲ καὶ ὁ δαιμόνιος Ἀριστοτέλης αἰτίαν δι' ἣν
ἐκεῖθεν μὲν ἰοῦσα ἡ ψυχὴ δεῦρο ἐπιλανθάνεται
                τῶν ἐκεῖ θεαμάτων
ἐντεῦθεν δὲ ἐξιοῦσα μέμνηται ἐκεῖ
                τῶν ἐνταῦθα παθημάτων.

The reason given by Aristotle is explained by an analogy: he
who falls ill often forgets even the most elementary knowledge
which he had acquired.

Prima facie it seems that the θεάματα cannot be anything else
but the ideas, which the soul has seen before it fell ill, i.e. became
embodied. This would clearly prove that at times Aristotle

---

common sense, has become unconscious of its nature. In a way, all our understanding
is limited by some unconscious assumptions as to what an author — any author —
could possibly have said or meant, by some unconscious assumptions that this or that
could not have been meant by anybody. It is such assumptions which make it more
than once impossible to understand what the author really said. Some of these
assumptions can be brought to light and thus deprived of their efficacy by confronting
them with current theories incompatible with them (though, they, in turn, may
lead to another set of impossibility assumptions). In other words, these references
do not serve to interpret Greek philosophy in a positive way. They rather, in a
purely negative fashion, try to prevent the ruling out of certain interpretations
because of their alleged impossibility or improbability. No consequence is valid
ab posse ad esse; but the implicit or explicit denial of a certain *posse* often blocks the
way to a perception of an *esse*. The establishment of such a *posse* often unblocks
the way. *Ab posse ad posse videre aliquid esse* seems to be sound procedure.
* I. Duering, "Aristotle and Plato in the mid-Fourth Century", *Eranos* 54 (1956)
109–120. It is therefore close at hand for Duering to assume that Aristotle, the
character in Plato's *Parmenides*, is identical with the historical Aristotle. On additional allusions to Aristotle in Plato's writings see esp. E. Salin, "Platon Dion
Aristoteles", in: *Robert Boehringer. Eine Freundesgabe* (1957) 525–542.

accepted the doctrine of anamnesis with its corollary, the doctrine of ideas.

Not so, counters Duering. The concept of θεάματα belongs to Proclus, not to Aristotle.

This seems a rather dogmatic assertion. It is barely possible that Proclus said: we forget the ideas which we have seen before our birth and the explanation is given by the fact mentioned by Aristotle [scil. in a different context], viz. that people falling ill forget what they have learned. This would leave us guessing what the context was in which Aristotle put forward his observation. But we know beyond any reasonable doubt that in the *Eudemus* Aristotle spoke of visions, similar to those of Plato's Er and that he emphatically described death as soul's returning home. This speaks strongly in favor of Jaeger's interpretation.

And there is now additional proof available — a passage of al-Kindi, rediscovered by Walzer * and now easily accessible in English translation in the collection of Ross **. According to al-Kindi Aristotle somewhere told the story of a Greek king whose soul was caught up in ecstasy, so that he remained in a trance-like condition for many days. When he came to himself, he told what he has seen in the beyond, viz. souls, *forms*, and angels.

If al-Kindi's source was ultimately some genuine writing by Aristotle, the problem as to whether he ever professed the doctrine of ideas would be settled beyond dispute. Now, precisely this was denied by Bidez. For, as al-Kindi continues with his story, he tells us that the king told to all his acquaintances how long each would live — and his prediction turned out to be true. This, says Bidez, is clearly an instance of the art of casting horoscopes. And with this Aristotle most certainly has nothing to do. Thus, the whole fragment is suspect ***.

But when writing these words Bidez must surely have forgotten that in the *Eudemus* Aristotle has his hero predict the (violent) death of the tyrant of Thessaly, Alexander (a prediction, which came true, thus establishing the veracity of Eudemus also with regard to the rest of his vision). Indeed it is difficult to imagine

---

* R. Walzer, "Un frammento nuovo di Aristotele", *Studi italiani di Filologia classica* 14 (1937) 125–137; G. Furlani, *Riv. trim. studi fil. e rel.* 3 (1922) 50–63.
** Aristotle, *Select Fragments* tr. by [W.] D. Ross, 1952 (*The Works of Aristotle tr. into English under the editorship of Sir David Ross*, vol. XII), p. 23, 11.
*** J. Bidez, *Les mages hellénisés* (1938) vol. I 247.

8 INTRODUCTION

that this or a similar kind of verification should have been absent
from any report on visions in trance.
Duering does not even mention the al-Kindi fragment. It would
be interesting to know what he would say of it.
2. The problem of the demonology in Aristotle and, therefore,
in the Academy appears in new light in W. Lameere, "Au temps
où F. Cumont s'interrogait sur Aristote", L'Antiquité Classique
18 (1949) 279–324. Is there really any reason not to translate the
words φύσις δαιμονία ἀλλ᾽ οὐκ θεῖα (De div. per somnum 2,
463b12–15) simply by: 'though nature is not full of gods [scil. as
Thales had it and as in his way Plato has it when he says that all
is full of souls, i.e. of gods: Nomoi X 899 B] it is full of spirits'
[pace P. Boyancé]? And should we not take a little more literally
the Symposion when it gives credit to spirits, intermediary between
gods and men, for the efficacy of μαντική, τῶν ἱερέων τέχνη, τέχνη
περὶ τὰς θυσίας τελετὰς ἐπῳδάς, μαντεία, γοήτεια (202 D) and even
goes so far as to say ὁ μὲν περὶ ταῦτα σοφὸς δαιμόνιος ἀνήρ, ὁ δὲ
ἄλλο τι σοφὸς ὢν ... βάναυσος (203 A)? Could any Neoplatonist
use stronger language? Or shall we say that Diotima being twice
removed from Plato cannot be taken as representing his views?
3. On the anticipation of the doctrine of the One-above-being
by Plutarch see H. Doerrie, "Zum Ursprung der neuplatonischen
Hypostasenlehre", Hermes 82 (1954) 331–342, esp. 332;339;342.

BIBLIOGRAPHICAL NOTE

The thesis of the fundamental difference between Platonism and Neoplatonism was presented with particular succinctness by E. Zeller,
Die Philosophie der Griechen, v. III/2⁵ (1923) 475–480; 496 f. More
recently, E. Hoffmann was its eloquent defender. In addition to his other
writings quoted in this book see his Platon (1950). Most recent is the
attempt to state the difference by E. v. Ivánka, "Die neuplatonische
Synthese", Scholastik 20–24 (1949) 30–38. For the opposite point of view
see e.g. J. Stenzel, Zahl und Gestalt² (1933) 128; P. Wilpert, "Platons
Altersvorlesung ueber das Gute", Philosophisches Jahrbuch 59 (1949) 1–13.
See also E. Bréhier, "Platonisme et néoplatonisme", Revue des Etudes
grecques 51 (1938) 489–498 = Études de Philosophie antique (1955) 56–64,
criticizing the "neoplatonic" interpretation of Plato in A.–J. Festugière,
Contemplation et vie contemplative selon Platon² (1950); C. J. de Vogel,
"On the Neoplatonic Character of Platonism and the Platonic Character
of Neoplatonism", Mind 62 (1953) 43–64.
The most exhaustive study of the system of Plato as presented by
Aristotle is known to be L. Robin, La Théorie platonicienne des Idées
et des Nombres d'après Aristote (1908). One aspect of the results of his

study Robin summarized (598–602) by saying: *Aristote nous a mis sur la voie d'une interprétation néoplatonicienne de la philosophie de son maître* (600); words which could well serve as the motto of this book.

The assertion that the only source of Aristotle's (and of all other Academics') knowledge of Plato were the latter's dialogues, together with the other that they all and Aristotle misinterpreted Plato's doctrines has recently been put forward by H. Cherniss, *Aristotle's Criticism of Plato and the Academy*, v. I (1944); cf. *idem, The Riddle of the Early Academy* (1945), esp. 33;43;59.

On the neoplatonic character of the philosophy of Xenocrates see R. Heinze, *Xenokrates* (1892), esp. 118–123; on Speusippus see E. Frank, *Plato und die sogenannten Pythagoreer* (1923), esp. 128–134; 239–261; on Hermodorus see P. Merlan, "Beitraege zur Geschichte des antiken Platonismus. I", *Philologus* 89 (1934) 35–53, esp. 42 f.; P. Wilpert, "Neue Fragmente aus peri tagathou", *Hermes* 76 (1941) 225–250; *idem, Zwei Aristotelische Schriften ueber die Ideenlehre* (1949), esp. 183–194; J. C. de Vogel, "Problems Concerning Later Platonism", *Mnemosyne* 1949, 197–216; 299–318; [A.–J.] Festugière, *La Révélation d'Hermès Trismégiste*, v. IV² (1954) 307–314. On the religious coloring of the Academy in addition to Heinze see also P. Boyancé, "Sur l'Abaris d'Heraclide le Pontique", *Revue des Etudes anciennes* 36 (1934) 321–352; *idem*, "Xenocrate et les Orphiques", *ibid.* 50 (1948) 218–231. On Academic interest in occult phenomena see e.g. R.Walzer, "Un frammento nuovo di Aristotele", *Studi italiani di Filologia classica* 14 (1938) 125–137.

On Agatharchides (the Anonymus Photii) see O. Immisch, *Agatharchidea* (1919); cf. Ueberweg-Praechter¹² 65, n. 1;480;518;157*; K. Reinhardt, art. Poseidonios, *RE* XXII/1 (1953) 763–768; on Moderatus see E. R. Dodds, "The Parmenides of Plato and the Origin of the Neo-Platonic One", *Classical Quarterly* 22 (1928) 129–142; P. Merlan, "Ueberfluessige Textaenderungen", *Philologische Wochenschrift* 1936, 909–912; A.–J. Festugière, *op. cit.* (above) 38–40. On Eudoros see Ueberweg-Praechter¹² 531; H. Doerrie, "Der Platoniker Eudoros von Alexandreia", *Hermes* 79 (1944) 25–39.

On Posidonius in addition to the literature quoted in ch. II of the present book see also W. Theiler, *Die Vorbereitung des Neuplatonismus* (1930).

On the relation between the Academy, Pythagorism, Neopythagorism, in addition to the work by Frank quoted above see A. Schmekel, *Die Philosophie der mittleren Stoa* (1892) and C. Baeumker, *Das Problem der Materie in der griechischen Philosophie* (1890); also P. Merlan, "Beitraege zur Geschichte des antiken Platonismus. II." *Philologus* 89 (1934) 197–214; *idem*, "Die Hermetische Pyramide und Sextus", *Museum Helveticum* 8 (1951) 100–105.

On pre-Neoplatonism, in addition to the book by Theiler quoted above see esp. Ueberweg-Praechter¹² 524–556 and R. E. Witt, *Albinus and the History of Middle Platonism* (1937); on different schools in Neoplatonism (and on Iamblichus' position within Neoplatonism) see K. Praechter, "Richtungen und Schulen im Neuplatonismus", *Genethliakon fuer C. Robert* (1910) 100–156 (but cf. J. Bidez, "Le Philosophe Jamblique et son école", *Revue des Etudes grecques* 32 [1919–1921] 29–40).

On the problem of the "neoplatonic" interpretation of the *Parmenides* see the survey in F. M. Cornford, *Plato and Parmenides* (1939) V–IX; 131–134.

On Plato's system as presented in Aristotle see e.g. W. D. Ross, *Aristotle's Metaphysics*, 2 vv. (1924), v. I, p. XLV–LXXI. In its brevity remarkable is E. Lask, *Gesammelte Schriften*, 3 vv. (1923–1924), v. III 36–38.

On Aristotle's Platonism see W. Jaeger, *Aristoteles*[2] (1955).

On Iamblichus, *De communi mathematica scientia* we find a few lines or words in Zeller III/2[5] 758–760; T. Whittaker, *The Neo-Platonists*[2] (1928) 225–228; G. Mau and W. Kroll, art. Iamblichus in *RE*; Ueberweg-Praechter[12] 612–617; K. Praechter, "Richtungen und Schulen im Neuplatonismus" (see above) 128.

Examples of works written with sympathy for excessive realism: H. Bett, *Johannes Scotus Erigena* (1925), esp. 109–115; G. R. G. Mure, *Aristotle* (1932); G. R. G. Mure, *An Introduction to Hegel* (1940); N. Hartmann, *Aristoteles und Hegel* in: *Kleinere Schriften*, v. II (1957) 214–252, esp. 229–244.

Appendix

AD BIBLIOGRAPHICAL NOTE

1. On the general plan of Iamblichus' work on Pythagorism see P. Tannery, *Pour l'Histoire de la Science Hellène* (1887) 372–374 and "Sur l'arithmétique pythagoricienne", in: *Mémoires scientifiques*, v. II (1912) 179–201.

2. A particularly penetrating discussion concerning the difference between the mysticism of Plato and that of Plotinus can be found in P. Friedlaender, *Plato*, v. I (1958) 82–84. According to Friedlaender, in Plato the climactic experience does not imply the soul's becoming one with the supreme object of contemplation, whereas in Plotinus such an identification does take place. But from the *Epinomis*, whoever its author, can easily be seen how close such an identification is to Plato (or a Platonist). It is necessary, says the *Epinomis*, to espy the One that links all the μαθήματα (τὴν ὁμολογίαν οὖσαν μίαν ἁπάντων). And this link (δεσμὸς εἰς πάντων scil. of arithmeticals, geometricals, harmonicals, astronomicals — see below, p. 89) will be revealed to the learner who εἰς ἓν βλέπων μανθάνῃ (991 A; 992 A). Such a learner will after his death have overcome the plurality of sensations and μιᾶς τε μοίρας μετειληφότα μόνον καὶ ἐκ πολλῶν ἕνα γεγονότα, εὐδαίμονα τ᾿ ἔσεσθαι (992 B). How far are we here from the formula μόνος πρὸς μόνον or its alternative εἰς πρὸς ἕν (or ἕνα)?

Admittedly, the *Epinomis* does not speak of such a 'unification' in this life, whereas Plotinus does. But clearly the contemplation of the One results in the soul itself becoming what she contemplates, viz. One. Thus, contrary to what Friedlaender asserts, there is within the orbit of Platonism space for the identification of the contemplator with the object of his contemplation. Cf. also W. Jaeger, "The Greek Ideas of Immortality", *Harvard Theological Review* 52 (1959) 135–147, esp. 144 f. (in its ascent through knowledge the soul gradually becomes what it knows).

I. SOUL AND MATHEMATICALS

When Festa edited Iamblichus, *De communi mathematica scientia* * (subsequently referred to as *Isc*) in his Preface (p. IX) he noticed its similarity to the First Prologue of the Proclus commentary on Euclid ** and in the apparatus pointed out the literal coincidences and parallels. We are going to discuss one aspect of this similarity.

Both Iamblichus and Proclus are "realists" (anti-abstractionists, conceptual realists, ontologists, excessive realists) with regard to mathematicals. They are convinced of the full subsistence of mathematicals (cf. also Proclus *In Eucl.* Def. XIV, p. 139, 22–26 Fr; 142,8 Fr). The realist-nominalist controversy usually concerns itself with non-mathematical universalia; we should not overlook, however, that here we have an example of "multiple" realism, i.e. a realism asserting the subsistence of more than one type of non-sensibles and universals. Thus in addition to and above the mathematicals we have in Iamblichus and Proclus intelligibilia, also fully subsisting. Below the mathematicals we find the sensibilia or the subject-matter of physics. Therefore, as a rule, Iamblichus and Proclus describe the mathematicals as intermediate, assuming a tripartition of being (*Isc* ch. XIV, p. 52, 6 F; 54, 2. 10–13 F). They are realistic "trialists". The intermediate character of mathematicals is stressed by Iamblichus time and again (*Isc* ch. I, p. 10, 8–24 F; ch. III, p. 14, 1–6 F; ch. XII, p. 46, 1–3 F; ch. XIII, p. 48, 26–27 F; p. 50, 14–25 F; ch. XIV, p. 51, 11 F; 54, 2–13 F; ch. XV, p. 55, 5–56, 4 F; cf. Proclus *In Eucl.* Prol. I, p. 3, 1–14, 12; 11, 26–12, 2 Fr; 19, 12 Fr; 35, 7 Fr). To the intermediate character of mathematicals corresponds the intermediate character of mathematical knowledge (*Isc* ch. I, p. 11, 10 F; ch. XXXIII, p. 95, 5–22 F) ***. In obvious connection with his trialism of being Iamblichus accepts also the tripartition of theoretical philosophy into theology, mathematics, and physics

---

* Iamblichi *De communi mathematica scientia liber* ... ed. N. Festa (1891).

** References are to Procli Diadochi *In primum Euclidis elementorum librum commentarii* rec. G. Friedlein (1873). F will stand for Festa, Fr for Friedlein.

*** On the intermediate character of mathematicals cf. K. Praechter, "Richtungen und Schulen im Neuplatonismus", *Genethliakon* ... *C. Robert* (1910) 100–156, esp. 132. More on it later.

(*Isc* ch. XV, p. 55, 8. 23 F; ch. XXVIII, p. 88, 19 F; ch. XXX, p. 91, 13. 24 F; ch. XXXI, p. 92, 19 F; 93, 2 F).

With their realism goes what we could call intuitionism. Mathematicals do not become objects of our knowledge by being abstracted by us from the sensibles in which they are embodied (*Isc* ch. V, p. 19, 19–20, 20 F; ch. VIII, p. 34, 9 F; ch. XXVIII, p. 89, 5 F; cf. Proclus *In Eucl.* Prol. I, p. 11, 26–14, 23 Fr). Rather they are known directly *. Regardless of whether knowledge of them begins with sensation, this knowledge most certainly does not stem from sensation (to use Kant's language). We even may ask whether we could "know" sensibilia at all without our knowledge of mathematicals. But whether or not the mathematicals are prior with regard to us, they are prior by nature (*Isc* ch. XXXIV, p. 97, 9 F). Significantly, mathematicals are called the object matter of recollection ** (*Isc* ch. XI, p. 44, 7 F).

The same holds true for the relation between the intelligibles and the mathematicals. The latter are "derived" from the former, not the other way around. And the intelligibles, too, are objects of direct "intuition". It is one of the great tasks of mathematics to train the eye of our soul in the perception of the intelligibles. This task mathematics can fulfill because its objects too can be "seen" if one trains oneself, while the untrained person has an eye that sees only the sensible.

* The mathematical realism of Proclus and — by implication — of Iamblichus is presented in N. Hartmann, *Des Proklus Diadochus philosophische Anfangsgruende der Mathematik nach den ersten zwei Buechern des Euklidkommentars dargestellt* (1909); A. Schmekel, *Die positive Philosophie in ihrer geschichtlichen Entwicklung*, 2 vv. (1938, 1914), esp. v. I 100–106, see below p. 40; A. Speiser, *Die mathematische Denkweise* ² (1945) 57–61; M. Steck, *Proklus Diadochus ... Kommentar* (1945) 1–152, passim. On the First Prologue see also P. Tannery, *La Géometrie grecque* (1887) 21. Neo-Kantians (like the early Hartmann) are in sympathy with anti-abstractionism, but not with intuitionism and realism; they are inclined to interpret intuitionism as apriorism (see below p. 77). It is only in Husserl that anti-abstractionism and intuitionism meet again; whether this combination implies excessive realism is a matter of controversy. Husserl himself answered the question in the negative. There is a sense in which abstractionism and intuitionism are not opposed: see A. Hufnagel, *Die intuitive Erkenntnis nach dem hl. Thomas von Aquin* (1932) 49 n. 4.

** Archytas fr. 3 Diels reads: δεῖ γὰρ ἢ μαθόντα παρ' ἄλλω ἢ αὐτὸν ἐξευρόντα ... ἐπιστάμονα γενέσθαι... ἐξευρεῖν δὲ μὴ ζατοῦντα ἄπορον καὶ σπάνιον, ζατοῦντα δὲ εὔπορον καὶ ῥάιδιον, μὴ ἐπιστάμενον δὲ ζητεῖν ἀδύνατον.

The last words are usually translated: "for him who does not know [how] to seek it is impossible to find". It is characteristic that Iamblichus interprets them as meaning: "for him who does not know it is impossible to seek; therefore there must have been a time when we knew — obviously before our birth" (*Isc* ch. XI, p. 45, 7 F). In other words, according to Iamblichus, Archytas taught the doctrine of anamnesis.

Now, how do Iamblichus and Proclus describe the three realms of being of which the mathematicals are the intermediate?

The two words most characteristic of the two outer terms are: indivisible and divisible (*Isc* ch. I, p. 10, 9 F; ch. III, p. 14, 4–6 F; Proclus *In Eucl.*, Prol. I, p. 3,14–4,8). Accordingly, mathematicals are a kind of mixture of the indivisible and the divisible, limit and the unlimited, one and many (*Isc.* ch. III, p. 12, 26–13, 9 F; ch. XII, p. 46, 1–6 F).

A series of predicates attaches itself to these two basic terms; particularly important are the terms "limited" and "unlimited" (*Isc* ch. III, p. 12, 22–24 F), and "intelligible" and "sensible" (*Isc* ch. XXXIII, p. 95, 5–6 F).

It is impossible for any one (and least of all for a neo-Pythagorean or Platonist) to read the description of the mathematicals and the two other realms between which they mediate, without being reminded of Plato's *Timaeus*. Here (35 A) in precisely the same words, the (world) soul is described as being intermediate between two other "realms" *. How, then, could Iamblichus and Proclus (cf. *The Elements of Theology*, prop. 190, p. 166 Dodds and his commentary a.l.) describe mathematicals in terms used by Plato to describe the world soul?

But the problem is even somewhat more complicated by the fact that in his psychogony Plato describes (in a highly baffling manner) the constitution of the world soul, using profusely mathematical terms (numbers, relations, circles). In other words, the soul itself looks like a mathematical entity.

---

* The correct interpretation of the *Timaeus* passage can be found e.g. in F. M. Cornford, *Plato's Cosmology* (1937) 60–66. The soul is a compound of intermediate essence (being, substance), intermediate identity, and intermediate diversity. "Intermediate" means in all three cases, intermediate between divisible and indivisible. (What Plato meant to say is: In the realm of the permanently changing no thing truly is, no thing is truly identical with itself, no thing is truly different from any other. In the realm of the eternally unchanging everything truly is, everything is truly identical with itself, everything truly differs from every other thing. This created cosmos of ours is neither completely changing nor completely changeless. It shows elements of both change and changelessness — i.e. disorder mastered, though not subdued completely, by order. This is due to the presence of the world soul, intermediate between being and becoming).

Cornford's interpretation is essentially that of Proclus, as Cornford himself points out. It is also that of Hermeias, who with great brevity and precision says: intermediate essence, intermediate identity, and intermediate diversity are the three elements of which the soul was made (*Hermiae Alexandrini In Platonis Phaedrum scholia* ed. Couvreur [1901], p. 123, 7–11). The agreement between Proclus and Hermeias may prove that both had this interpretation from Syrianus.

Certainly this was not overlooked by Iamblichus and Proclus. What did they think, when they described the mathematicals in the way in which Plato described the soul? How did they explain that Plato's soul so much resembles a mathematical entity?

Or, to make the problem simpler: since it is the soul which is described by Plato in the *Timaeus* as being an intermediate between the indivisible and the divisible in the realm of body, and since Iamblichus and Proclus use the same terms to describe the mathematicals, what is the relation between their mathematicals (intermediate) and Plato's soul (intermediate)?

After all, even a philosopher who does not *start* from a description of the mathematical in terms used by Plato to describe the soul may, simply on reading the *Timaeus*, ask himself: of what is Plato actually speaking? of the soul? or of mathematicals?

Indeed, we find this problem discussed in full in *Isc* and referred to in Proclus' commentaries on Euclid and on the *Timaeus* *.

It is remarkable that Iamblichus should discuss this problem in a work devoted to philosophy of mathematics — not to an interpretation of the *Timaeus* or to the study of the soul. It is remarkable that precisely the same problem is treated by Proclus in his commentary on the *Timaeus*. This proves clearly that it is more than a special problem. We can safely say: whoever within the orbit of Platonism accepts either the intermediacy of mathematicals or the intermediacy of the soul, will have to discuss the relation between the two intermediates **. Let us discuss Iamblichus first.

After having described the mathematicals as intermediate (*Isc* ch. I–II, p. 10, 10–24 F; 11, 3–15 F; 11, 25–12, 2 F), Iamblichus says (ch. III, p. 12, 22–13, 9 F) that the principles of mathematicals are the limited and the unlimited in the form appropriate to mathematicals, these principles being, in some form, omnipresent in all reality.

Incidentally, it is somewhat misleading to use these terms (see Plato, *Philebus* 24 A; R. G. Bury, *The Philebus of Plato*

---

* Procli Diadochi *In Platonis Timaeum commentaria* ed. E. Diehl, 3 vv. (1903–1906).
** On these and related problems cf. L. Robin, *La Théorie platonicienne des Idées et des Nombres d'après Aristote* (1908) 592–595; cf. 203–211 and 265 f.

[1897] and R. Hackforth, *Plato's Examination of Pleasure* [1945] a.l.; Bonitz, *Index Aristotelicus* s.v. Πυθαγόρειοι). We should think, "limit" and "unlimited" would be more appropriate (Plato, *Philebus* 23 C). The limited means obviously: figure considered from its circumference, not from its area or volume. We shall see later on (p. 38) why this is of some importance. For the time being we go back to Iamblichus.

"Are these principles also causes of motion [= change]?" Iamblichus goes on to ask (p. 13, 9 F) *.

A strange question. How does the problem of motion (change) come in at all in a philosophy of mathematics? And why, after all, should the limited and the unlimited be considered principles of motion (change)? Whatever the intrinsic reason, we find that according to Iamblichus some made these two principles principles of motion (change) — those, namely, who assume the existence of these two principles ἐν τῇ ψυχῇ καὶ τῆς ψυχῆς ζωαῖς καὶ δυνάμεσι (p. 13, 11 F).

Here for the first time some connection between the mathematical and the soul is established. The passage is difficult, but at least Iamblichus' objection is clear. It is better, he says, to posit the soul in a different sphere of being and to assume that the mathematical principles and the mathematical spheres of being are unmoved or unchanging (*ibid.*, lines 12–16; line 25; cf. *Isc* ch. IV, p. 18, 17 F).

This much is clear: Iamblichus interprets the assertions of his adversaries. These are (1) that the limited and the unlimited are principles of the soul; (2) that they [therefore] are principles of motion (change), soul being obviously considered as a principle of motion (change); (3) that, therefore, the mathematicals are or contain principles of motion (change). According to Iamblichus, this implies an identification of the soul with the mathematical to the extent that both would belong to the same sphere of being. He criticizes this identification; he prefers to keep the two spheres of being separated and to exclude motion (change) from mathematicals.

Before proceding further, a word of warning must be added. We cannot expect a consistent terminology. What one writer calls divisible and indivisible (partible and impartible) another

---

* Square brackets within a translation or a paraphrase indicate my additions.

may call unlimited and limited (or limit); a third, the same and the other; a fourth, one and multitude; a fifth, ungenerated and in the process of generation (or generated); a sixth, intelligible (or intellectual) and sensible, and so forth. It is obvious that we must understand the idea, whereupon we can easily see that all these pairs express one and the same dualism, though somewhat different points of view. Once we see this, we perceive clearly that the whole problem discussed by Iamblichus, whether the mathematicals are motive (see below), is connected with problems of the interpretation of the *Timaeus*.

One more word of warning. We distinguish plainly between a principle of motion (change) and what is moved (changing). This distinction is not always made in Greek. An orthodox Aristotelian would be careful to distinguish; but not so Iamblichus. "Mathematicals are unmoved (changeless)" often means for him that they are not principles of motion. Thus, whenever we use the adjective "motive" we use it as equivalent to: κινητόν, κινητικόν, κινοῦν, κινούμενον, i.e. changer, changeable, changing, leaving it to the context to decide which is meant.

We can now resume our discussion. Iamblichus says: we had better assume the soul to have a separate kind of existence. This means that in addition to the three spheres of being which we have met so far (and which we meet in *Isc* time and again) we have to assume a fourth one. Indeed this is stressed in chapters III and IV (p. 13, 13–15 F; p. 18, 13–20 F). These chapters leave us with the impression that instead of a tripartition we should assume at least a quadripartition of being.

Whatever the origin of the problem, the solution certainly is no longer within the framework of the *Timaeus*. In the *Timaeus* there is no place for a fourth sphere of being. Whether the intermediate is interpreted as soul or as a mathematical or as both, there can be no more than one such intermediate. This can be said with confidence.

Therefore the question is legitimate: how are we to reconcile the presuppositions of the problem with its solution? These presuppositions are: soul as intermediate; three spheres of being; problem as to the identity of the soul and mathematicals. They are still well within the problems of the *Timaeus*. But the solution is: mathematicals not motive; soul in a sphere of being different from mathematicals; four or more spheres of being. To answer this question we must resume our analysis of *Isc.* Ch. IV ended with the assertion that mathematical principles differ from the corporeals by being immaterial; from the intelligibles by their composite character; and from the principles of the soul by being unmoved. "The principles of life" (or to use Iamblichus' more circumstantial description, "the principles which one investigates with regard to life") is only another expression for soul; and thus the chapter reiterates the doctrine of four different kinds of principles, mathematicals differing from soul.

This seems to wind up the topic concerning the relation between mathematicals and the soul. Ch. V gives a survey of theorems common to all branches of mathematicals and makes it clear that "common" does not mean "abstracted" and in this sense later than the specific theorems but on the contrary designates what is prior to all specific cases. Ch. VI gives a series of excerpts from the *Republic* and the *Epinomis*. Ch. VII (identical with *In Nicomachi arithmeticam introductionem* p. 7, 3–9, 23 Pistelli and derived from Nicomachus) contains a discussion of the continuous and the discontinuous and introduces us to a quadripartite mathematics (arithmetics, geometry, music, astronomy; see below p. 89). Ch. VIII contains an exposition of Plato's quadripartite line and in connection with this an anti-abstractionist statement as to the way in which we come to know mathematicals, and a quotation from "Brotinos" on the difference between νοῦς and διάνοια together with a commentary on it, finally a quotation from "Archytas" on the quadripartite line with a commentary on it. None of these topics has anything to do with the relation between mathematicals and the soul.

But in ch. IX the problem emerges again.

However the point of view is this time completely different. The problem is not whether the mathematicals are motive; it is with what branch of mathematicals we should identify the soul. Iamblichus says:

"Let us discuss first the doctrine held by those who refer mathematics to the soul. .... *

---

* Or, as we could also say, utilizing the summary of this chapter (p. 4, 15–19 F): those who reduce the mathematical sphere of being to the soul.

It would not be reasonable to posit the soul as being just one branch [kind] of mathematicals ... Therefore the soul should not be defined either as [1] idea of the all-extended [three-dimensional] or as [2] self-motive number or as [3] mathematical, subsisting harmony [attunement] nor as anything else of this kind specifically, but rather all this should be intertwined together, because the soul is, it is true, idea [form] of the numerable [determinable by number] but it also subsists according to numbers comprising harmony; and *all* the symmetries occurring in mathematics should be listed as belonging in common to the soul; as a result, then, the soul coexists simultaneously with the geometrical, arithmetical, and harmonical proportion, so that the soul is identical with [all] formulas of analogies [λόγοι κατ' ἀναλογίαν] ..." (p. 40, 9–41, 1 F).

"And, to sum up the whole doctrine, we think that the soul exists in relations common to *all* mathematicals .... The concept [definition] of the soul contains the complete fullness of mathematics" (p. 41, 24–42, 6 F).

Iamblichus rejects, then, the identification of the soul with any single branch of mathematicals. Therefore we should not describe the soul as idea (form) of the all-extended (three-dimensional). It is clear, and will become even more so, that whoever described it in this way, identified it with geometricals. The word "extended" sufficiently indicates it. We should not describe the soul as a self-moved number. It is clear that he who described it in this way, identified it with arithmeticals. And we should not describe it as subsisting mathematical attunement (harmony). Whoever does so, would identify it with harmonicals (such as the arithmetical, geometrical, and harmonical proportion). And no similar descriptions are admissible which would identify the soul with a special part of mathematicals instead of making it a compound of all of them, because the soul is an idea (form) of the numerable (see below p. 19), i.e. has a geometrical nature; its existence is number-like, i.e., it has an arithmetical nature; and these numbers contain ratios, i.e., the soul has also a harmonic nature — in short, the soul exists according to relations common to *all* branches of mathematics; he who says "soul" expresses mathematics in its fullness. And the presupposition is that there are three such branches: arithmemetic, geometry, harmonics (cf. also *Isc* ch. IX, p. 40, 24–25 F, where three "analogies", the geometric, the arithmetic, and the harmonic, are enumerated, and p. 41, 5–15 F, describing the "debt" of the soul to arithmeticals, geometricals, and harmonicals).

There is one word in our passage which needs some explanation: numerable (ἀρίθμιος). It is a difficult word. Sophonias (*In libros Aristotelis de anima paraphrasis*, p. 131, 17 Hayduck), who copied the passage, changed it to number (ἀριθμός: ἰδέας οὔσης ἀριθμοῦ). But it is obvious that Iamblichus intended to give a description of the soul which would be a summing up of the three descriptions mentioned by him. According to him, what is wrong with these descriptions is only their one-sidedness; and the only suggestion made by Iamblichus is a description sufficiently many-sided. Therefore, his own description must contain all three partial descriptions. The words "in accordance with *numbers* comprising attunement (harmony)" correspond with the two descriptions self-moved [self-changing] *number* and *mathematical* attunement (harmony). Therefore "idea (form) of the numerable" must correspond to "form of the all-extended", and "numerable" must correspond to "all-extended".

How is this possible? Ἀρίθμιος means "numerable"; how could it mean "extended"? But ἀρίθμιος does not mean anything else but ἀριθμητός, which is simply "body" as numerable (cf. e.g. Moderatus in Stob. I, Pr, 8, p. 21, 19–21 Wachsmuth) or in other words — geometrical quantity or the geometrical "stuff" *.

In Latin, too, "numerabilia" can designate the geometrically extended as subject to number (see e.g. Cassiodorus, *Inst.* p. 151, 21 f.; 152, 1 Mynors).

However, we also have an excellent commentary on our passage in one of the excerpts from Iamblichus' *On the Soul*, preserved in Ioannes Stobaeus **.

"After this I am going to review those who posit the essence of the soul as mathematical essence.

---

* But even regardless of the details of this passage, the much longer passage ch. IX, p. 41, 6–15 F makes it obvious that according to Iamblichus the soul unites in itself the three aspects of mathematicals.

** On this passage cf. P. Merlan, "Ueberfluessige Textaenderungen", ♯ 3, *Philologische Wochenschrift* 1936, 909–912, esp. 912; [A. J.] Festugière, *La Révélation d'Hermès Trismégiste*, v. III (1953) 179–182.

Now, one kind of mathematicals is [formed by] figure (which is the limit of extension) and by this extension itself. The Platonist Severus defined the soul in these very terms, while Speusippus [defined it] as idea [form] of the all-extended ... [fr. 40 Lang].

Number is still another kind [of mathematicals]. Indeed, some Pythagoreans find "number" without any qualification to be a fitting description of the soul. Xenocrates, however, [defined the soul] as a self-moved [self-changing] number. Moderatus [defined it] as comprising ratios ...

Let us further consider attunement (harmony), ... viz. mathematical. Moderatus defined the soul by it ..." (Iambl. in Stob. I 49, 32, p. 363, 26–364, 20 Wachsmuth).

The similarity of the two Iamblichus passages is palpable. In both the basic question is: with what branch of mathematicals should we identify the soul? With the help of the second passage we can find who identified the soul with arithmeticals alone, with geometricals alone, with harmonicals alone.

Let us consider those, says Iamblichus, who think that the essence (substance) of the soul is mathematical. There are three branches (kinds) of mathematics: arithmetic, geometry, and harmonic, and accordingly we find definitions of the soul in terms of arithmetic, geometry, or harmonic.

Examples of the first are Xenocrates and Moderatus. The former speaks of the soul as a self-moving [self-changing] number; the latter, as of a number containing ratios (proportions). Examples of the second are Speusippus and Severus. The former describes the soul as form of the all-extended threedimensional; the latter, as limit of the extended (dimensional). An example of the third is Moderatus again *.

In *On the Soul* these three main mathematical interpretations of the soul are simply reported by Iamblichus. Not so, however, in *Isc*. We saw that here Iamblichus considered them to be one-sided and wanted to replace them by one expressing the identity of the soul with all the branches of mathematics. "Neither Speusippus, nor Xenocrates, nor Moderatus", says

---

* It is obvious that in a definition like "the soul is number comprising harmony" (or "the soul subsists according to a number which comprises harmony", etc.) we either can stress the number element or the attunement element. Hence, Iamblichus can quote Moderatus twice.

Iamblichus in *Isc* in effect: "Only by combining the three do we get an adequate description of the soul". In short, while the identity of the soul and mathematicals was denied in *Isc* ch.s III and part of IV, this identity is virtually proved in ch. IX. It is wrong to identify the soul with *a* mathematical; it should be identified with *the* mathematical.

The whole problem is well known to Proclus, too *. His solution is rather similar to that of Iamblichus. Of the two passages in which he deals with it, one resembles the passage in Iamblichus' *On the Soul*. In his commentary on Euclid Proclus defends (p. 12, 9–18, 4 Fr) the realistic point of view in various ways. He objects particularly to the theory of abstraction. Where does the soul receive its knowledge of mathematicals? Not from itself, nor from the νοῦς alone. And it was proved before that it cannot receive it from the sensibles (it is remarkable how here the three spheres of being are presupposed). The only possibility left is: the soul receives it jointly from the νοῦς and from itself. After all, the soul is "iconically" all that the νοῦς is "paradigmatically". Therefore Plato is right when he constructs the soul of *all* mathematical branches [kinds] and divides it numerically and binds it by proportions and harmonical ratios and places the erstwhile principles of figures in it ... and makes the circles in it move in an intellectual motion. Thus, *all* mathematicals exist primarily in the soul ... and the soul is the fullness of all mathematicals ...

The soul has its essence ** in these branches of mathematicals ... (p. 16, 16–17, 6 Fr).

Having made sure that the soul should be identified with all branches of mathematics — i.e. arithmetics, harmonics, geometry, astronomy (on this order and on the emergence of a fourth branch of mathematics see below p. 89), Proclus now adds some words of caution. We quote them, because some of the most characteristic terms reappear in them establishing a closer connection between Proclus and Iamblichus.

"Neither should we take the number as [applied] to it to be a multitude of monads, nor should we interpret [the phrase] 'idea of the extended' as [meaning a] body ..." (p. 17, 7–9 Fr).

---

* See in this connection A. Speiser, *Die mathematische Denkweise*[2] (1945) 58 f.
** I suggest the verb "to essence" (the soul essences).

"In the soul are present the live and intelligent paradigms of the phenomenal [1] numbers, [2] figures, [3] proportions, and [4] motions ..." (p. 17, 9–11; 15–21 Fr).

"Thus, the mathematical relations constituting the souls in their fulness are essential and self-moved ..." (p. 17, 22–24 Fr).

Further and in a different context, "the motion peculiar to mathematics is neither local nor motion as change ...; it is lifelike [vital]" (p. 18, 22–24 Fr).

In other words, Proclus insists that though the soul has been said to be a number [i.e., an arithmetical], it is not a number containing a multiplicity of units. Though it has been said that the soul is ἰδέα τῶν διαστατῶν [i.e., a geometrical, τῶν διαστατῶν ἰδέα corresponding to σχῆμα], it is not a body [by which Proclus means both geometrical body having geometrical extension and sensuous body having extension in the ordinary sense of the word] *. Though soul has been described in terms of ratios [i.e., as harmonical] these ratios are not only relations; they subsist and are self-moved (on motion in connection with harmonicals see below p. 29). Though the soul has been described in terms of motion (i.e., as an astronomical, having been designated as containing a plurality of circles) this motion, being mathematical, is neither spatial motion nor change.

And Proclus is obviously none too sure that to make the soul motive (via mathematicals as motive) is strictly Platonic **. In a different context he notices that sometimes Plato seems to make the soul itself motive, sometimes he lets the soul receive its motive character from the realm of intelligibilia (p. 32, 7–10 Fr). Indeed, it is well known that of the five genera in the *Sophist* (being, sameness, otherness, motion, rest) only the first three appear in the *Timaeus*.

Thus, the identification of the soul with all branches of mathematics — the pleromatic character of the soul — is stressed by both Iamblichus and Proclus. Both do it within the frame of a philosophy of mathematics; both move well within the orbit of the *Timaeus*.

---

* On the difference between these two kinds of extension as insisted upon by Aristotle see below p. 98.

** On the problem of the motive character of the soul, cf., for the time being, K. Mras, "Macrobius Kommentar zu Cicero's Somnium", *SB der Berl. Ak., Philos.-hist. Kl.*, 1933, 232–286, esp. 274 f.

The second Proclus passage (cf. above p. 21) is similar to the passage in *Isc*. In his commentary on the *Timaeus*, Proclus says: We should not interpret the intermediacy of the soul (between the divided and undivided; cf. *In Tim*. 35 A, 187 E, v. II 155, 25 Diehl) as the soul being partly somatic, partly asomatic, as Eratosthenes did, nor should we define it in terms of geometrical extension, as Severus did (186 E, v. II 152, 25–28 Diehl). The objections to Eratosthenes and Severus are treated together, obviously because of the reason given above on p. 22, i.e. that the soul is neither a sensible nor a geometric body. Continuing, Proclus returns to the problem of the mathematical nature of the soul and says:

"Of our predecessors who make out the essence of the soul to be mathematical, because the soul is intermediate between physicals and superphysicals, some say that the soul is number and make it out to be of the monad, as being indivisible, and of the unlimited dyad, as being divisible; some others, taking the soul to be a geometrical entity, construct it of point and extension.

Of the former opinion are men like Aristander and Numenius and very many other interpreters; of the latter opinion is Severus" (*In Tim*. 35 A, 187 A, v. II 153, 17–25 Diehl).

And having distinguished between the discontinuous (the element of arithmetic) and the continuous (the element of geometry), he sums up by saying:

"With regard to the soul both coincide (συντρέχει), the unification and the differentiation ... Therefore the substance of the soul is not merely arithmetical or the soul would not be continuous; nor is it [merely] geometrical, or the soul would not be differentiated. But the soul is the one and the other at the same time ...

[Furthermore], by being arithmetical, the soul possesses substantially [i.e., in the form of being, not in the form of knowing] harmonics ... by being geometrical the soul possesses astronomy, because the circles in the soul are both moved and unmoved ... [Therefore the soul is] a substantial bond of [all branches of] mathematics [the soul not only knows mathematics, the soul *is* mathematics]" (*In Tim*. 36 B, 213 D–E, v. II 238, 16–239, 6 Diehl).

The connection with the *On the Soul* passage is evident; Proclus enumerates the opinions identifying the soul with single branches of the mathematicals. We also know his objections: "number", when referring to the soul, must not mean a number consisting of monads, extension must not mean "geometrical" extension. The end-result of this whole discussion regarding the mathematical nature of the soul we find a little later: the soul is arithmetical, geometric, harmonic, and astronomic and knows the corresponding branches of mathematics — the soul contains *all* the branches of mathematics — the stress being on "all". To describe these branches, in the two passages we find all the phrases familiar from Iamblichus: *all* branches of mathematics; number; harmonic ratio; figure; fullness of all branches of mathematics; the idea (form) of things extended; point (corresponding to limit) and extension (cf. *In Tim.* 36 B, 213 E, v. II 239, 6–16 Diehl).

We now return to Iamblichus. *Isc* still continues the discussion of the problem concerning the relation between mathematicals and the soul in ch. X. The content of this chapter is stated in the summary * (p. 4, 20–24 F) in following words: In what way does the soul [or, more precisely: the sphere of being "soul"] consist of all branches of mathematics? By what kind of distinction could one mark off the mixture [of mathematicals] within the soul? Does the soul contain the complete reality of [the objects of] mathematics or is there some additional principle of them to be taken into consideration?

In other words, it is taken for granted, the soul consists of all branches of mathematicals. The problem still left is to find out what each of these branches contributes to the soul so as to make it one soul and how, on the other hand, in spite of the unity of the soul (or the unity of mixture), the diversity of the several branches still is preserved. And another problem still left is whether there are any mathematicals outside the soul or whether the soul contains in itself all the mathematical reality.

Now, when we turn from the summary to what is marked off in Festa's edition as chapter X, corresponding to the summary # 10, we may have some doubts as to the agreement between

---

* On the summaries (κεφάλαια) in Iamblichus see H. Oppermann in *Gnomon* 5 (1929) 545–558 esp. 552 f.; L. Deubner, "Bemerkungen zum Text der Vita Pythagorae des Iamblichos", *SB der Berl. Ak., Philos.-hist. Kl.*, 1935, 612–690; 824–827, esp. 689 n.; 690; 690 n. 2.

the summary and the actual content. The last question of the summary (whether there are any mathematicals outside the soul) is indeed being discussed in ch. X; but all the preceding questions seem to be discussed in the second part of ch. IX (p. 41, 5–42, 6 F). In this section Iamblichus relates the different branches of mathematics to different aspects of the soul. Its "determinate" and "defining" character the soul receives from numbers (its "unitary" λόγος from the number One); for its capacity to discharge itself into the realm of the extended the soul is indebted to geometricals; its capacity to establish harmony, order in motion, and common measure in what is incommensurable and to elevate accord to concord (symphony to eumetry) comes to the soul from harmonicals (and this is the reason why the soul can perceive harmony, being itself harmony and its essence consisting of numbers and other similar mathematical measurables).

It may be, therefore, that the division between ch.s IX and X is not in complete agreement with the summary — either as the result of somebody's slip of the pen, marking off ch. X at the wrong place or some slight inconsistency between outline and its execution (or content and subsequent summary), likely to occur in any writer.

But in the present context the question of the composition of the two chapters is entirely secondary. What is important is to see that the whole inspiration of ch.s IX and X is completely different from that of ch.s III and IV. In the latter, the soul and mathematicals were said to belong to different spheres of being; in the former, the soul becomes virtually indistinguishable from a mathematical entity. It is a mathematical entity of its own kind, to be sure, by being an arithmetical, a geometrical, and a harmonical at the same time, but a mathematical entity it still is. All these identifications of the soul and the mathematicals may ultimately be a correct or a mistaken interpretation of the *Timaeus*; in any case the net result is a division of being into three spheres, the middle sphere being described in such a way as to obliterate virtually any difference between soul and mathematicals. It is this tripartition of being which occurs in Iamblichus most frequently; but we saw that ch.s III and IV lead to a quadripartition of being with the soul being distinguished from mathematicals (whereas ch. VIII leads to still another quadripartition, viz. that corresponding to Plato's quadripartite line, i.e. into intelligibles, mathematicals, sensibles, and images). The unity of Iamblichus' book is most precarious as we can already see and as we shall see time and again.

Let us now resume our discussion of ch. X.

In spite of the mathematical constitution of the soul already established the question can still be asked: is the soul the product of the combination of the three branches of mathematicals? Or are the three branches, on the contrary, products of one soul? In other words, is the diversity of the branches prior to the unity of the soul or is the unity of the soul prior to the diversity of the three branches?

Iamblichus rejects both alternatives. The first would deprive the soul of its status which is to be the principles of mathematicals, make the branches of mathematics a scattered plurality, and the soul an almost accidental product of their concurrence, and have other odd consequences. The second would make the soul the cause of mathematicals and introduce a difference between the two according to the principle that the cause is superior to and different from its effects. What is left is the third alternative: neither is prior to the other. The soul coincides (concurs) with the mathematicals (συντρέχει πρὸς αὐτά — one is almost tempted to translate: the soul and mathematicals form one single team of runners — only we must not imagine these runners to exist independently from the team) and coexists with them (συνυφέστηκεν) with the paradoxical result of an uncomposed and undivided mixture. A complete interpenetration of the mathematicals and the soul takes place so that the soul gives complete unity to the different branches of mathematicals and in turn abandons itself to all and several of them. There are no mathematicals outside the soul. But the unity of the soul does not prevent its differentiation *. The last question of the summary (whether mathematicals have any principle in addition to the soul) has been answered in the negative.

---

* A good parallel illuminating the point of Iamblichus' discussion would be provided by the question: "Is the organism prior to its parts or are the parts prior to the organism?" with the subsequent answer that neither is the case; that the whole organism is indivisibly in its parts and in turn exists only in virtue of the plurality of them. The organism is not the result of its parts; nor is it the cause of them.

To sum up: ch.s III and IV stress the difference between the mathematical and the soul. They do not fit into the tripratition of being into intelligibles, mathematicals, and sensibles. Ch.s IX and X virtually abolish any difference between the soul and mathematicals, and particularly stress the fact that the soul should be identified with all branches of mathematicals rather than with one alone. They are therefore compatible with the tripartition of being. In both respects i.e., in identifying the soul with all branches of mathematicals rather than with a single one and in keeping the tripartition of being, the two chapters agree with a number of passages in Proclus.

For the present purpose it is not all-important to ascertain to what extent Iamblichus and Proclus themselves were ready to accept a complete and unconditional identification of the soul with mathematicals. What matters is that both discuss this identification as a serious interpretation of the relation between the two. It is sufficient for our purpose to assume that both say in substance: if the soul is to be identified with the mathematicals, it must not be identified with just one branch of it, it should rather be identified with all — three or four — branches.

In other words, the question asked on p. 16 how to reconcile the presupposition of the problem (tripartite being) with its solution (offered in ch. III in the form of a quadripartition of being, differentiating between soul and mathematicals) should be answered by saying that it is only ch. s IX and X with their virtual identification of the soul and mathematicals which are consistent with the original assumption of a tripartite being, whereas ch.s III and IV are indeed inconsistent with it. And these ch.s IX and X are in better agreement with Proclus than are ch.s III and IV, because Proclus does not say that the difference between soul and mathematicals consists in the former being motive, the latter being not.

But is it not unfair to Iamblichus to charge him with such inconsistence? Is it possible to assume that he should not have noticed the contradiction between ch. III and IV on one hand, ch.s IX and X on the other?

The answer to the first question is that *Isc* is quite obviously a series of excerpts from different authors rather than Iamblichus' own work. It seems what he did was to entrust a scribe with copying passages indicated by him, on loose sheets and patching them up into a whole by introductions, summaries, changes of a word every now and then, etc. It is obvious that no particular consistency can be expected to result. Nor should it be expected: Iamblichus' book is comparable to a selection from sources rather than to an exposition of the views of one author. It is not quite a florilegium; but it is not meant to be an original either. To a certain extent Iamblichus assumes the responsibility for his sources; but he does not have to make them appear entirely consistent.

An example well known already reveals immediately the kind of Iamblichus' editorial activity. One and the same passage (as we know today, taken from Aristotle's *Protrepticus*) appears in his *Protrepticus* and in *Isc.* In the former it is part of ch. VI, p. 38, 3–41, 2 Pistelli. In the latter it is part of ch. XXVI, p. 81, 7–83, 2 F. Unhesitatingly, by cuts and replacing some words of Aristotle by his own, Iamblichus adapts the original text for his purpose, but he does not mind using the same passage as a whole twice in two different books. Once more we have the inpression that Iamblichus intends to produce something which is neither an original nor a florilegium.

Besides, it appears that Iamblichus is not quite insensitive to the contradiction between ch.s III and IV on one hand, ch.s IX and X on the other. In fact, he avoids in ch.s IX and X anything which would make either the soul or the mathematicals appear to be motive. We shall see this better when we investigate once more the relation between the identifications of the soul with mathematicals as present in Proclus and Iamblichus.

The most outstanding difference between the two is as indicated. Iamblichus' mathematics in ch.s IX and X is tripartite, containing only arithmetics, geometry, and harmonics (acoustics), with astronomy wanting. Proclus' mathematicals are quadripartite, with astronomy included *. Now, it was Nicomachus

---

* On the subdivisions of mathematics see P. Tannery, *La Géométrie grecque* (1887) 38–52; W. D. Ross, *Aristotle's Metaphysics* (1924) ad Γ 2, 1004a8 (v. I 259). It is well known that in addition to a quadripartition we find also an entirely different division of mathematics in Proclus, reported by him as that of Geminus (cf. J. G. van Pesch, *De Procli fontibus* [1900] 87–113, esp. 97). Mathematics is divided into two parts, which today would be called pure and applied. Pure mathematics contains arithmetics and geometry, leaving astronomy and acoustics to applied mathematics (*In Eucl.*, Prol. I, p. 38, 1–12 Fr; on the designation of acoustics as canonics see p. 40, 22 Fr).

(see below p. 89) who justified the quadripartition of mathematics by basing it on the principle that mathematics is science
of quantity, quantity being either discreet or continuous, discreet
quantity being either per se (arithmetics) or in relations (acoustics
or harmonics), continuous quantity being either unmoved
(geometry) or in motion (astronomy). This quadripartition
Iamblichus reports after Nicomachus in *Isc* ch. VII, p. 30,
19–31, 4 F (cf. also *Isc* ch. V, p. 18, 27–19, 1 F) and it is the
same quadripartition which Proclus is ready to accept in both
his commentary on the *Timaeus* (e.g. *In Tim.* 213 C, v. II 238, 14
Diehl) and in his commentary on Euclid (see above p. 21 ; 23). But
of course nobody should in one and the same breath assert that
mathematics contains the four branches enumerated above and
also that mathematicals are unmoved. On the other hand, he
who accepts a tripartition of mathematics with the exclusion
of astronomy can, indeed he should, cling to the interpretation
of mathematicals as being unmoved.

Because in ch.s IX and X Iamblichus accepts a tripartite
mathematics, his mathematicals are unmoved. Accordingly,
the problem of the motive character of the soul is entirely sup-
pressed. We see this with particular clarity in two places. In *Isc*
ch. IX he quotes (p. 40, 16–17 F) Xenocrates' definition of the
soul as self-moving (self-changing) number to reject it as one-
sided. But though he professes to suggest a definition based
on the principle of κοινῇ συμπλέκειν πάντα (p. 40, 19 F, i.e.,
πάντα τὰ γένη of mathematicals [p. 40, 12–13 F]; cf. Stob. I
49, 32, p. 363, 26–365, 4 Wachsmuth, presenting also three
mathematical γένη, i.e., arithmeticals, geometricals, and harmonicals) in this "synthetic" definition we miss the word
αὐτοκίνητος, i.e. the synthetic definition contains part of the
definition of Xenocrates (number) and omits another (related
to motion). Furthermore, describing the aspect of the soul for
which the soul is indebted to harmonicals he says that the soul
has the power of harmonic *motion* (p. 41, 12–13 F), but the stress
is entirely on "harmonic" — he almost could have said that the
soul is not the source of motion but rather of whatever is orderly
in the motions of the universe. In other words, there is not a
hint in ch. IX that the soul is moved nor should there be one,
because in this chapter the soul is identified with tripartite

mathematics, excluding astronomicals. To this extent Iamblichus may have tried to avoid too flagrant a contradiction between ch.s III and IV on one hand, ch.s IX and X on the other. He does it at the cost of suppressing the question of the motive character of the soul, though he does not succeed completely. At the end of ch. X we read that the soul will be differentiated in accordance with its different δυνάμεις, ζωαί, and ἐνέργειαι (p. 43, 8–10 F). This immediately reminds us of the argument of those who tried to make mathematicals motive, according to *Isc* ch. III. Some, says Iamblichus here, will perhaps grant motion to the principles of mathematicals (i.e., the limited and the unlimited) — viz. those who posit these principles in the soul and the ζωαί and δυνάμεις of the soul (p. 13, 9–12 F). On reading the passage in ch. X quoted above, one feels inclined to ask: is the mention of ζωαί and δυνάμεις as peculiar to the soul an indication that the mathematicals of which it consists are indeed moved? No clear answer can be found in ch. X — we are left feeling that the relations between motion and mathematicals, motion and the soul, mathematicals and the soul as presented in ch.s III and IV, and again in ch.s IX and X are in several respects inconsistent.

Let us now sum up the results of the foregoing discussion. Both Iamblichus and Proclus describe the mathematicals (which they take to subsist) as intermediate. The realms between which they mediate are often described in terms of the divisible and the indivisible. Both are aware of the "intermediacy" of the soul, though Proclus stresses it more than Iamblichus. Both deal with the problem whether methematicals and the soul are identical — Iamblichus arguing sometimes pro, sometimes contra; Proclus assuming identity. In connection with this question both assert the identity of the soul with *all* branches of mathematics — three in Iamblichus, four in Proclus. These assertions are closely linked with the motive or nonmotive character of mathematicals. Proclus asserts the former, Iamblichus sometimes the former, sometimes the latter. The solution is closely connected with the problem of a tripartite mathematics without astronomy, or a quadripartite one, including astronomy.

This much is immediately clear: *Isc* is based on different sources, in which some of the problems treated above were decided in different ways *. Iamblichus did not bother to reconcile contradictory opinions. As a result, his mathematicals sometimes include, sometimes exclude motion; his mathematics is sometimes tripartite, sometimes quadripartite.

We now have a substantial number of key terms. They are a safe guide through the tangle of many problems. This will become obvious in what follows; but even now we can see how easy it is to discover the different sources from which Iamblichus drew, once we have a clear insight into the difference (and what it implies) between a tripartite and a quadripartite mathematics.

And we can conclude this chapter with a synopsis of the passages involving the basic contradiction as to the motive or non-motive character of mathematicals.

Isc ch. III, p. 13, 12–15 F
It is better to assume that the mathematical principles and the mathematical sphere of being [οὐσία] are nonmotive.

Isc ch. IV, p. 18, 14–18 F
The mathematical principles are nonmotive.

Isc ch. XIII, p. 50, 18–19 F
Mathematicals differ from the realm of becoming by their nonmotive nature.

Isc ch. XV, p. 55, 14–15 F
Mathematics prepares for theology also by being a contemplation of things stable and nonmotive.

Isc ch. XXIV, p. 75, 18–19
Mathematics is concerned

Isc ch. VII, p. 30, 25–31, 2 F
Geometry ... received as a helpmate the spheric [astronomy] which is the instrument of knowledge of continuous quantity in motion.

Isc XII, p. 47, 6–16 F
Most men believe that the branches of mathematics are nonmotive and that the objects of their knowledge are nonmotive; this, however, is a wrong opinion. For there are branches of mathematics investigating the number of motion ... and the incorporeal circular motions of the soul with which the heavenly revolutions coexist .... In such investigations astronomy and harmonics are contained.

Isc ch. XIX, p. 63, 23–64, 13F
The mathematician deals

---

* Cf. Zeller III/2⁵ (1923) 759.

with a kind of nature stable and void of motion.

Isc ch. XXVI, p. 81, 11–12 F

Things belonging to the non-motive mathematical kinds are limited and ordered.

Isc ch. XXVIII, p. 89, 2–8 F

The mathematical ratios are nonmotive, corresponding to the character of mathematicals, which are exempt of motion.

with theologicals, noeric mathematicals, the self-moved sphere of being, and the eternal ratios (wherein they define the self-moved number), with the heavenly bodies and motions, etc.

Isc ch. XXVII, p. 86,14–15F

In mathematics some things are completely nonmotive, others (in acoustics and astronomy) are motive.

The source of the first right-side passage is Nicomachus, *Intr. arithm.* I 3, 1; p. 6 f. Hoche (cf. Festa's adnotation a.l.); there can hardly be much doubt that the left-side passage is from some other source. They contradict each other and the same holds true for the rest of the two columns.

Appendix

1. The contradiction between ch. III and ch. IX of *Isc* is only apparent, according to Loenen *. This he proves by saying that the same (apparent) contradiction must have, at least implicitly, been present in Posidonius. For he, on one hand, identified the soul with mathematicals but on the other must have known that the soul according to Plato was motive. How then does Loenen resolve the apparent contradiction? By assuming that Iamblichus when speaking of the motive soul means soul in the ordinary sense of the word, whereas when he speaks of non-motive mathematicals he still can identify them with the soul, viz. with the soul as idea (ideal soul). This distinction, says Loenen, should be of great interest to students of Plato.

Loenen's explanation is a classic example of an *ad hoc* hypothesis. There is not the slightest hint of the doctrine of a double soul in *Isc*. As to what Posidonius *must* have known about the

---

* J. H. Loenen, *Mnemosyne*, S. IV, vol. X/1 (1957) 80–82.

relations between mathematical and the soul with regard to the problem of motion, we know nothing.

2. The relation between the two chapters of *Isc* has in a very interesting manner been interpreted by Kohnke *. These two chapters, says Kohnke, not only contradict each other. They closely correspond to each other like thesis and antithesis. It is therefore to be assumed that both appeared in one and the same work whose author first presented the doctrines and then proceeded to refute them. And Kohnke even guesses that this author was nobody else but Posidonius.

I am not quite sure that the fact that the two chapters correspond to each other (Kohnke is right on this point) is best explained by his hypothesis. After all, Iamblichus could have excerpted ch. III of *Isc* from the work in which it originally appeared and ch. IX from the work in which it was refuted. Kohnke might object that I attribute too much to the diligence of Iamblichus. I see no way on which to arrive at certainty. But if Iamblichus did what Kohnke suspects him of having done, it would illustrate the kind and scope of his editorial activity.

Incidentally, if Kohnke guessed correctly and both chapters are from Posidonius, this would explain the presence of the phrases ψυχῆς ζωαὶ καὶ δυνάμεις appearing in ch. III, p. 13, 11 F and ch. IX, p. 43, 9 F. They could be rooted in the concept of ζωτικὴ δύναμις (*vis vitalis*), which we connect with Posidonius (see K. Reinhardt, art. Poseidonios, *RE* XXII/1 [1953] 648 f.).

3. The importance of the term συντρέχειν to designate the unity of distinct natures or the distinction in spite of unity: *Symbolum Chalcedonense* (e.g. in P. Schaff, *The Creeds of Christendom* [1877, later reprints] 62).

4. On the meaning of Iamblichus' 'authorship' see below, p. 156–8.

---

* F. W. Kohnke, *Gnomon* 27 (1955) 157–164.

II. POSIDONIUS AND NEOPLATONISM *

Both Iamblichus and Proclus are well aware that when they discuss the relation between soul and mathematicals they are treating a traditional problem. Both know that their solution concerning the identification of the soul with *all* kinds of mathematicals (three in Iamblichus, four in Proclus) is not the only one offered by philosophers. In both the Iamblichus passages we find representatives of three points of view: those who identify the soul with the arithmetical, those who identify it with the geometrical, those who identify it with the harmonical. Proclus enumerates representatives of only two points of view (arithmeticals and geometricals), and there are only two names (Severus and Moderatus) common to both lists. But both obviously feel that they are contributing to the solution of a traditional problem. The question is legitimate: How far back can we trace the problem?

The answer is contained in Plutarch, *De animae procreatione in Timaeo* (Plutarchi *Moralia*, ed. C. Hubert, v. VI [1954]). Here we read:

"Some [scil. Xenocrates] think that the mixing of the indivisible with the divisible substance means nothing else but the procreation of number ... But this number [scil. the product of these two factors] is not yet soul, for it lacks active and passive motion. However, soul was procreated by admixing 'the same' and 'the other', of which the latter is principle of movement and change, the former principle of rest" (ch. II, 1012 D).

Thus we have Xenocrates' definition of the soul as selfmoved number. And this Plutarch takes to mean: The essence (substance) of the soul is number (ch. III, 1013 D).

Let us comment on this.

First of all, we find here the report that Xenocrates interpreted the psychogony as arithmogony. In terms of our problem, he identified the world-soul in Plato's *Timaeus* with just one branch of mathematics: numbers.

In connection with this, he defined the soul as number.

---

* This chapter continues some of the ideas presented previously in: P. Merlan "Beitraege zur Geschichte des antiken Platonismus", *Philologus* 89 (1934) 35–53; 197–214 and *idem*, "Die Hermetische Pyramide und Sextus", *Museum Helveticum* 8 (1951) 100–105.

Immediately he seems to have added: the soul undoubtedly is principle of motion in Plato. Therefore, the number with which Plato's world-soul is to be identified must be defined as motive.

Hence the definition: the soul is self-moved number.

But there remained one more question. Which of the ingredients of the mixture constituting the soul (soul having been defined as number) is responsible for its motive power?

Xenocrates singled out the two terms "sameness" and "otherness" *. They, he said, made the soul to be motive number.

In the Plato passage in question there is, to be sure, not the slightest trace of the assertion that the soul is motive by being composed of sameness and otherness.

But this makes Xenocrates' interpretation all the more characteristic. He was the first (or among the first) to interpret Plato's world-soul as motive number (or, as we could also say, as number containing the source of its change within itself). It is this identification which serves as a background for Iamblichus' query: how is it possible to identify the soul with mathematicals without admitting the principle of motion to mathematicals? Xenocrates unhesitatingly did it at least to the extent of making some of the mathematicals move, these moving mathematicals being identified by him with the soul; others, among whom is the author used by Iamblichus in *Isc* ch. III and part of IV, objected.

It is interesting to notice that Aristotle also faces this problem. Generally, his mathematicals are nonmotive: the passages *De caelo* III 6,305a 25–26 and *De motu animalium* I 1,698a 25–26 are particularly characteristic. But in a passage like *Met.* A 8,989b 32–33 he would add cautiously "except astronomicals"; or he would introduce sciences intermediate between mathematics and physics (cf. p. 62 n.), dealing with objects that are semi-mathematicals and subject to motion.

We now resume the discussion of Plutarch.

[1] Men like Posidonius "did not remove [the soul] from matter very far. [2] They took the phrase 'divided about the bodies' to mean 'substance [οὐσία] of the limits'. They mixed them with

---

* Cf. Arist., *Met.* K 9, 1066a 11: there are some who characterize motion as otherness (or inequality or non-being); see also *Physics* III 2, 201b 19–21, with Ross' commentary a.l.

the intelligible, and [3] said of the soul, that it was idea [form] of the all-extended [cf. Speusippus fr. 40 Lang], existing according to number which comprises harmony.

[4a] For on one hand, mathematicals are placed between the first intelligibles and the sensibles, [4b] while, on the other hand, the soul shares eternity with the intelligibles, passibility [change-ability] with the sensibles, [5] so that it is fitting that [its] substance should be intermediate" (ch. XXII, 1023 B).

What does this mean? Posidonius identified the world soul with mathematicals. He did so, because on the one hand, the soul is described by Plato as participating in the eternity of the first intelligibilia and of the changeableness of the sensibilia. This proves that the essence of the soul is intermediate. On the other hand, still according to Posidonius, the mathematicals have their place between the first intelligibilia and the sensibilia.

In other words, Posidonius said: In Plato's *Timaeus* the soul is intermediate between intelligibilia and sensibilia. The mathematicals [and here we must add: in Plato, according to Posidonius] are intermediate between intelligibilia and sensibilia. Therefore, Posidonius said, soul equals mathematicals.

This resulted in the definition: the soul is idea (form) of the all-extended, being constituted according to number comprising attunement. The similarity of this definition with the definitions in Iamblichus and Proclus is obvious.

What is most interesting in this definition is that it presents the first attempt to identify the soul not with one branch of mathematicals, but with three. Once more: "idea (form) of the all-extended" stands for geometricals; "number" represents arithmeticals; "number comprising harmony" represents the ratios (proportions) or the musicals.

The whole definition explains, and is explained in turn by, the two passages in Iamblichus' (*Isc* and *On the Soul*) and the Proclus passages quoted above (p. 21–24). What is absent in Posidonius' definition is any explicit reference to the problem of motion and we do not know whether he treated it at all. All the other elements of Iamblichus' discussion can easily be found in Posidonius' definition. The main difference between Posidonius-Iamblichus and Proclus is that the former assume a tripartite mathematics, the latter assumes a quadripartite one *.

How did Posidonius arrive at his assertion that the world-soul is intermediate between intelligibilia and sensibilia? He did it by interpreting Plato's phrases: "the undivided" and "what is divided about the bodies" as standing for "intelligibilia" and for "essence [substance] of the limits" respectively.

It seems clear, therefore, that Posidonius' essence (substance) of the limits stands for the sensible (divided), just as does Plato's "that which is divided about the bodies". Plato's phrase is hardly anything more than a circumlocution for the world of change, body extended, etc. Admittedly, it is an ambiguous phrase; in *Enn.* IV 2 Plotinus interpreted it as meaning the limits which have become divided only by being embodied **. But Plotinus' interpretation is erroneous and simply the result of his tendency to keep the soul as free from pollution by the body as possible (cf. H. R. Schwyzer, "Zu Plotins Interpretation von Platons Timaeus 35 A", *Rheinisches Museum* 84 [1935] 360–368, esp. 365–368). The result of his interpretation is a quadripartition (IV 2, 2, 52–54 Bréhier): the eternal (undivided, one), the indivisibly divided (soul, one-and-many), the divisibly undivided (embedded forms, many-and-one), the divisibly divided (body, many). Is this still Plato's *Timaeus*? Plato's cosmogony implies only three kinds of being: that of the eternal that of the soul, and that of the temporal, changing, extended, i.e. divided bodily. And Posidonius remained true to this tripartition. If we do not assume this, the whole idea of intermediacy, so clearly the backbone of Posidonius' interpretation, would lose its basis.

But can ἡ τῶν περάτων οὐσία ever stand for anything but πέρατα? Is it not to pervert the letter by interpreting it as

---

* On the exclusion of astronomy from mathematics in Posidonius see E. Bréhier, "Posidonius d'Apamée, théoricien de la géométrie", *Revue des Etudes grecques* 27 (1914) 44–58 (= *Études de Philosophie antique* [1955] 117–130). On the nonmotive character of geometricals in Posidonius see A. Schmekel, *Die positive Philosophie in ihrer geschichtlichen Entwicklung* 2 vv. (1938, 1914), v. I 105 f.

** Cf. F. M. Cornford, *Plato's Cosmology* (1937) 63. See, however, also P. Shorey, "The Timaeus of Plato", *American Journal of Philology* 10 (1889) 45–78, esp. 51 f., and *idem*, "Recent Interpretations of the Timaeus", *Classical Philology* 23 (1928) 343–362, esp. 352. But here as in so many cases the question of the correct interpretation of Plato is less important than the question how he was actually interpreted.

meaning that which is within the πέρατα? the extended? the divided?

Not so, if we simply take it to be a subjective genitive. Τῶν περάτων οὐσία is the kind of being which "has" or "accepts" limits — just like "that which is divided about the bodies" or "the limited" in Plato (cf. above p. 15).

Our assertion is confirmed by the Proclus passage where, as an obvious equivalent of Posidonius' "idea of the all-extended" (p. 36) we read: idea of extended things. "The extended things" are Posidonius' οὐσίαι; "idea" corresponds to "limit". Τῶν περάτων οὐσία we could almost translate "*property* of the limits".

Furthermore, Plutarch accuses Posidonius (or rather his followers) of being too materialistic in their description of the soul — or more literally, of having brought the soul in too close proximity to matter. How did Posidonius do it? By mixing the intelligible with "them", meaning limits; "them" being obviously Plutarch's somewhat careless reference to "the substance of the limits". One of these two elements must be the expression of Posidonius' materialism. It cannot be "the intelligible"; so we are left with "the substance of the limits", and this must mean bodies. Otherwise Plutarch's criticism would be completely unfounded. Οὐσία is the πεπερασμένον without its limits; "the substance of limits" is anything which has received, or can receive, a limit. Limit alone, without some genitive, is limit without the limited. This is the way in which Posidonius, according to Proclus (*In Eucl.* p. 143, 8–21 Fr), used the word "form", "figure". The substance of the limits can not mean simply limit. Nor can it mean "essence of the limits". None of these translations would explain Plutarch's reproach of materialism.

It is hardly necessary to remind the reader that for a Stoic the equation οὐσία = ὕλη is ready at hand (see *SVF*, Index s.v. οὐσία) and that also Timaeus Locrus opposes the ἀμέριστος μορφή to μεριστὴ οὐσία, i.e. form which is indivisible to οὐσία = matter which is divisible (ch. IV; v. IV 409 Hermann) *.

We can now sum up what Posidonius did.

1. He continued along a line of interpreting the *Timaeus* started

---

* Cf. the discussion of this topic in E. R. Goodenough, "A Neo-Pythagorean Source in Philo Judaeus", *Yale Classical Studies* 3 (1932) 115–164, esp. 125 f.

in the Academy: towards identification of Plato's world-soul with mathematicals. Xenocrates was one of the first to do it — he identified the soul with number *. Speusippus did something similar: he identified the soul with the geometrical. The source of our knowledge of this fact is Iamblichus (see above p. 20). Geometricals, says Iamblichus, are one of the branches of mathematicals; they are made up of form and extension, and Speusippus, one of the men who define soul by mathematicals, defined the soul as idea (form) of the all-extended. Idea stands clearly for form. The Iamblichus reference seems absolutely precise, makes perfect sense, and seems entirely trustworthy (see below p. 43). As reported by him, Speusippus identified the soul with a geometrical (cf. fr. 40 Lang).

It seems, then, that also Posidonius found Speusippus as identifying the soul with another branch of mathematicals. Finally in Moderatus (if he preceded Posidonius) or some member of the Academy, he found the soul identified with mathematical harmony.

2. In interpreting the *Timaeus* Posidonius made use of the Platonic tripartition sensibilia, mathematicals, intelligibilia. He found it where Aristotle had found it or in Aristotle (*Met.* A 6,987b14 and many other passages; cf. Ross, *Aristotle's Met.* a.l. [v. I 166–168]). He combined it with the tripartition of the *Timaeus*: and as he already found a tendency to identify the world soul with mathematicals (a tendency which originated, it seems, quite independently from the other tripartition), he combined the two tripartitions, thus arriving at the equation: soul = intermediate = mathematicals.

Therefore, to the extent to which we find the identification: soul = intermediate = mathematicals in Iamblichus or Proclus, they follow Posidonius. Iamblichus, with his identification of the soul with three branches of mathematicals, follows him more closely than does Proclus. From Posidonius a straight line leads to Iamblichus and Proclus.

Did Posidonius interpret the mathematicals realistically? We can answer this question with only a modicum of certainty. We know that Posidonius insisted on defining "figure" in terms

---

* Cf. K. Praechter, art. Severus 47 in *RE* II A 2 (1923), esp. p. 2008 with n. ***.

of circumference rather than included area or volume (cf. Proclus *In Eucl.* p. 143, 6–17 Fr.; Hero *Definitiones* 23, p. 30, 8–11 Heiberg). But, contrary to what Schmekel (*op. cit.*, above p. 37 n., v. I 100–106) says, this does not speak either for or against Posidonius' realism. More decisive is the passage in Diogenes Laertius VII 135 where Posidonius is credited with the assertion that the geometric surface exists in our thoughts and in reality at the same time. He was quite obviously at variance with other Stoics quoted by Proclus *In Eucl.* Def. I, p. 89 Fr (*SVF* II 488) who asserted that the limits of bodies existed only in our thoughts. In other words, there was at least a strain of mathematical realism in Posidonius *.

Into which of the different pictures of Posidonius of more recent years does our description of Posidonius fit best? Undoubtedly into that of W. Jaeger (*Nemesius von Emesa* [1915]). He presented him as the protagonist of the bond-and-intermediacy idea. Such a man must be sympathetic to the idea of an intermediate. Earlier than anybody else, he is likely to discover the intermediate place of Plato's world-soul (described in mathematical terms) on one side, the intermediate place of mathematicals in Plato as reported by Aristotle on the other side, and to identify these two intermediates.

This, then, seems to be established beyond doubt: Posidonius did influence Neoplatonism. The sector in which he did it (interpretation of the *Timaeus*; identification of Plato's world-soul with mathematicals) may seem small; we shall see later how important it was **.

And now a few words on Speusippus' and Xenocrates' identification of the soul with one particular branch of mathematics. The report of Iamblichus according to which Speusippus defined the soul as the idea of the all-extended has recently been scrutinized by H. Cherniss (*Aristotle's Criticism of Plato and the*

---

* Cf. L. Edelstein, "The Philosophical System of Posidonius", *American Journal of Philology* 57 (1936) 286–325, esp. 303; also P. Tannery, *La Géométrie grecque* (1887) 33 n. 2; H. Doerrie, "Ὑπόστασις", *Nachrichten der Ak. d. Wiss. Göttingen, I. Philol.-hist. Kl.*, 1955, p. 35–92, esp. p. 57.
** On Posidonius in the Middle Ages cf. also R. Klibansky, *The Continuity of the Platonic Tradition During the Middle Ages*² (1950) 27.

Academy v. I [1944] 509–512). He is inclined to consider it untrustworthy, or at least unintelligible. According to him, it implies that Speusippus considered the soul to be a mathematical entity, while Aristotle said (*Met.* Z 2,1028b21–24) explicitly that Speusippus distinguished sharply between magnitude and the soul.

Why Cherniss should trust unconditionally Aristotle's report is not quite clear. This report is obviously highly critical of Speusippus and interested in presenting him as a "disjointer" of being. Even so, as the difference between soul and geometricals is, according to Aristotle himself, not much greater than the difference between numbers and geometricals (the soul following immediately the geometricals), we must allow the possibility that Aristotle stressed the difference and left the similarity unmentioned. It is true that "idea of the all-extended" sounds almost like the definition of a geometrical solid; and we can only guess, how, then, the soul differs from any other geometrical solid. Does "idea of the all-extended" imply motion? Is this the reason why the soul is a branch of mathematics rather than a mathematical *tout court*? We do not know; but still the contradiction between Aristotle's report and the mathematical interpretation of Speusippus' definition does not seem to be particularly serious. It may amount to the difference between "mathematical entity" and "what is closest to a mathematical entity". How close is closest?

But let us suppose that the definition as reported and interpreted by Iamblichus is incompatible with Aristotle. What would follow? Do we have to reject it or wind up with an *"ignoramus"* as to its true meaning? This is hardly necessary. Perhaps Speusippus expressed himself ambiguously; perhaps he changed his opinion; perhaps he was flatly contradicting himself. After all, he survived Plato only by some eight to nine years (Diogenes Laertius IV 1; cf. F. Jacoby, *Apollodors Chronik* [1902] 313) *; It is difficult to assume that he "gave up" the theory of ideas

---

* It seems that insufficient attention is being paid to this fact. The majority of the philosophic works of Speusippus must have been written during Plato's lifetime, and it is very difficult not to see in his appointment as Plato's successor the latter's approval. Even if some non-philosophic considerations determined Plato's decision, he still could not have thought of Speusippus as professing a doctrine of which he, Plato, disapproved. Cf. E. Frank, *Plato und die sogenannten Pythagoreer* (1923) 239.

from the very beginning of his philosophic career, of which he spent the greatest part in the Academy. Speusippus must have changed or contradicted himself in this respect, too.

Having rejected the mathematical interpretation, Cherniss suggests that it meant perhaps a defense of the *Timaeus* against Aristotle: the soul is not a magnitude, as Aristotle has asserted, but idea of the body just like Aristotle's εἶδος *. And Cherniss quotes some passages proving that Aristotle identified πέρας and εἶδος of the extended body.

Now, Cherniss' whole discussion culminates in the assertion that Aristotle never suggests that the Platonists called the soul a form; and he obviously considers this silence to be another proof that they actually did not do so. But if Speusippus, according to Cherniss, said: the soul in the *Timaeus* is an εἶδος — just as you, Aristotle, make her an εἶδος — does not this mean that he called the soul a form? Or would Cherniss deny that εἶδος as used by Aristotle to designate the soul should be translated "form"? In the paper by P. Merlan, "Beitraege zur Geschichte des antiken Platonismus", *Philologus* 89 (1934) 35–53; 197–214 to which Cherniss refers, it is said (206) that the interpretation of Speusippus (and Xenocrates) ** therein suggested seems to blur the difference between the Peripatetic and the Academic definitions of the soul and the attempt is there made to show that the difference between the Aristotelian soul as εἶδος and the Academic soul as ἰδέα = form was perhaps indeed not so great as is usually assumed. Does not Cherniss confirm this fully by his interpretation of Speusippus' definition? And if so, does he not contradict himself? After reading his keen discussion one is almost tempted to sum it up by saying: perhaps one of the main differences between the Academic and the Peripatetic interpretations of the soul was that the former tended towards the identification of forms of *all* bodies with the soul (mathematical forms being the most outstanding representatives of form),

---

* Cf. H. Cherniss, *The Riddle of the Early Academy* (1945) 74.
** With regard to Xenocrates, Cherniss (511) says that Merlan's attempt to identify the soul with intermediate mathematicals results in the impossible identification of the δοξαστόν with the μαθηματικόν; and he kindly explained (orally) that such an identification is impossible because, mathematicals being the highest sphere of being in Xenocrates, the coordination of δόξα with mathematicals would leave ἐπιστήμη without any subject matter. But why should not ἐπιστήμη concern itself with the *principles* of mathematicals? Cf. also below, p. 44.

while Aristotle limited the equation soul = form by describing the soul as the form of *living* bodies alone *. In any case, if, according to Cherniss, Speusippus said: Plato meant the soul in the *Timaeus* to be an ἰδέα = εἶδος, how can Cherniss say that the Platonists never called the soul an idea or form?

But perhaps it would be appropriate to explain how ἰδέα = εἶδος could mean both form and essence. The form (figure, shape, contour, outline) of a thing is (1) what keeps it apart from all other things — the boundary between it and its surroundings; (2) the framework which remains stable though the matter constantly changes — this framework being either rigid, or "elastic" as in the case of living organisms. In other words, it is the form by which everything remains identical with itself and different from every other thing. Thus, the form represents the element of being (stability) as opposed to the element of becoming. The form, then, is the equivalent of the presence of the idea in the thing. To the extent to which a thing has form, it participates in the idea. It is easy to see that this interpretation can equally well be applied to any quality, e.g., the just, the beautiful, etc., though in such cases form loses its visibility and becomes an abstract boundary.

One further word of warning must be added. A reader of Cherniss may be misled into believing that it was only some modern interpreter who said that Speusippus' definition meant to make the soul a *mathematical* entity (in fact, it is not quite clear whether Cherniss doubts just this or only whether Speusippus could have made it an *intermediate* mathematical). We must not forget, however, that it is only in Iamblichus that we find the definition of Speusippus; and Iamblichus says explicitly that this definition was meant to give geometrical status to the soul. It seems risky to accept from Iamblichus the words of Speusippus and reject his interpretation on the ground that it seems to contradict Aristotle. After all, the presumption is that Iamblichus read the words of Speusippus in their context; and he quite obviously had no interest in misinterpreting them (as Aristotle had). The whole Iamblichus

---

* Cf. e.g. N. Hartmann, "Zur Lehre vom Eidos bei Platon und Aristoteles", *Abh. der Berl. Ak., Phil.-hist. Kl.*, 1941 p. 19= *Kleinere Schriften*, v. II (1957) 129–164, p. 145, on the role of mathematics and biology respectively in Plato and in Aristotle.

excerpt in Stobaeus (I 49, 32, p. 362, 24–367, 9 Wachsmuth) makes the impression of a solid piece of work *; several times, he makes it clear that he knows the difference between a report and an interpretation very well (see e.g. I 49, 32, p. 366, 9 Wachsmuth).

Perhaps another word of criticism may here be added. According to Cherniss, Xenocrates could not have made the soul a mathematical entity because of its "intermediate" position, since he identified numbers and ideas. True, the latter is precisely what Theophrastus said (*Met.* I 3, p. 2 Ross and Fobes), if the reference is to Xenocrates; but the same Theophrastus says a little later (III 12, p. 12 Ross and Fobes) that Xenocrates "derives" everything — sensibles, intelligibles, mathematicals, and also divine things — from the first principles (fr. 26 Heinze). Intelligibles and mathematicals are kept apart (the Ross-Fobes rendering: "Objects of sense, objects of reason *or* mathematical objects, and divine things" is an interpretation not a translation; cf. their discussion of this passage on p. 56 f; for the simple translation see Ross, *Aristotle's Met.* p. LXVI or LXXV) **. If "the divine things" are astronomicals, we here simply have Aristotle's pattern (sensible-perishable, sensible-imperishable, eternal — however with the latter subdivided into mathematicals and intelligibles) ***. It seems therefore unwarranted to deny altogether the possibility of intermediate mathematicals in Xenocrates. It is characteristic that Theophrastus mentions Xenocrates' name only in the second of the two passages quoted above; in the first he perhaps relies on Aristotle alone. But even Aristotle never quoted Xenocrates by name as the one who identified ideas with numbers. It may well be that Aristotle was not absolutely sure of his interpretation of Xenocrates.

* And an ambitious one at that. Iamblichus obviously tries to replace what he considers an inadequate outline underlying Aristotle's presentation of the opinions of his predecessors in *De anima*.

** The interpretation of Ross and Fobes aims at the reconciliation of fr. 5 and fr. 26 Heinze. In the former, Sextus Empiricus, *Adv. math.* VII 147 reports that Xenocrates assumed three spheres of being (things outside the heavens, accessible to νοῦς and ἐπιστήμη; the heavens, accessible to both αἴσθησις and νοῦς, the mixture of which is equivalent to δόξα; and things within the heavens, accessible to αἴσθησις; these three spheres corresponding to the three μοῖραι). In fr. 26 Heinze Theophrastus mentions four entities (αἰσθητά, νοητά, μαθηματικά, θεῖα). But is this reconciliation necessary? Is it not more likely that Xenocrates suggested different divisions of being in different contexts?

*** Cf. P. Merlan, "Aristotle's Unmoved Movers", *Traditio* 4 (1946) 1–30, esp. 4 f.

We should not overlook either that Xenocrates might have identified ideas and numbers, but kept geometricals apart. This, indeed, seems to be the gist of Arist. *Met.* θ 2, 1028b24 (fr. 34 Heinze with Asclepius a.l.). Of the five remaining Aristotelian passages gathered by Heinze only one says that the man whom we suppose to have been Xenocrates identified ideas with mathematicals *tout court*; the rest speak of numbers. The only passage which seems to say that Xenocrates denied the difference between ideas and magnitudes (*Met.* M 6, 1080b28; fr. 37 Heinze) admits of a different interpretation. When Aristotle says that Xenocrates believes in mathematical magnitudes but speaks of them unmathematically, we should perhaps accept the first part of this assertion at its full value and discount the second as implying a criticism. All this should make us cautious. It is risky to assert positively that Xenocrates was *always* or *ever* a dualist (or a trialist only in the sense in which Aristotle was a trialist, by subdividing the sphere of the sensibles into perishables and imperishables).

It is not easy to see why Cherniss finds it so strange that some scholars tried to "reconcile" (the quotation marks are his) Plato and Xenocrates, ascribing to the former the doctrine that soul is number (572). All he says against this reconciliation is that Aristotle never ascribes this doctrine to Plato and considers it as peculiar to Xenocrates. Just how convincing is this argument? Is it not clear, on the contrary, that Xenocrates *interpreted* Plato as having said precisely that? And was his interpretation so thoroughly mistaken?

Cherniss interprets Plato's system as teaching the intermediacy of the soul between ideas and phenomena (606; cf. 407–411) *.

---

* Cf. 442,453. Cherniss faces the following dilemma. Aristotle asserts (*Met.* Z 2,1028b18–24) that Plato knew only three spheres of being, ideas, mathematicals, and sensibles, whereas Speusippus knew more than three, viz. sensibles, soul, geometricals, arithmeticals. Either Cherniss accepts the part referring to Plato as trustworthy (in spite of *Tim.* 30 B). Then there was no place for a soul in Plato's system as mediating between ideas and sensibles and Cherniss' interpretation of Plato would be erroneous. Or he considers Aristotle's presentation of Plato's system to be erroneous or perhaps an illegitimate translation of the epistemological intermediacy of mathematicals as suggested by Plato's *Republic* VII, into ontic intermediacy (see, however W. D. Ross, *Plato's Theory of Ideas* [1951] 25 f.; 59–66; 177) — then he should not rely on his presentation of Speusippus. The way out seems to be to assume that (1) Aristotle's presentation of Plato is correct because in Plato's system the soul can be identified with the mathematical; (2) in presenting Speusippus Aristotle interprets differences within the realm of the mathematical (arithmeticals, geometricals, soul)

According to him there is no function left for God in Plato's system; as to the νοῦς, it is part of the soul (and the ideas are outside of it). Thus there remain only three spheres of being (or whatever Cherniss would call them). He would not deny that Aristotle time and again repeated that Plato assumed three spheres of being: ideas, mathematicals, sensibles. How far is Cherniss from Aristotle?

Cherniss accepts Cornford's interpretation of the *Timaeus* (cf. above p. 13 note). He would not deny that Aristotle described the mathematicals as having a "mixed" character: they share eternity with the ideas, multiplicity with the sensibles. Are eternity and multiplicity anything else but aspects of indivisibility and divisibility, respectively? How far is Cherniss from Aristotle?

Still it cannot be maintained that there is no difference at all between his and Aristotle's interpretation. But this difference can be reduced to just one statement: the soul is motive according to Cherniss, the mathematicals are not (579 f.).

In other words, Cherniss can object to the identification of the soul with mathematicals only for the same reason for which the author used as source in *Isc* ch. III objected. But there is no reason for him, either, to deny that the soul is *some kind* of mathematical entity and, *together with other mathematical entities*, intermediate.

Thus, as we said, the wording in the *Timaeus* was an invitation to identify soul and mathematicals *. Speusippus and Xenocrates availed themselves of this invitation — at least partly.

Posidonius accepted Aristotle's tripartition and Speusippus' definition of the soul as being Platonic. We know the results.

One step remained to be taken: to make the mathematicals motive. This is precisely the step which Cherniss refuses to take. But how wrong is this step? Who could say that it is not in the spirit of Plato (cf. Zeller II/1⁵ 781 n.l)? Only if we accept unconditionally Aristotle's assertion (cf. p. 35) that all mathematicals are nonmotive (an assertion in the name of which Galilei's application of mathematics to physics was opposed)

---

as if they were absolute differences, because he is interested in presenting the views of Plato and Speusippus as entirely different, which they, however, are not.
  * Cf. E. Zeller, II/1⁵ (1922) 780–784, esp. 784 n. 1.

can we do it. But should we not expect Aristotle to stress and overstress the nonmotive character of mathematicals — the same Aristotle who so emphatically denied the presence of any motive entity in Plato's system? Cherniss criticizes him severely for having failed to see that in Plato's system the soul is motive; is it so impossible to assume that, with regard to mathematicals too, Aristotle took for granted what neither Plato nor orthodox Platonists would have conceded as obvious? To be sure, the identification of soul with mathematicals is not pure and un-alloyed Platonic doctrine; but it could be good Academic doctrine. Especially, this equation cannot be called un-Platonic because of the motive character of the former, the nonmotive character of the latter.

This leads to still another question. How great is the difference between the definition of the soul by Xenocrates (self-moved or self-changing number) and that of Speusippus (idea of the all-extended)? Both definitions stress the mathematical character of the soul, though one stresses more the arithmetical, the other more its geometrical aspect (cf. Zeller, *ibid.*, p. 784 n.l). Considering the fact that Plato describes his world-soul in terms of numbers first, in terms of circles afterwards, there is nothing surprising in the difference, nor in the similarity, of the two definitions. Iamblichus compares them from this point of view; and on reading the whole passage (I 49, 32, p. 364, 2–10 Wachsmuth) instead of dissecting it into single δόξαι one can hardly doubt the correctness of his interpretation. Just as Xenocrates asserted that Plato's psychogony is actually arithmogony, Speusippus might have asserted that it was schemagony. Now, to prove that Xenocrates' self-moving number has nothing to do with figure, Cherniss (p. 399 n. 325) quotes Cicero, *Disputationes Tusculanae* (I 10, 20, fr. 67 Heinze): *Xenocrates animi figuram et quasi corpus negavit esse, verum numerum dixit esse.* Cherniss does not translate *"verum"*; but it seems obvious that it means "still", not "on the contrary", so that Xenocrates is made to say by Cicero: though the soul should not be described as a geometrical figure or solid (*quasi corpus* = geometrical body or volume, as differing from *corpus* = tangible body), *still* it is a number — i.e. we here have the difference between two branches of mathematics, with Xenocrates giving preference to arithmetic, whereas someone preferred geometry.

And it may very well be that with regard to the problem of making mathematicals (arithmeticals or geometricals) motive, the difference between Xenocrates and Speusippus can be brought down to this: according to the former the soul, i.e. a self-changing number, is *part* of the realm of mathematicals, according to the latter we should not make any of the mathematicals motive, but rather posit moved mathematicals = soul as a separate sphere of being, following the unmoved mathematicals rather than being part of them.

In short, the report of Iamblichus, according to which both Speusippus and Xenocrates identified the soul with a mathematical (whether they did it interpreting the *Timaeus* or professing their own doctrine is immaterial in the present context), is unobjectionable. And there is nothing in the *Timaeus* to rule out this identification as completely un-Platonic *.

We can now return to the problem of how the mathematical character of the soul (in other words, the soul being an idea as mathematical form) is related to the Aristotelian soul as εἶδος of a living body. Perhaps the following interpretation may be suggested. For Aristotle the soul becomes a form of the body (i.e. no longer a subsistent entity) within the same train of thought which led him to give up excessive realism in mathematics **. Mathematicals for Aristotle no longer subsist;

---

* There is no more reason to expect that the doctrines of the *Timaeus* concerning the soul should be compatible with the ones in the *Phaedrus*, than to do so with regard to the structure of the universe and its history as presented in the *Timaeus* on one hand and the *Politicus* on the other.

** On relics of Plato's treatment of mathematics ("*existenzableitende Mathematik*") in Aristotle cf. F. Solmsen, "Platos Einflusz auf die Bildung der mathematischen Methode", *Quellen und Studien zur Geschichte der griechischen Mathematik* ... Abt. B: Studien 1 (1931) 93–107; see on this problem also *idem, Die Entwicklung der aristotelischen Logik und Rhetorik* (1929), esp. 79–84; 101–103; 109–130; 144 f:, 223; 235–237; 250f. Solmsen's interpretation, particularly his analysis of the *Analytica Priora* and *Posteriora* has recently been criticized by W. D. Ross (*Aristotle's Prior and Posterior Analytics* [1949] 14–16). To the extent to which Ross' criticism refers to the problem of the chronological order within Aristotle's *Analytics* it does not concern us here. But what is of interest in the present context is Ross' assertion that "the doctrine of the *Posterior Analytics* is not the stupid doctrine which treats numbers, points, planes, solids as a chain of genera and species ..." (p. 16). Now, whether the relation of point to line, etc. can be stated precisely in terms of genus and species

and therefore the soul cannot subsist either, because soul and mathematicals coincide. Whether he was ready to accept the complete denial of the subsistence of the soul (i.e. the complete denial of its immortality and pre-existence) is a well-known matter for controversy. If the above suggestion is accepted, if the giving up of mathematical realism is another aspect of the same development which led him to give up what could be called psychical realism, we should expect a strong tendency to assume for the soul only the same kind of subsistence, pre-existence, and post-existence which Aristotle was ready to grant to mathematicals — whatever their subsistence might have meant to him. Jaeger boiled down the change in Aristotle's

in our customary sense of the word is certainly doubtful. But what matters is just this: number is prior to the point, point to the line, etc. — and in this, only in this sense of the word is what is prior at the same time more general (or universal). The line implies the point etc., not the other way round. It is perhaps a strange but hardly a stupid doctrine to say that you "derive" the line from the point by "adding" something — this process of addition resembling somewhat, but being completely different from the determination of a genus by a specific difference. And it is precisely this doctrine of "derivation" by "addition" that can be found in the *Analytics*. In *An. Post.* I 27, 87a31–37 Aristotle says: Among the reasons why one science is more exact than another is also this that one is ἐξ ἐλαττόνων, the other, less exact, ἐκ προσθέσεως. And he adds: λέγω δ' ἐκ προσθέσεως, οἷον μονὰς οὐσία ἄθετος στιγμὴ δὲ οὐσία θετός· ταύτην ἐκ προσθέσεως. On the whole problem cf. also A. Trendelenburg, *Logische Untersuchungen* 1 (1870), v. I, ch. VII, esp. 271–297.

In other words: monad plus position results in a line. This is precisely the Academic *Existenzableitung* in mathematics. It will ultimately lead to the derivation of physical bodies from solids. Because the point is less determined than the line, it is more real and precedes the line. It is only from our point of view that what is less determined than the concrete individual in space and time is the universal. To understand the method of *Existenzableitung*, however, we have to look at it from a completely different point of view. The more determined a thing is, the less real it is, the less determined, the more real. And if the point is less determined than the line and in this sense of the word more universal, it is obvious that universal, when used in this context, cannot mean what we term the universality of genera and species. Plotinus, *Enn.* VI 2, 3, 17–18 Bréhier; 10, 15–23 Bréhier; 35–43 Bréhier; 11, 41–45 Bréhier should be compared.

From an abstractionist point of view all this makes no sense. The geometrical point is "abstracted" not from the geometrical line, but from a physical "point". The line is not derived from the point, it is abstracted from a physical "line". And, of course, only physical points and lines are real, i.e. οὐσίαι, the mathematical points and lines are simply the results of abstraction. This abstractionist point of view is undoubtedly that of another Aristotle; but in the passage quoted above, Aristotle speaks as an Academic would and derives the line from the point etc., by a process different from the process by which a genus "becomes" a species and so on. Indeed, he even designates the monad and the point as οὐσίαι. On reading Ross' commentary a.l. one almost has the feeling that Ross is somewhat embarrassed by it. His explanation of why Aristotle here uses the term οὐσία is certainly weak enough.

The whole problem of "derivation" will become clearer in ch. VII. For the time being we limit ourselves to the assertion that Aristotle's *Analytics* contain relics of mathematical realism, just as Solmsen had asserted.

psychology to the formula: from the soul as εἶδός τι to the soul as εἶδος τινός (Aristoteles[2] [1955] 44). The same formula can be used to describe the change in the status of mathematicals — from realism to moderate realism. Objecting to Jaeger, Cherniss (op. cit. 508) turned attention to the fact that even in Met. M 2, 1077a32–33 the soul still is considered to be εἶδος and μορφή τις. However, first of all Cherniss overlooks that this assertion may be hypothetical (οἷον εἰ ἄρα ἡ ψυχὴ τοιοῦτον) *; but let it be supposed that Cherniss is right. This would only prove that Aristotle was somewhat dubious as to the relation between his former and his more recent conception of the soul — just as in Met. E 1, 1026a15 he is still somewhat dubious as to the entire status of mathematicals. All this, including the passage just quoted by Cherniss, once more proves how orthodox-Academic the equation soul = mathematicals is. Aristotle says in Met. M 2: Lines cannot subsist (or: be οὐσίαι) as forms, the way soul does (or, according to the above interpretation: the way the soul is supposed to do). The very fact of comparing lines with forms and souls shows how easily Aristotle switches in his thoughts from mathematicals to the soul. What we see happening in the Metaphysics, we see even better in De anima: in II 3,414b28 we find a detailed (and puzzling) comparison of the problems involved in the definition of the soul and in that of a geometrical figure. We could perhaps say: without this equation soul = mathematicals as a background, it would be hardly comprehensible why Aristotle elaborates the comparison between soul and geometrical figure in such detail.

A comparison of two Simplicius passages is also instructive.

He says on Xenocrates (In Arist. De an. 404b27, p. 30, 4 Hayduck and 408b32, p. 62, 2 Hayduck, fr. 64 Heinze):	And he says on Aristotle's Eudemus (In Arist. De an. 429a10, p. 221, 25 Hayduck, fr. 46 Rose, fr. 8 Walzer):
By his definition of the soul as self-moved number Xenocrates	[Stressing] the intermediacy of the soul between the undivided

Continued on page 51

---

* In F. Nuyens, L'Evolution de la Psychologie d'Aristote (1948) we find a curiously self-contradictory interpretation of this phrase. On p. 173 n. 76 he approves (quite correctly) of the translations of Tricot (comme l'âme, si bien l'âme est bien telle en effet) and Ross (as the soul perhaps is). But his own translation is (173): comme c'est sans doute bien le cas pour l'âme.

intended to point out its intermediacy between ideas and the
realm shaped by ideas (and its
ἴδιον).

and the divided and the fact
that the soul shows characters
of both the shape and the
shaped [ὅρος and ὁριζόμε-
νον] ... Aristotle defined the
soul as a form (εἶδός τι).

In other words, in his *Eudemus* Aristotle was according to
Simplicius very close to the mathematical interpretation of the
soul.

After the identification of the soul with the, or with a, mathematical was once made, there was no limit to combinations, some
of which could become extremely fanciful. Of course, it was
not easy to surpass the fancifulness of Plato's *Timaeus* and its
strange mixture of poetic metaphors and mathematical formulas,
culminating in a concept which cannot be grasped either by
imagination or by thought — a soul which is a circular strip
consisting of a mixture of being (essence), identity, and diversity,
this mixture being "marked" (whatever this may mean) according
to some ratios or intervals. But it was always possible to simplify
Plato's fancies, still preserving the main idea, viz. the identification of the soul with some specific geometrical *, or number,
or ratios. One such combination has been preserved in Sextus
Empiricus and Anatolius-Iamblichus.

Anatolius, περὶ δεκάδος, p. 32
Heiberg ∼ Iamblichus, *Theolo-
goumena arithmeticae* 23–24 ed.
V. de Falco (1922), p. 30, 2–15

Sextus   Empiricus,   *Adv.
math.* IV 5–8 ∼ VII 95–100

Οὐ μόνον δὲ τὸν τοῦ σώματος
ἐπέχει λόγον τετράς, ἀλλὰ καὶ
τὸν τῆς ψυχῆς· ὡς γὰρ τὸν ὅλον
κόσμον φασὶ κατὰ ἁρμονίαν διοικεῖσθαι, οὕτω καὶ τὸ ζῷον ψυχοῦσθαι. δοκεῖ δὲ καὶ τελεία
ἁρμονία ἐν τρισὶ συμφωνίαις
ὑφεστάναι ... [i.e. the fourth,

ὥστε ἐν τῷ 'τετάρτῳ' ἀριθμῷ
τὸν τοῦ σώματος περιέχεσθαι
λόγον· καὶ μὴν καὶ τὸν τῆς
ψυχῆς· ὡς γὰρ τὸν ὅλον κόσμον
κατὰ ἁρμονίαν λέγουσι διοικεῖσθαι
οὕτω καὶ τὸ ζῷον ψυχοῦσθαι.
δοκεῖ δέ ἡ τέλειος ἁρμονία ἐν
τρισὶ συμφωνίαις λαμβάνειν τὴν

Continued on page 52

---

* Cf. Lydus, *De mensibus* II 9: the soul is a rectangle, a circle, a sphere.

the fifth, and the octave] ...
ὄντων δὲ ἀριθμῶν τεσσάρων τῶν
πρώτων ... ἐν τούτοις καὶ ἡ τῆς
ψυχῆς ἰδέα περιέχεται κατὰ τὸν
ἐναρμόνιον λόγον ... εἰ δὲ ἐν τῷ
δ' ἀριθμῷ τὸ πᾶν κεῖται ἐκ ψυχῆς
καὶ σώματος, ἀληθὲς ἄρα καί, ὅτι
αἱ συμφωνίαι πᾶσαι κατ' αὐτὸν
τελοῦνται.

ὑπόστασιν ... ἀλλὰ γὰρ τούτων
οὕτως ἐχόντων, καὶ κατὰ τὴν
ἀρχῆθεν ὑπόθεσιν τεσσάρων ὄντων
ἀριθμῶν ... ἐν οἷς ἐλέγομεν καὶ
τὴν τῆς ψυχῆς ἰδέαν περιέχεσθαι
κατὰ τὸν ἐναρμόνιον λόγον ...

Both passages try to explain why the number four "corresponds to" or "contains the formula of" both the body and the soul. As far as the body is concerned, the reason is obvious: the pyramid is the first body and the pyramid corresponds to the number four, because four points are necessary and sufficient to form this kind of solid (cf. Iamblichus, *ibid.*, 18, p. 22, 10 Falco; 62, p. 84, 11 Falco; Sextus, *ibid.*). Somewhat more complicated is the proof that the four corresponds also to the soul. First, Sextus and Iamblichus equate the harmony which governs the universe with the soul of the living being — in other words, they assert that the soul is essentially harmony. Secondly, they explain that perfect harmony contains three intervals, the fourth, the fifth, and the octave. But these three intervals are based on the ratios $3/4$, $2/3$, and $1/2$, i.e., on ratios formed by numbers all of which are contained in the number four. Thus the four contains the fundamental intervals and is in this sense of the word perfect harmony; but the same, i.e. being perfect harmony, is true of the soul too. Therefore, the four "corresponds to" both body and soul.

All this can be expressed in the condensed form: the four "is" pyramid in the realm of the extended, it "is" soul in the realm of the non-extended. Still simpler: 4 = pyramid = soul. If we read this equation backwards, we see immediately that it amounts to the identification of the soul with an arithmetical (the four), a geometrical (the pyramid), and at the same time is based on the assumption that it is "composed" of three specific harmonies (intervals).

What is the source of Sextus and Anatolius-Iamblichus? In his investigations concerning mainly Iamblichus V. de Falco ("Sui Theologoumena Arithmeticae", and "Sui trattati aritmologici di Nicomaco ed Anatolio", *Rivista Indo-Greca-Italica* 6 [1922] 51–60 and 49–61) suggested that this source might have been among others Posidonius who in his commentary on Plato's *Timaeus* commented on the number four. Now, whether it was in a formal commentary or simply in some comments on Plato's *Timaeus*, de Falco seems to have well established his thesis that Posidonius commented on the four in such a way as to make it correspond to a pyramid and the soul at the same time; this would jibe perfectly with his definition of the soul as quoted by Plutarch (above p. 36). But perhaps it is again possible to go one more step back *. In the well known quotation from Speusippus (*Theologoumena arithmeticae* 61–63, p. 82, 10–85, 23 Falco) Iamblichus reports that in his little book on Pythagorean numbers Speusippus in the first half of it devoted some space to a consideration of the five regular solids. It is almost impossible to imagine that in this consideration the equation four = pyramid did not occur, just as it occurs in the second half of his book (p. 84, 11 Falco). Perhaps it is not too risky to assume that it also contained the equation pyramid = soul or at least some words making it easy for an imitator to proceed to this equation. Perhaps it contained the definition (fr. 40 Lang) soul = "idea" of the all-extended, quoted by Iamblichus. It could very well have been among the sources of Posidonius or at least have inspired him and others to identify the soul with some mathematical. The equation soul = pyramid sounds very crude, but so does the whole discussion concerning the number ten, preserved for us by Iamblichus in the form of a literal quotation from Speusippus (fr. 4 Lang).

In any case and whatever the ultimate source, the equation soul = the three fundamental harmonies = pyramid = number four, as found in Sextus Empiricus and Anatolius-Iamblichus, is another characteristic example of the attempts to identify the soul with three branches of mathematics.

---

* Or two steps, if we accept the theory of F. E. Robbins, "Posidonius and the Sources of Pythagorean Arithmology", *Classical Philology* 15 (1920) 309–322 and *idem*, "The Tradition of Greek Arithmology", *ibid.*, 16 (1921) 97–123, esp. 123 (cf. K. Staehle, *Die Zahlenmystik bei Philon von Alexandreia* [1931] 15) according to which there is behind Posidonius some arithmological treatise composed in the 2nd century.

For modern thinking, the identification of soul and mathematicals probably sounds somewhat fantastic *. But perhaps
it can be explained in rather simple terms. When we speak of
soul (or intelligence, νοῦς, etc.), semiconsciously we take the
word to designate something subjective — consciousness, etc. —
as opposed to the objects of consciousness. But this is not the
only possible point of view **. Reasonableness and reason may
very well be interpreted as two *aspects* of one and the same
reality (whether or not we are going to use the term Absolute,
Absolute Identity, etc. for it) — reasonableness as reason in
its self-alienation and reason as reason having become conscious
of itself. Indeed, can it be denied that in *some* sense of the word,
reason *is* what it thinks, or that the objects are what they are
thought to be? If we assume that the universe has a reasonable
structure, we can express this conviction by saying that it has
a soul, intelligence, etc. Now, the best proof that the universe
has a reasonable structure is that it is amenable to mathematical
calculation ***.

In other words, it seems to be helpful to approach Greek
philosophy by way of Schelling, or even, to a certain extent,
Kant. The latter turned our attention to the problem of applicability of mathematics to reality ****. To be sure, he explained
it in terms of his theory of the *a priori* and formal element of our
knowledge and of his Copernican turn, certainly a most un-Greek
explanation. But this is precisely the point where Schelling
(and, in his Schellingian phase, Hegel) stepped in: reason is
applicable to the universe because the universe is (objectively)
reasonable. When Plato says that the world-soul *causes* by her
thinking the reasonable motions of the universe, this is tanta-

---

Cf. also A. Delatte, *Etudes sur la littérature pythagoricienne* (1915), esp. 206–208 and
idem, "Les doctrines pythagoriciennes des livres de Numa", *Bull. de l'Académie R. de
Belgique (Lettres)* 22 (1936) 19–40, tracing back the revival of Pythagorism to the
beginning of the 2nd century B.C.
* See e.g. W. D. Ross, *Plato's Theory of Ideas* (1951) 213.
** Cf. H. Heimsoeth, *Die sechs groszen Themen der abendlaendischen Metaphysik*[3]
(1954) 90–130, esp. 92f.; 118; E. Bickel, "Inlocalitas", p. 9 ,in: *Immanuel Kant.
Festschrift zur zweiten Jahrhundertfeier seines Geburtstages. Hg. von der Albertus-
Universitaet in Koenigsberg i. Pr.* (1924).
*** Cf. C. F. von Weizsaecker, *The History of Nature* (1949) 20.
**** The extent to which this problem still is with us can be seen e.g. in V. Kraft,
Mathematik, Logik und Erfahrung (1947). Cf. also O. Becker, "Mathematische
Existenz", *Jahrbuch fuer Philosophie und phaenomenologische Forschung* 8 (1927)
439–809, esp. 764–768; M. Steck, *Grundgebiete der Mathematik* (1946) 78–95.

mount to the assertion that there *are* reasonable motions in the universe, which can be known *.

Thus, it may be appropriate to conclude this chapter by a quotation from Schelling's *Ueber das Verhaeltnis der bildenden Kuenste zur Natur* (1807):

For intelligence (*Verstand*) could not make its object what contains no intelligence. What is bare of knowledge could not be known either. To be sure, the system of knowledge (*Wissenschaft*) by virtue of which nature works, is unlike that of man, which is conscious of itself (*mit der Reflexion ihrer selbst verknuepft*). In the former thought (*Begriff*) does not differ from action, nor intent from execution (*Saemtliche Werke*, 1. Abt., v. VII [1860] 299).

Appendix

1. The most recent presentation of Posidonius is that of K. Reinhardt in *RE* XXII/1 (1953). Here on the passage in question (Posidonius in Plutarch) see p. 791 (cf. M. Pohlenz, *Die Stoa*, vol. II [2nd ed., 1955], p. 215). To reconcile this passage with their interpretation of Posidonius both Pohlenz and Reinhardt must assume that the passage is strictly interpretative and does not imply that Posidonius shared the views which he credited Plato with.

2. For accepting the testimony of Iamblichus in preference

---

* Cf. e.g. E. Hoffmann, "Platonismus und Mittelalter", *Vortraege der Bibliothek Warburg 1923–1924* (1926) 17–82, esp. 54 f. (but see also 72–74). Also J. Moreau, *L'Ame du monde de Platon aux Stoiciens* (1939) should be compared. However, Moreau insists on the non-realistic interpretation of both the soul and mathematicals (50–53) and, in his *La Construction de l'Idéalisme platonicien* (1939), on not separating mathematicals from ideas as a separate sphere of being (343–355). J. Stenzel, *Metaphysik des Altertums* (in: *Handbuch der Philosophie* I [1931]) 145 and 157 uses the formula "metaphysical equivalence" to describe Plato's system. This is hardly anything else but Schelling's principle of identity — the Absolute precedes both being and consciousness. Cf. also N. Hartmann, "Das Problem des Apriorismus in der Platonischen Philosophie", *SB der Berl. Ak.* 1935, 223–260, esp. 250–258 = *Kleinere Schriften*, v. II (1957) 48–85, esp. 74–83. In R. G. Bury, *The Philebus of Plato* (1897) we find Platonism interpreted as Schellingian pantheism (LXXVI f.); and a similar interpretation is that in R. D. Archer-Hind, *The Timaeus of Plato* (1888) 28 — however his interpretation of the particular as "the symbolical presentation of the idea to the limited intelligence under the conditions of space and time," (*ibid.*, p. 35) is unduly subjectivistic.

(or, as I should chose to say, in addition) to that of Aristotle and thus assuming that Speusippus (sometimes at least) identified the soul with a mathematical (geometrical) I was more than once criticized *. Unfortunately my critics limit themselves simply to the statement that Aristotle is more trustworthy than Iamblichus. One wonders how they arrived at this conclusion. One wonders specifically whether they ever read the whole passage in which it appears or limited themselves to reflecting on just this one fragment. As the whole passage has now been translated and provided with an extensive commentary ** it is, I think, easy to see that as a historian of philosophy Iamblichus is not given to reading his own ideas into authors whose doctrines he simply set out to present. On the contrary, Iamblichus here makes the impression of a reporter, completely neutral with regard to the authors whom he quotes. Why, precisely, should we distrust him when he contradicts (or seems to contradict) Aristotle?

Besides, I did not evade the problem of reconciling the report of Aristotle (certainly never a neutral reporter he) with that of Iamblichus. Shouldn't my critics, instead of flatly rejecting the testimony of Iamblichus, try to explain why he should have committed the error they charge him with?

3. Perhaps some semi-systematic reflections will be considered pertinent.

To most modern readers the assertion that the soul is (or resembles) a geometrical will sound unintelligible. But if a modern philosopher should say that the geometrical structure of the crystal is its soul, we may dissent, we may find his assertion fantastic, but would we say that we don't 'understand' what he means? I don't think so.

And our attitude (if we so like, understanding in the same way in which a psychiatrist understands his patient) would hardly change if the philosopher now continued and said that the universe should be interpreted as a giant crystal.

If we now instead of the crystal as a *product*, think of the *process* of crystallization, it is easy to understand that the geo-

---

* Esp. by G. de Santillana, *Isis* 40 (1957) 360–362 and G. B. Kerferd, *The Classical Review* 69 (1955) 58–60.
** [A.-J.] Festugière, *La Révélation d'Hermès Trismégiste*. III. *Les Doctrines de l'âme* (1953) 177–264, esp. 179–182.

metrical structure of the crystal could be thought of as motive rather than as a result brought about by the process.

Now, it is well known that in the 20th century attempts were made to explain biological processes in terms of what could be called a motive form and which the author of such an explanation, Driesch, called an entelechy.

Considering all this, the definition of the soul as form of the all-extended (the three-dimensional, space) should loose much of its strangeness. Moreover, its close relation to Aristotle's classic definition of the soul as entelechy of a living body should become obvious.

BIBLIOGRAPHICAL NOTE

The two passages in Plutarch (on Xenocrates and Posidonius) and Speusippus' definition of the soul have very frequently been discussed. Here are some items:
A. Boeckh, *Ueber die Bildung der Weltseele im Timaeos des Platon* (1807) repr. in: *Gesammelte kleine Schriften*, v. III (1866) 109–180, esp. 131 f; Th. Henri Martin, *Etudes sur le Timée de Platon*, 2 vv. (1841), v. I 375–378; A. Schmekel, *Die Philosophie der mittleren Stoa* (1892) 426 f.; 430–432; R. M. Jones, *The Platonism of Plutarch* (1916) 68–80, esp. 73 n. 12; 90–94 — his own paraphrase of ἡ τῶν περάτων οὐσία is "the basis of the material world", with a refutation (93 f.) of G. Altmann, *De Posidonio Platonis commentatore* (1906), who interpreted it as *geometricae formae*; L. Robin, *Etudes sur la Signification et la Place de la physique dans la philosophie de Platon* (1919), repr. in *La Pensée hellénique* (1942) 231–366, 52–54; R. M. Jones, "The Ideas as the Thoughts of God", *Classical Philology* 21 (1926) 317–326, esp. 319; A. E. Taylor, *A Commentary on Plato's Timaeus* (1928) 106–136, equating ἡ τῶν περάτων οὐσία with extension; P. Merlan, "Beitraege zur Geschichte des antiken Platonismus. II. Poseidonios ueber die Weltseele in Platons Timaios", *Philologus* 89 (1934) 197–214; H. R. Schwyzer "Zu Plotins Interpretation von Platons Tim. 35A", *Rheinisches Museum* 84 (1935) 360–368, equating after Posidonius ἡ τῶν περάτων οὐσία with μεριστὴ οὐσία (363); J. Helmer, *Zu Plutarchs "De animae procreatione in Timaeo"* (1937) 15–18; L. Edelstein, "The Philosophical System of Posidonius", *American Journal of Philology* 57 (1936) 286–325, esp. 302–304; P. Thévenaz, *L'Ame du monde, le Devenir et la Matière chez Plutarque* (1938) 63–67, with a polemic against my equation ὕλη = μεριστόν = πέρατα = τὸ πάντη διαστατόν on p. 65; K. Praechter, art. Severus 47 in *RE* II A 2 (1923).

Of the more recent literature on Posidonius only W. Jaeger, *Nemesios von Emesa* (1915) need to be mentioned in the present context. For everything else see K. Reinhardt, art. Poseidonios in *RE* XXII/1 (1953).

For discussions concerning the status of mathematicals in Plato's philosophy see particularly L. Robin, *La Théorie platonicienne des Idées et des Nombres d'après Aristote* (1908) 479–498; J. Moreau, *La*

Construction de l'Idéalisme Platonicien (1939), esp. 343–366 (according to him they differ by their mode, not by their essence and they are inconceivable unless thought); *idem, L'Ame du Monde de Platon aux Stoiciens* (1939), esp. 43–53; F. Solmsen, *Die Entwicklung der aristotelischen Logik und Rhetorik* (1929) 79–84; 101–103; 237; 250; E. Frank, "The Fundamental Opposition of Plato and Aristotle", *American Journal of Philology* 61 (1940) 34–53; 166–185, esp. 48–51.

In many respects my identification of Plato's world-soul with the mathematicals is a return to F. Ueberweg, "Ueber die Platonische Weltseele", *Rheinisches Museum* 9 (1854) 37–84, esp. 56; 74; 77 f. Cf. also J. Moreau , *Réalisme et idéalisme chez Platon* (1951) with the criticisms by H. D. Saffrey in *Revue des Sciences Théologiques et Philosophiques* 35 (1951) 666 f.

III. THE SUBDIVISIONS OF THEORETICAL PHILOSOPHY

There is still another interesting aspect connected with the realistic treatment of mathematicals by Iamblichus and Proclus. We mentioned several times that they both accepted a tripartition of being. We noticed that Iamblichus connected with this tripartition of being a tripartition of philosophy into theology, mathematics, and physics (cf. above p. 11). We know that these two tripartitions are "Aristotelian", i.e. that they can be found in Aristotle's *Metaphysics* and *Physics*. The tripartition of being is, as a rule, reported by Aristotle as Platonic (*Met*. A 6, 987b14–16; 28–29; Z 2,1028b19–21; K 1,1059b6–8; but see also *Met*. K 1, 1059a38–1059b2; *Phys*. III 5,204a35–204b2 with Ross' note a.l.); the tripartition of theoretical philosophy he professes as his own doctrine.

Now it is obvious that this tripartition of philosophy fits the preserved writings of Aristotle very badly, as was stressed e.g. by Zeller (II/2⁴ [1921] 179–181). It is strange that it should so often be overlooked that it has its roots in what Aristotle reports to have been Plato's tripartition of being (see P. Merlan, "Aristotle's Unmoved Movers", *Traditio* 4 [1946] 1–30, esp. 3–6), and A. Mansion (*Introduction à la Physique Aristotélicienne*² [1945] 122–195) summed up the situation by saying that the tripartition of theoretical philosophy into physics, mathematics, and theology makes sense only within the framework of Platonism, while it makes hardly any sense in the non-Platonic phase of Aristotle's philosophy *. In what follows some details will be added to his interpretation.

First of all, let us establish the connection between the Aristotelian and the Platonic tripartition.

The two classic passages on the tripartition of speculative knowledge into theology, mathematics, and physics are in *Met*. E 1,1026a6–19 and K 7,1064b1–3 (together with *Phys*. II 2,193b22–36; 194b14; cf. *Nic. Eth*. VI 9, 1142a17–18).

It is easy to guess that this tripartition is the outgrowth of

---

* Cf. also E. W. Strong, *Procedures and Metaphysics* (1936) 288 n. 38. The whole book is very important for the topic of the present investigation in that it shows the survival of this tripartition down to the 18th century.

what Aristotle reports so often to have been Plato's tripartition of being (οὐσία) into ideas (intelligibles), mathematicals, and sensibles. But it is not even necessary to guess; *Met.* Γ 2, 1004a2 provides the connecting link. There are as many parts of speculative philosophy as there are spheres of being (οὐσίαι), says Aristotle. In this one sentence we have Plato and Aristotle combined.

Thus, the tripartition of speculative philosophy corresponds to three spheres of being, one of which are mathematicals interpreted realistically. But Aristotle finally gave up this interpretation. He did so with some hesitation; the words "unclear" and "perhaps" in *Met.* E 1,1026a9 and 15 express this hesitation. *Met.* K 7,1064a33 denies subsistence to mathematicals without hesitation (perhaps only because it is shorter and has less time for niceties). And other parts of the *Metaphysics* are very outspoken in the non-realistic interpretation of mathematicals. Inasmuch as the hesitation seems to have started early it is not surprising to find in Aristotle passages proving that he himself had misgivings about the tripartition which accorded mathematics a place between physics and theology. Thus in *Met.* Z 11, 1037a14 mathematics seems to be either forgotten or displaced from its position between physics and theology; and in E 1, 1026a19 instead of the order physics — mathematics — theology we find mathematics — physics — theology (see below, p. 76).

Even more interesting is another unique passage. In *Phys.* II 7, 198a29–31 the three realms of being are described as the theological, the astronomical, and the physical. The theologicals are imperishable and changeless, the astronomicals imperishable and changeable, the physicals perishable and changing. This tripartition is obviously much more in tune with Aristotle's non-realistic interpretation of mathematicals and recommended particularly by his tripartition expressed in *Met.* Λ 1, 1069a30; 6,1071b3. Here the three realms of being are described as that of the imperishable and unmoved; of the imperishable in motion; and of the perishable in motion, implying a division of philosophy into theology, astronomy, and physics.

It is remarkable how Alexander Aphrodisias faces the text in *Met.* Γ 2,1004a2 (*In Metaph.* p. 250 f. Hayduck) so clearly establishing the link between Plato and Aristotle and so clearly Platonic in character. On reading him one almost feels that the text is extremely unpleasant to him. He dodges the question as to what the different οὐσίαι and, therefore, the parts of philosophy, are. In the end he suggests that one of these οὐσίαι could be imperishable but movable; that is, he draws from the unique passage in *Physics*, quoted above and implying that astronomy rather than mathematics would be the intermediate branch of theoretical philosophy. Indeed, we can not blame, but should praise, Alexander for his sensitiveness. Where he can eliminate mathematics as a full-fledged branch of theoretical philosophy from Aristotle's system, he does it *.

On the other hand, it is sufficient to read St. Thomas' discussion concerning the unmoved character of mathematicals in his commentary on Boethius *De Trin.* 2 (*q.* 5, *art.* 3, *ad octavum*) to see how puzzled he was by the very passage in *Physics*, used by Alexander to interpret the passage in *Metaphysics*. To extricate himself from the difficulty he follows the lead of Avicenna. He separates astronomy from arithmetic and geometry and makes it one of the intermediate sciences between mathematics and physics (*q.* 5, *art.* 3, *ad quintum*); furthermore he asserts, after Averroes, that the tripartition in *Physics* refers exclusively to things and not at all to knowledge (*ibid.*, *ad octavum*; cf. *In II Phys.*, *lect.* *II*). This device makes it possible to designate the objects of mathematics as either unmoved or moved and to make the two tripartitions appear to be consistent. More will soon be said on this topic. For the time being it is sufficient to observe that Alexander Aphrodisias tried to preserve the Aristotelian (i.e. moderately realistic) character of Aristotle's tripartition of theoretical philosophy by giving preference to the *Physics* passage, obviously because he felt that the tripartition in *Metaphysics* was Platonic (excessively realistic with regard to mathematicals). St. Thomas, as shall presently be seen, reinterpreted the tripartition in *Metaphysics* so as to deprive it completely of its Platonic character; he therefore did not have to interpret it in the light of the *Physics* passage **.

---

* See also the tripartition in Rabbi Gershon Ben Shlomoh d'Arles, *The Gate of Heaven* (tr. and ed. by F. S. Bodenheimer), Jerusalem, 1953, p. 86 f.; but cf. H. A. Wolfson, "The Classification of Science in Medieval Jewish Philosophy", *Hebrew Union College Jubilee Volume* (1925) 263–315, esp. 283.

** Cf. H. A. Wolfson, *ibid.* partic. on Avicenna, p. 299 f.; *idem*, "Additional Notes",

Aristotle himself in the end denied the subsistence of mathematicals, but obviously through some kind of inertia kept the
three branches of knowledge (cf. W. Jaeger, *Aristoteles* ²[1955]
225), whether or not he attempted to replace this tripartition by
another more consistent with his own philosophic system.
The wisdom of this conservatism may be doubted. With the
correspondence of the three spheres of philosophy to the three
spheres of being gone, there was no reason to keep mathematics
as a branch of knowledge between theology and physics. As
a result, even in Aristotle himself the tripartition is inconsistent
within itself. We are going to discuss the two passages exhibiting
this inconsistency.

The first is *Met.* E 1,1026a11–16. Physics, says Aristotle,
deals with objects which are ἀχώριστα (on this term see below)
and in motion; mathematics with objects which are unmoved
but not subsistent (χωριστά) though mathematics considers them
as subsistent; theology (first philosophy) with objects that
subsist (χωριστά) and are unmoved. It is quite obvious that
this tripartition is false, because it is based on two principles:
ratio essendi and *ratio cognoscendi*. Physicals and theologicals
differ from each other by their modus of existence, the former
being moved, the latter being unmoved (on the meaning of the
difference between ἀχώριστα and χωριστά see below). But mathematicals differ from physicals not by any particular modus of
existence; in fact, they have no existence of their own. They
differ from them only *formaliter*, to use the scholastic term,
i.e. by the way they are being considered. This way is often
described by Aristotle as the way ἐξ ἀφαιρέσεως, which usually
is being translated by "abstraction". In other words, what we
have before us is not a true tripartition. It is rather a dichotomy,
with one of the members subdivided. The dichotomy is "moved-
unmoved"; the member "moved" is subdivided. Physicals
are moved and are being considered as moved; mathematicals
are moved but are being considered as unmoved.
    All commentators or followers of Aristotle who on one hand

---

Hebrew Union College Annual 3 (1926) 371–375, esp. 374. On intermediate sciences
in Aristotle see e.g. W. D. Ross, *Aristotle's Prior and Posterior Analytics* (1949)
63; A. Mansion, *Introduction à la Physique Aristotélicienne*² (1945) 186–195.

accepted his tripartition, on the other hand his moderate realism, find themselves involved in the same difficulty.

But in addition to being a hybrid of moderate realism and of excessive realism the passage contains one more flaw. The physicals are described in it as ἀχώριστα (1026a14). This is quite obviously a mistake. They should be described as χωριστά. Strangely enough, nobody noticed it before A. Schwegler (*Die Metaphysik des Aristoteles*, v. IV [1848] 14–16). True, once it was done, Schwegler's emendation was almost unanimously accepted by all scholars (see e.g. Ross, *Arist. Met.* a.l.; H. Cherniss, *Aristotle's Criticism of Plato and the Academy*, v. I [1944] 368 f.; and W. Jaeger, *Aristoteles*[2] [1955] 225 with n.l). What Aristotle really intended to say was: physicals subsist, but they are moved; mathematicals are at least being considered as unmoved, but they do not subsist; theologicals alone subsist and are unmoved. This would still be a faulty tripartition, as noticed above, but it would at least be a clear one. But almost as if one fault had to engender another, the word χωριστόν was replaced by ἀχώριστον — as Jaeger explained, by a reader who took χωριστόν to mean "immaterial" (which physicals, of course, are not), and made the change to ἀχώριστα in his copy from which it found its way in all our manuscripts. Perhaps it would be simpler to assume with D. R. Cousin, "A Note on the Text of Metaphysics 1026a14", *Mind* 49 (1940) 495–496 that it was a mistake of Aristotle himself, but this is immaterial in our context. Whatever the reason — the net result is an utterly confused passage.

However, the assertion that Aristotle's tripartition is ultimately Platonic must still be defended against a possible objection. Physics, in Aristotle, is the *science* of the sensible; but can there be a *science* of the sensible for a Platonist? Indeed, P. Duhem (*Le Système du monde*, v. I [1913] 134–150) asserted that the introduction of physics as a branch of knowledge analogous to mathematics or theology is a complete reversal of Plato's views by Aristotle. But to agree with Duhem's assertion we should have to assume that neither the discussion in the *Phaedo* 96 A ff. nor the whole *Timaeus* (including its physiology) is part of wisdom according to Plato or that Plato would have denied that the subject matter treated by him in these works is the realm of the sensible *. Plato rejects the current theories, by which the realm of the sensible is explained; he introduces a new one, based on the theory of ideas, philosophy of numbers, and teleological considerations; he certainly would stress that physics is not the supreme branch of wisdom. It cannot be denied, however, that physics has a place in Plato's theoretical philosophy, though perhaps it did not have it there from the very beginning of Plato's activity. The extent to which Plato was ready to reconsider his early evaluation of the world of flux, can best be seen from the passage in *Timaeus* 46 E–47 E, with its eulogy of sensation, which makes possible astronomy and music theory. The trend towards physics as a science inherent in Plato's philosophy, together with the corresponding trend to bridge the χωρισμός between ideas and the realm of the sensible, is strong even in Plato's dialogues and was probably even stronger in the Academy and its oral discussions **.

We have submitted Aristotle's tripartition to severe criticism. Is there no way to defend it at least to a certain degree? Indeed there is. Let us assume that what Aristotle actually meant to say was this. First philosophy is a theoretical science; I admit that both physics and mathematics are theoretical sciences so that they could claim the title of first philosophy; however, I must deny the validity of their claim. In other words, Aristotle did not mean to put forward a tripartition of theoretical science — rather he found and used it as a starting point for his dis-

---

* On the presence of ordinary scientific theory in the *Phaedo* myth see P. Fried-laender, *Plato*, v. I (1958) 262–277; also C. Mugler, *Platon et la recherche mathématique de son époque* (1948) 273–283. Particularly interesting is the "rehabilitation" of Plato's physics by Lautman. See esp. A. Lautman, *Symétrie et dissymétrie* and *Le problème du temps* (1946), esp. 11 and 22–24; *Bulletin de la Société française de Philosophie* 1946, 1–39 (*La Pensée mathématique*). Cf. below p. 201. We must not forget the introduction of the term ἐπιστημονικὴ αἴσθησις by Speusippus (on this concept see also A. J. Neubecker, *Die Bewertung der Musik bei Stoikern und Epikureern* [1956] 13–15) nor the passages in Plato leading up to it; cf. J. Stenzel, *Studien zur Entwicklung der Platonischen Dialektik von Sokrates zu Aristoteles* (1931), Index s.v. *doxa*, in spite of H. Cherniss, *Aristotle's Criticism of Plato and the Academy*, v. I (1944) 475; cf. also E. Hoffmann, *Platon* (1950) 144 f. For Plato's attitude toward natural science see also P. Shorey, "Platonism and the History of Science", *American Philosophical Society, Proceedings* 66 (1927) 159–182.

** In addition to J. Stenzel, *Studien zur Entwicklung der platonischen Dialektik* (1931) 54–122; *idem, Zahl und Gestalt²* (1933), esp. 119; 123–125, also A. Rey, *La Maturité de la Pensée scientifique en Grèce* (1939) 272–296 and F. Solmsen, *Plato's Theology* (1942) 75–97 are examples of contemporary interest in this problem. Cf. also C. J. de Vogel, "Examen critique de l'interprétation traditionelle du Platonisme", *Revue de Métaphysique et de Morale* 56 (1951) 249–268, esp. 255.

cussion of the essence of metaphysics, but never thought seriously of making it part of his own doctrines. "There are three theoretical sciences" for him means, then: "there are three theoretical sciences in existence" and it does not mean "there are three theoretical sciences *in rerum natura*".

But this defense is less an interpretation of what Aristotle actually said than an assertion that he should have said it. Aristotle introduces the tripartition in his own name. Therefore, we have still to discuss other interpretations which would amount to a defense of what Aristotle actually said.

The best seems to be this. The tripartition, as Aristotle found it, was based on the material distinction (to use a scholastic term) between the objects of physics, mathematics, and metaphysics. But Aristotle turned it (or at least was on the verge of turning it) into a tripartition based on the formal distinction: metaphysics, physics, and mathematics have the same material object (reality in its totality) but approach it from a different point of view. More specifically, the tripartition is based on grades of abstraction. Physics abstracts from what St. Thomas called *materia signata* (*individualis*) *sensibilis*, its object being not this stone now, but the stone. Mathematics abstracts from the *materia communis* (*sensibilis*), leaving only the *materia intelligibilis* to its objects. Metaphysics abstracts from all matter, even *materia intelligibilis*.

This interpretation of the Aristotelian tripartition is frequently called Thomistic. In what follows we are going to prove three things. First, the interpretation is historically incorrect. Second, it would be an entirely unsatisfactory interpretation of metaphysics. Thirdly, it is not St. Thomas' interpretation.

First. It is true that Aristotle said that science (ἐπιστήμη) is always of what is general (καθόλου) while sensation is of the individual (e.g. *Anal. Post.* I 31, 87b28–39; but cf. also *ibid.* II 19, 100a17 and *Met.* M 10, 1087a18–25) *. But there is nothing in his writings to indicate that this difference between sensation and knowledge was applied by him to explain the difference between physical knowledge and sensation. There

* Cf. e.g. Zeller II/2⁴ (1921) 198 f., esp. n. 6; 309 f.; H. Cherniss, *Aristotle's Criticism of Plato and the Academy*, v. I (1944) 236–239; 338–351; most succinctly G. R. G. Mure, *Aristotle* (1932) 186–189.

is no hint in Aristotle that the transition from the latter to the former takes place on the basis of the process of abstraction. If we assume that our term abstraction corresponds to Aristotle's term ἀφαίρεσις (we shall deal with this problem later) we must say that Aristotle has never said that we reach objects of physics by ἀφαίρεσις from the objects of sensation. There is further no hint in Aristotle to indicate that he thought of the objects of physics as being in any sense ἐξ ἀφαιρέσεως, while he repeated this of the objects of mathematics time and again (see e.g. *De an.* I 1, 403a10–15). It can with certainty be said that Aristotle has never asked himself how to combine his tripartition of theoretical philosophy with his interpretation of the difference between sensation and science. His assertion that objects of mathematics exist only as objects of abstraction, Aristotle defends against Platonists (and/or Pythagoreans) who asserted their subsistence. It should be perfectly obvious that if Aristotle ever meant to deny the full subsistence of physicals, he would have said so supporting it at least with as many arguments as he produced to prove the non-subsistence of mathematicals. But the idea that only objects of sensation fully subsist while objects of physics exist only ἐξ ἀφαιρέσεως is not present in Aristotle.

What does Aristotle imply when he says that science is never of the individual? In the two passages quoted above in which Aristotle deals with this question *ex professo*, the implication is that sensation informs us of the ὅτι only, while it is only through science that we learn the διότι. This means that science tells us that this specific phenomenon is a case falling under a general rule (law) — in this sense of the word science deals with a καθόλου. But Aristotle does not say that the καθόλου of any science is the object of anything like an abstracting intuition. What the mathematician sees are objects only ἐξ ἀφαιρέσεως. But he "sees" them and they become the terms of mathematical propositions. However, the catholicity of physical science is not based on the intuition of a "general", "universal" object; it is based on the subsumption of the specific case under a "general", "universal" rule. This stone now falls according to a rule valid for all individual stones at all times, not for an abstract stone which the physicist "sees" by abstracting it from the individual stone. In modern terms: Aristotle assumed abstractive intuition as the presupposition of mathematics, but he never thought of abstractive intuition in physics. A passage like *De caelo* III 7,306a17 seems to indicate that the subject matter of physics simply coincides with the objects of sensation. A passage like *Nic. Eth.* VI 9, 1142a17–21 clearly proves that, at least sometimes, Aristotle considered ἀφαίρεσις as the method of mathematical knowledge alone, opposing it to the knowledge of both physics and theology, as these were based on experience *. And in *De part. anim.* I 1, 641b10 we find the flat assertion that physics does not deal with anything ἐξ ἀφαιρέσεως. All this sums up to the clear insight that it would be entirely un-Aristotelian to assume that for him objects of physics exist *only* (this "only" is the crucial point between him and the Academy regarding the mathematicals) as objects of abstraction.

The only passage which could be interpreted as containing the assertion that physics uses the method of abstraction is *Phys.* II 2, 193b35. The Platonists separate (χωρίζουσι), says Aristotle, physicals, though they are *less* separable than mathematicals. Here Aristotle seems to state by implication that physicals, too, are objects of abstraction (if we assume χωρίζειν to be here the equivalent of "to abstract"). But the context proves that what Aristotle says is: in speaking of ideas of sensible things the Platonists overlook that they speak of them as if they, i.e. the ideas of sensible things (not any objects of physics), could exist separately, though they cannot — even less than mathematicals can exist separately from sensibles.

Secondly. Even if we suppose that it is admissible to designate the physical objects as existing (only) ἐξ ἀφαιρέσεως, this would still be insufficient to make the Aristotelian tripartition consistent. Physics and mathematics would indeed differ from sensation in using the method of abstraction to avail themselves of their objects, these objects thus having no subsistence. But what would become of metaphysics? Unless we deny that

---

* Cf. other passages mentioned in L. M. Régis, "La philosophie de la nature", *Etudes et Recherches* ... I. Philosophie. Cahier 1 (1936) 127–158, esp. 130 n.l. But it must be admitted that there is also an opposite tendency in Aristotle. See the discussion in G. R. G. Mure, *Aristotle* (1932) 207 and cf. below p. 74.

in Aristotle the objects of metaphysics are the unmoved movers (or some other separate οὐσία or οὐσίαι), we shall have to admit that the metaphysical objects do not exist ἐξ ἀφαιρέσεως only. On the contrary, they and just they have full subsistence, being pure actualities (while the objects of sensation are permeated by potentiality). But if they do not exist so, the method of abstraction cannot be applied to them. In other words, even if we admit that physicals can be described as objects of abstraction, the doctrine of the degrees of abstraction would still be unable to justify the tripartite division of theoretical philosophy, with metaphysics as one of the three. To the extent to which metaphysics deals with unmoved movers (separate οὐσία), the method of abstraction does not apply to it.

Does Aristotle's metaphysics deal with any objects in addition to the unmoved movers? If we answer in the affirmative, can the method of abstraction be applied at least to them? We shall discuss this problem later in ch. VII.

Thirdly. The doctrine of the degrees of abstraction as corresponding to the three theoretical philosophies is not Thomistic at all, in spite of the fact that it is frequently presented as such by French and English interpreters. We prove this by concentrating especially on the *Summa theologiae* *. We do this for two reasons. The first is that with regard to St. Thomas' commentary on Boethius' *De Trinitate* (of which we shall presently speak) the un-Thomistic character of the doctrine of the three degrees was proved by L. B. Geiger ("Abstraction et séparation d'après Saint Thomas in De Trinitate q. 5 a.3", *Revue des Sciences Philosophiques et Théologiques* 31 [1947] 3—40). The second reason is the manner in which Geiger's interpretation has been criticized by M.-V. Leroy ("Le savoir spéculatif", *Revue Thomiste* 48 [1948] 236–339; Annexe: Abstractio et separatio d'après un texte controversé de saint Thomas), who clinched his argument by the question: if St. Thomas does not teach in his commentary on Boethius the doctrine of the degrees of abstraction, how shall we explain that in all writings posterior to this commentary he does teach it without reserve? In what follows it will be shown that there is no doctrine of degrees of abstraction in St.

---

* For what follows cf. P. Merlan, "Abstraction and Metaphysics in St. Thomas' *Summa*", *Journal of the History of Ideas* 14 (1953) 284–291.

Thomas' *Summa theologiae* either — at least not in the sense assumed by Leroy. By so doing, the correctness of Geiger's analysis of the commentary on Boethius will be confirmed.

What the *Summa* teaches is this: By the third degree of abstraction (i.e. by abstraction from *materia signata sensibilis*, from *materia communis* and *sensibilis*, from all matter including the *materia intelligibilis*) we grasp such objects as *ens, unum, potentia, actus*, etc. All these objects can exist also without any matter (while physicals and mathematicals cannot); by which is meant that they apply also to (are present in, are predicable of) immaterial substances. Only in this sense of the word are they immaterial, which, of course, is quite different from the immateriality of God, the angels, etc. Furthermore, the *Summa* stresses that we cannot reach disembodied forms (immaterial substances) superior to the soul, such as God and the angels, by the method of abstraction. The assertion to the contrary the *Summa* considers to be an erroneous doctrine of Avempace (Ibn Bagga). The doctrine is erroneous because these immaterial substances are neither forms nor universals; thus they can be reached neither by *abstractio formae* nor by *abstractio universalis* (I *q.* 88, *art.* 2, *Resp. Dic.*).

It is true, the *Summa* stresses that the only way leading to some (inadequate) knowledge of these immaterial substances starts from objects of sensation. This starting point is common to different ways: one leading to physicals and mathematicals, another to such objects as *ens, unum*, etc., a third to immaterial substances. But this third way is different from the other ways in that it is not the way of abstraction. It is rather described by St. Thomas in such terms as: *per comparationem ad corpora sensibilia, per excessum* or *per remotionem* (I *q.* 84, *art.* 7, *ad tertium; q.* 88, *art.* 2, *ad sec.*); by some kind of *similitudines* and *habitudines ad res materiales* (I *q.* 88, *art.* 2, *ad primum*).

In other words, the method of abstraction is applicable to metaphysics only to the extent to which metaphysics treats *forms* common to material and immaterial substances (later called transcendentals). As far as metaphysics deals with immaterial substances, it requires a method different from the method of abstraction.

As sometimes the sentence *impossibile est intellectum* . . .

aliquid intelligere ... nisi convertendo se ad phantasmata (I q. 84, *art.* 7, *Resp. Dic.*) is quoted to prove that abstraction is the only method by which we can come to know anything above the sensibles, it should be stressed that this sentence occurs in the topic indicated by the title of *q.* 84: *Quomodo anima ... intelligat corporalia.* The knowledge of immaterial substances is treated *ex professo* only in *q.* 88 (title: *Quomodo anima humana cognoscat ea quae supra se sunt*), and throughout this *quaestio* the applicability of abstraction to immaterial substances is denied.

If we consider it legitimate to designate metaphysics dealing with immaterial substances such as God, angels, as *metaphysica specialis*, while designating metaphysics dealing with such objects as *ens, unum, potentia, actus,* as *metaphysica generalis,* we should say in brief: In his *Summa* St. Thomas teaches that the method of abstraction is inapplicable to *metaphysica specialis* * (cf. below).

It will only be Geoffrey of Fontaines who shall say:

> *secundum statum vitae praesentis non est nisi unus modus intelligendi omnia, sive materialia ... sive immaterialia ... scilicet per abstractionem speciei intelligibilis virtute intellectus agentis, mediante phantasmate. (Quodl.* VI, *q.* 15 in: M. Wulf, "L'intellectualisme de Godefroi de Fontaines d'après le Quodlibet VI, q. 15", *Festgabe ... Clemens Baeumker* [1913] 287–296, esp. 294).

But this is not what St. Thomas said and should not be presented as his doctrine **.

---

* This is made completely clear in some presentations of St. Thomas other than those in French or English. An older example is K. Werner, *Der heilige Thomas von Aquino* (1858–1859): abstraction in metaphysics is insufficient as metaphysics deals not only with the most universal but also with the most real which must be reached by a way different from that of logical universalization. This other way Werner correctly calls (though hardly describes) *separatio* (v. II 157, n.l). A more recent example is M. L. Habermehl, *Die Abstraktionslehre des hl. Thomas von Aquin* (1933) 58–60.

** We find the above results fully confirmed when we read St. Thomas' *Expositio super Boetium De Trinitate.* Commenting on Boethius' tripartition (on which see below) St. Thomas declares that only physics and mathematics make use of abstraction, the former mainly of *abstractio universalis,* the latter of *abstractio formae.* The method used in theology, says St. Thomas, should be called *separatio* rather than *abstractio*; *separatio* being clearly the intellectual method underlying all discursive thinking (*q.* 5, *art.* 3, *Resp.*). Again Avempace is quoted (*q.* 6, *art.* 4, *Resp.*) as having committed the mistake of assuming that the quiddities of immaterial substances are

Thus in any case, i.e. whether Thomistic or not, the attempt to defend the tripartition by transforming degrees of being into degrees of abstraction would succeed only at the cost of a radical transformation of its meaning in Aristotle.

We still have to make sure of one more thing. Throughout our discussion we assumed that Schwegler was right in changing the ἀχώριστα in *Met.* E 1, 1026a14 to χωριστά. But even if we decided to keep the ἀχώριστα, the whole passage in question would not gain. If we keep ἀχώριστα, the meaning can obviously be only "material", while χωριστά would designate immaterial things. But this would still amount to a dichotomy: material — immaterial, either with the former subdivided into material and being considered as such (physicals), and materials but not being considered as such (mathematicals), or with the latter subdivided into things being considered as immaterial and being immaterial (theologicals) and things being considered as immaterial but not being immaterial (mathematicals). Again the *ratio essendi* and the *ratio cognoscendi* would be mixed up.

But is there any possibility of denying the correctness of Schwegler's criticism? Is it possible at all to defend the ἀχώριστα? Let us make sure once more that as far as logic is concerned Schwegler was right.

Because the subject matter of metaphysics is described by Aristotle as ἀκίνητα and χωριστά, the claim of physicals to be the subject matter of metaphysics can be refuted on one of three grounds — quite independently of what χωριστόν or ἀχώριστον means. Physicals may be unfit to function as subject matter of metaphysics (1) because they are neither χωριστά nor ἀκίνητα (or, positively, because they are both ἀχώριστα and κινητά); (2) because they are ἀκίνητα but not χωριστά; (3) because they are χωριστά but not ἀκίνητα. We can rule out (2) immediately,

---

adequately expressed in the quiddities of sensible things so that one could abstract them. And again one branch of metaphysics only is credited with dealing with *ens, substantia, potentia, actus* (*q.* 5, *art.* 4, *Resp.*) all of which can obviously be reached by abstraction; while another branch of metaphysics deals with beings which never exist *in materia et motu* (though it considers them only *tamquam principia subiecti*) so that they cannot obviously be abstracted from matter. The method appropriate to *metaphysica specialis* St. Thomas describes in terms of *excessus, remotio, via causalitatis* (*causa excellens*) — and he refers to Ps. Dionysius (*q.* 6, *art.* 2, *Resp.*; cf. St. Thomas, *Opusculum* VII, *Expositio super Dionysium De div. nom.*, ch. VII, *lectio* 4).

physicals never being described by Aristotle as ἀκίνητα. Thus
line 14 must be equivalent to (1) or (3). But we must rule out
(1) because in line 14 of our passage Aristotle says: physics deals
with ἀχώριστα indeed, *but* they are not ἀκίνητα. This contradicts (1). If Aristotle meant to say of the physicals that they
were ἀχώριστα he should have said: Physics deals with things
that are both ἀχώριστα and κινητά. What he says is however
something else. Unless we translate the words ἡ μὲν γὰρ φυσικὴ
περὶ ἀχώριστα μὲν ἀλλ' οὐκ ἀκίνητα by "physics deals with things
which are not material *nor* unmoved" ἀχώριστα is impossible.
But who would be bold enough to assert that this is a possible
translation? *

Thus we are left with (3) — it is what Aristotle should have
written.

In the second passage, *Met.* K 7, 1064a30–b3 the same difficulties reappear. At first blush, the passage is smoother. Physicals
are described as moved and neither χωριστόν nor ἀχώριστον is
used for them. Theologicals are described as χωριστά and ἀκίνητα.
Mathematicals are described as μένοντα ἀλλ' οὐ χωριστά. The
whole inappropriateness of this division comes out when we ask:
in what sense are the mathematicals unmoved? Of two things
one, either they are unmoved or they are being considered as
unmoved. In what sense are they οὐ χωριστά? Either they are
οὐ χωριστά or they are being considered as οὐ χωριστά. Now, if
μένοντα means "being unmoved", οὐ χωριστά must mean "not
being χωριστά". This makes no sense, because if mathematicals
are οὐ χωριστά, they must be moved. If, however, μένοντα
means "being considered as μένοντα", "οὐ χωριστά" must also

---

* A rhetorical question, I admit, because there is somebody bold enough to have
done just this. We find the ἀχώριστα defended as logically possible in E. Trépanier,
"La philosophie de la nature porte-t-elle sur des séparés ou des non-séparés?",
Laval Théologique et Philosophique 2 (1946) 206–209. The answer to his question is:
if "séparé" means "immaterial", physics deals with what is "non-séparé". But
"séparé" cannot mean immaterial in our passage because μέν, ἀλλ' οὐκ never can
mean "et non", as he suggests, without actually writing down the text together with
his translation. Had he done it, he would, I am sure, have realized his mistake. He
was misled by phrases like ἐκεῖ ἀλλ' οὐκ ἐνταῦθα where ἀλλ' οὐκ can indeed be
translated by "et non" ("and not"), but only because this French or English phrase
has full adversative force in this context ("et non" = "mais non" "and not" =
"but not"). In a phrase like "I am not rested and not (= nor), feeling well", "and
not" must be translated by μηδέ, not by ἀλλ' οὐκ.

mean "being considered as οὐ χωριστά" and mathematicals clearly lose any ontic status. By describing them as μένοντα Aristotle created the false impression that the tripartition is consistently based on ontic qualities. In E 1 he makes it clear that mathematicals may have no ontic status by saying that mathematics considers them as if they were subsistent and unmoved.

One more thing must be added. In any case it is highly misleading to describe both physicals and metaphysicals as χωριστά. Metaphysicals are χωριστά, because they exist separated from physicals (like Plato's ideas), physicals are χωριστά because, according to Aristotle, only particulars subsist. In other words, to say of metaphysicals that they are χωριστά, presupposes the possibility of the subsistence of disembodied forms — precisely what Aristotle denied when he criticized Plato —, while to say that physicals are χωριστά presupposes Aristotle's own theory that only particulars, i.e. embodied forms, exist *.

The whole discussion started by a reference to Mansion. It can now be summed up in the form of a criticism of some parts of his interpretation.

1. Mansion takes it for granted that Aristotle said of the object of metaphysics (conceived to be either being-as-such or immaterial being) that it is grasped by abstraction. But there is no passage in Aristotle which would support Mansion's thesis. It is obvious that he reads Aristotle in the light of later interpretations, particularly that of St. Thomas' commentary on Boethius, on which see below.

2. Mansion takes it for granted that the objects of physics are seized by an act of abstraction. Again there are no texts to support his interpretation. And it even seems that Mansion is on the verge of realizing it — but instead he criticizes Aristotle for not having properly elaborated his doctrine of the difference between physics and mathematics, calling it an abortive attempt of Aristotle (169). His very terminology proves the un-Aristotelian character of his attempt to state the difference between physicals and mathematicals in terms of degrees of abstraction. He calls

---

* Cf. H. Cherniss, *Aristotle's Criticism of Plato*, v. I (1944) 368 and 371 f.

physicals "choses sensibles pensées" or speaks of "un sensible élevé à l'ordre intelligible" (138 f.; 176).

Nothing indicates the distance between Aristotle and a doctrine asserting that physicals are objects of abstraction better than Aristotle's treatment of the so called intermediate sciences, i.e. astronomy, optics, mechanics (cf. Mansion 186–195). Aristotle is aware that all these sciences abstract in a way similar to the abstraction used in mathematics. But instead of proceeding from here to any general statement concerning physics, he uses this similarity only to clarify the mathematical character of these intermediate sciences. Precisely to the extent to which they use abstraction they are not physical sciences (cf. also *De an.* I 1, 403a12–14 on builders and physicians). Mansion himself states the reason. Aristotle's nature in its main bulk is not amenable to mathematical (quantitative) treatment and therefore the concept of a mathematical physics is absent from Aristotle's thought.

In other words, Mansion sees very well that the doctrine of the difference between mathematicals and physicals in terms of degrees of abstraction is un-Aristotelian; but instead of blaming interpreters for trying to find it in Aristotle, he blames Aristotle for not having done what he, according to those interpreters, set out to do *.

3. Mansion takes it for granted that the subject matter of St. Thomas' metaphysics can be grasped by abstraction. As the preceding discussion should have proved, this is unwarranted.

Thus, the whole tripartition of speculative knowledge in Aristotle is inconsistent and the result of a half-hearted attempt to keep the Platonic division of being. In addition, the classical passage expounding it, is disfigured by a textual mistake.

But it so happened that just this tripartition, mostly incorporated into a more general division of philosophy, was repeated and commented upon innumerably many times **. Some representative examples will suffice to characterize the results.

---

* Cf. also G. R. G. Mure, *Aristotle* (1932) 202 n. 3, esp. his discussion of *Met.* M 3,1078a5–9. This passage proves immediately that if Aristotle had developed the germs of a general theory of abstraction present in his writings, he would have arrived at an indifferent plurality of abstractive sciences, coordinate with mathematics.

** Cf. J. Mariétan, *Problème de la classification des sciences d'Aristote à St. Thomas*

We found (above p. 60 f.) Alexander (p. 251, 34–38 Hayduck) reluctant to accept the tripartition of being into theologicals, mathematicals, and physicals, and favoring the tripartition into theologicals, astronomicals, and physicals instead. No such doubts beset Ps. Alexander*. In his commentary on E 1, 1025b18–1026a6 and again on K 7, 1064a10 the former division is accepted. In the first of these two passages Ps. Alexander describes physicals as κινητά and ἀχώριστα, mathematicals as ἀκίνητα and χωριστά, theologicals as ἀκίνητα and χωριστά (p. 445, 19–446, 3 Hayduck) — though within the very same passage mathematicals are described also as not χωριστά (with manuscripts disagreeing as to whether the physicals were not only by a mistake described as χωριστά on p. 445, 12 Hayduck; cf. also p. 446, 35–447, 3 Hayduck). In the second passage Ps. Alexander describes mathematicals as unmoved and χωριστά by our thinking (p. 661, 2–9 Hayduck).

All this amounts either to a dichotomy ἀχώριστα-χωριστά meaning material-immaterial, with the former subdivided into moved and unmoved; or to another dichotomy moved-unmoved with the former subdivided into "and considered as moved" and "and considered as unmoved" or the latter subdivided into "immaterial-material" (or some other patching up); and χωριστός means sometimes immaterial, sometimes abstracted, etc. The chaos is obvious.

Ammonius ** stresses that mathematicals can be described either as separated (mentally) or as not separated (in fact;

(1901); L. Baur (ed.), *Dominicus Gundissalinus De divisione philosophiae* (1903) 316–397. Some other items: M. Grabmann, *Die Geschichte der scholastischen Methode*, 2 vv. (1909, 1911), esp. v. II 28–54; S. van den Bergh, *Umrisz der muhammedanischen Wissenschaften nach Ibn Haldun* (1912) 12–16; J. M. Ramírez, "De ipsa philosophia in universum, secundum doctrinam aristotelico-thomisticam", *La Ciencia Tomista* 26 (1922) 33–62; 325–364; 28 (1923) 5–35; 29 (1924) 24–58; 209–222; J. Stephenson, "The Classification of the Sciences According to Nasiruddin Tusi", *Isis* 5 (1923) 329–338; H. Meyer, "Die Wissenschaftslehre des Thomas von Aquin", *Philosophisches Jahrbuch* 47 (1934) 171–206; 308–345; 441–486; 48 (1935) 12–40; 289–312; M. Clagett, "Some General Aspects of Physics in the Middle Ages", *Isis* 39 (1948) 29–44, esp. 30–36; L. Gardet and M. M. Anawati, *Introduction à la Théologie musulmane* (1948) 97–134; I. Husik, *Philosophical Essays* (1952) 164 f.
* An investigation of all doctrinal differences between Ps. Alexander and Alexander would be worthwhile. On one of them see P. Merlan, "Ein Plotinos-Zitat bei Simplikios und ein Simplikios-Zitat bei Ps. Alexandros", *Rheinisches Museum* 84 (1935) 154–160. See also P. Moraux, *Alexandre d'Aphrodise* (1942).
** No attempt will be made to quote the Aristotle commentators in the proper chronological order.

In Porph. Isag. p. 11, 30–12, 8 Busse). At the same time he reports (*ibid.* p. 10, 15–11, 5 Busse) that some philosophers made mathematics *precede* physics. It is easy to see why this was done and how. Once there is no intermediate sphere of being, mathematics cannot keep its place between physics and theology. It is bound to be squeezed out and will acquire propaedeutic status rather than be part of philosophy *. Aristotle himself started this trend. In *Met.* E 1, 1026a6–11 he discusses the three branches in the order: physics, mathematics, theology. But after having criticized the claims to highest wisdom of the two first of them, he lists them now in E 1, 1026a19 in the order: mathematics, physics, theology (cf. above, p. 60). Ammonius, sensitive to the fact that mathematicals have no ontic status peculiar to them, preserved also the obvious consequences of this awareness.

The clear insight into the duality of principles underlying the tripartition we find also in David, *Prolegomena* p. 57, 9–58, 25 Busse and Ps. Galenus, *De partibus philosophiae,* p. 6, 11–16 Wellmann **. Intelligibilia subsist and are thought, without matter; geometricals exist only in matter but are considered by us as immaterial; sensibilia exist in matter and are considered by us together with their matter. What is particularly interesting to see, is that David and Ps. Galenus give full credit for this tripartition to Aristotle, opposing him to Plato who, according to Ps. Galenus, assumed only two divisions of knowledge. Here, indeed, the Platonic root of the tripartition is not only forgotten; it is denied.

In their denial of the subsistence of mathematicals Alexander, Ammonius, Ps. Galenus are Aristotelians. How does a Platonist handle the same tripartition? A typical example of a confused Platonist is Albinus. In his *Didascalicus* ch. III 4, p. 11 Louis the three parts of theoretical philosophy are theology, physics including astronomy, and mathematics. But in ch. VII, p. 41–47 Louis physics seems to have left astronomy to mathematics

---

* It is precisely for this reason that e.g. the predecessors (e.g. David, *Prol. phil.* p. 5, 9 Busse) of Averroes excluded mathematics (along with logic) from philosophy proper. Cf. L. Gauthier, *Ibn Rochd* (1948) 49–51; H. A. Wolfson, "The Classification of Science in Medieval Jewish Philosophy", *Hebrew Union College Jubilee Volume* (1925) 305.

** Cf. L. Baur, *Gundissalinus De divisione philosophiae* (1903) 337 n. 2.

dealing with motion and including music. At the same time mathematics is interpreted as a purely propaedeutic branch of knowledge. It is obvious that Albinus is unable to make up his mind whether mathematicals are motive or not and whether they do not deserve to be treated as a branch of philosophy if they subsist or whether they subsist.

As we have seen, both Iamblichus and Proclus never hesitate to ascribe full subsistence to mathematicals, so that in them because of their mathematical realism *, the tripartition is fully legitimate.

The most natural starting point for a discussion of medieval interpretations of the tripartition is Boethius. In *De Trinitate* ch. 2 we read:

Nam cum tres sunt speculativae partes, naturalis, in motu inabstracta ἀνυπεξαίρετος *(considerat enim corporum formas cum materia, ... quae corpora in motu sunt ...), mathematica, sine motu inabstracta (haec enim formas corporum speculatur sine materia ac per hoc sine motu, quae formae cum in materia sint, ab his separari non possunt), theologica, sine motu abstracta atque separabilis ** ...*

In the form of a synopsis:

Physicals	Mathematicals	Metaphysicals
in motu	*sine motu = speculata sine motu*	*sine motu*
inabstracta = considerata cum materia	*inabstracta = speculata sine materia*	*abstracta*
ἀνυπεξαίρετα, i.e. non subtracted	*non separabilia =* necessarily imbedded in matter	*separabilia,* i.e. not imbedded in matter

One look at this synopsis shows complete chaos. *Inabstracta*

---

* A famous instance of the survival of this realism we find in Kepler, *Harmonice mundi* (1619), book IV, ch. I, with long excerpts from Proclus *In Eucl.*, First Prologue (the parallel passages in Kepler and Proclus can easily be found in M. Steck, *Proklus Diadochus ... Kommentar zum Ersten Buch von Euklids "Elementen"* [1945]). It is beyond the scope of the present work to discuss E. Cassirer, *Das Erkenntnisproblem*, v. I³ (1922) 337 f., who interprets Proclus' and Kepler's conceptual realism as Kantian apriorism.

** The text quoted is that of the Rand-Stewart edition in the Loeb Library.

as applied to physicals means *considerata cum materia*; but as applied to mathematicals it means *speculata sine materia*. *Separabilis* means really *separatum* = *immaterial*. Epistemonic and ontic points of view are in a hopeless tangle. The introduction of a new term, ἀνυπεξαίρετος, obviously meant to replace the troublesome ἀχώριστα, only adds to the confusion. It means "existing in matter", but then it should also be applied to mathematicals instead of the *non separabilia*.

Boethius' writing became the object of many commentaries. In all of them we find some attempts to make the tripartition more consistent. We limit ourselves to some examples.

We begin with Johannes Scotus (Eriugena) *. According to him, mathematicals (like number) are immaterial, but mathematics considers them only in matter (*Commentum Boethii De Trinitate* in E. K. Rand, "Johannes Scottus", *L. Traube's Quellen und Untersuchungen zur lateinischen Philologie des Mittelalters* 1 [1906] 34, 25) **. This is either a simple mistake or an almost complete return to Platonic realism. Mathematicals seem to subsist. But if Johannes Scotus really intended such a return, certainly he was ill advised to say that mathematics considers mathematicals as imbedded in matter. This amounts to a strange distortion of both the abstractionist and the non-abstractionist point of view. Johannes Scotus seems to be the victim of Boethius' double term *inabstracta* and *inseparabilia* for mathematicals.

It is instructive to compare Thierry's and Clarenbaldus' commentaries ***. It is, indeed, quite obvious for them that mathematicals cannot be called ἀχώριστα in the same sense in which physicals are. They take it for granted that the method by which the former become objects of knowledge is abstraction, while there is no abstraction in physics. How, then, could Boethius call the mathematicals *inabstracta*? Thierry (?) in *Librum hunc* does not really try to solve the difficulty. After having repeated several times that mathematics operates by abstraction (p. 8 * 11. 19. 30 Jansen), while physics does not

---

* In this connection see on him J. Handschin, "Die Musikanschauung des Joh. Scotus", *Deutsche Vierteljahrschrift f. Literaturwiss. und Geistesgesch.* 5 (1927) 316–341.
** The question of its true author (Scotus or Remigius of Auxerre?) is immaterial in the present context.
*** In: W. Jansen, *Der Kommentar des Mag. Clarenbaldus von Arras zu Boethius De Trinitate* (1926).

abstract, he describes theologicals as abstract, meaning by this "existing without matter" (p. 9 * 7 Jansen) and leaves it to the reader to reconcile the two meanings of "abstract".

It is of some interest to see how the same confusion which changed the χωριστά to ἀχώριστα in Aristotle repeats itself in Thierry. On p. 9 * 20.21 Jansen the words *abstracta* and *inabstracta* are mixed up. *Abstracta* is used to designate physicals, *inabstracta* to designate theologicals. Jansen emends the passage by interchanging the two terms; but it seems he corrects the author rather than the scribe. Somehow the idea that the theologicals are *inabstracta*, in the sense of having subsistence and being more than objects of abstraction, and the idea that physicals may be designated as objects of abstraction (an idea which will be later developed by St. Thomas) "came through" and misguided Thierry's quill.

More critical is Clarenbaldus. In his commentary on Boethius he asks the question why Boethius should call mathematicals inabstract? He did so, says Clarenbaldus, to indicate that they inhere in matter and to distinguish mathematics from theology (p. 56 * 15 Jansen).

Different is the interpretation of Gilbertus Porreta (*Commentaria in librum De Trinitate*). In him, mathematics becomes knowledge of *all* forms (e.g. *corporalitas, color, latitudo*); its subject matter is, therefore, co-extensive with that of physics. Only, the latter considers its objects as they are (embodied in matter), the former considers them not as they are (abstracting from matter). Theologicals *non modo disciplina, verum etiam re ipsa abstracta sunt* (*PL* 64, 1267C; 1268 B–C). But a mathematics the subject matter of which are *all* forms is clearly not Aristotle's mathematics which deals only with mathematicals in the ordinary sense.

In Radulfus de Longo Campo (c. 1216) we find another attempt to reinterpret the whole tripartition. According to him, the three branches have one thing in common: their objects are invisible. Theology considers invisible substances, physics invisible causes, mathematics invisible forms (M. Grabmann, *Geschichte der scholastischen Methode*, 2vv. [1909,1911], v.II 49) *.

---

* There may be a certain similarity between this interpretation and the one of David al-Mukammas (see on him D. Neumark, *Geschichte der juedischen Philosophie des Mittelalters*, 4 vv., v. I [1907] 469 f.; 612 f.; v. II [1928] 215–219; J. Guttmann,

The weakness of this attempt is obvious: There is no principle underlying this partition, as the series: substances, causes, forms is based on none. Nevertheless, one thing is remarkable about Radulfus' interpretation. According to him, the object matter of none of the three branches of knowledge is accessible to the senses. In other words, a gulf separates physics from sensation. The tripartition of philosophy becomes inextricably connected with a basic epistemological problem. This basic problem is: how many types of knowledge are there in addition to and above sensation? If abstraction is the method found even in physics and if abstraction is the method of mathematics — does it perhaps follow that abstraction is the only method leading to any knowledge above the level of sensation? Is also theology (metaphysics) based on just another application of the method of abstraction? We obviously are ready to discuss St. Thomas in whom all these questions found their answers. But before doing so, let us devote some words to one author, preceding St. Thomas: Dominicus Gundissalinus. He claims to quote our Boethius passage but he certainly quotes it in a most peculiar way.

> *Et ob hoc dicit Boëcius, quod phisica est inabstracta et cum motu, mathematica abstracta et cum motu, theologia vero abstracta et sine motu* (De div. phil., p. 15 Baur).

As we see, Gundissalinus instead of quoting, quietly corrects Boethius in two ways. Whatever the reason, he describes mathematicals as moved; and perceiving that it is difficult to designate both physicals and mathematicals by any one and the same term (e.g. both either as *abstracta* or as *inabstracta*) corrects Boethius for a second time. But one type of confusion is eliminated only to make way for another: both mathematicals and theologicals are described as *abstracta*. The terms ἀνυπεξαίρετος and *separabilis-inseparabilis* Gundissalinus simply drops.

We can now turn to St. Thomas. His *Expositio super Boetium De Trinitate* is undoubtedly one of the high-marks of medieval philosophy *.

Die Philosophie des Judentums [1933] 85–87) as quoted in Judah ben Barzilai, according to H. A. Wolfson, "The Classification of Science in Mediaeval Jewish Philosophy", *Hebrew Union College Jubilee Volume* (1925) 263–315: "Philosophy is the knowledge of all things according to the measure of their forms [mathematics], the secret of their nature [physics], and the veracity of their impartation [theology?]" 271; cf. 296.

* Cf. M. Grabmann, *Die Werke des hl. Thomas von Aquin*³ (1949) 358–360.

St. Thomas seemingly accepts Boethius' tripartition of speculative philosophy. But he changes its meaning considerably. A brief indication will be sufficient as this matter has been discussed above in detail. St. Thomas makes the tripartition consistent by basing it entirely on cognitive differences (grades of abstraction, i.e. physics abstracts from individual matter, mathematics from all sensible matter, formal metaphysics from all matter; *q.* 5, *art.* 2, *Resp.*, *ad primum*; *art.* 3, *Resp.*, *ad quartum*; *art.* 4, *Resp.*). The price of this consistency is a double one. First, the status of the physicals is different from their status in Aristotle. Second, there is no place for special metaphysics within this new tripartition. From now on the choice was: either to keep the tripartition and interpret the meaning of special metaphysics in such a way that it would ultimately be reducible to general metaphysics, or to keep special metaphysics as a branch distinct from general metaphysics and abandon the tripartition. As all neat divisions are extremely convenient for school and didactic purpose, the first alternative became widely accepted *.

We still have to ask: is the dichotomy general and special metaphysics justified from Aristotle's point of view? This question will be answered in chapter VII.

It is interesting to see how the insight into the incorrectness of the Aristotelian tripartition expresses itself ultimately in Maritain. Maritain tried to interpret the tripartition of knowledge in terms of degrees of abstraction; but if we simply take a look at his synopsis of degrees of knowledge we see immediately that mathematics is no longer coordinated with theology and physics (J. Maritain, *Distinguer pour unir*[5] [1946] 69–93, esp. 79 = *Distinguish to Unite* [1959] 35–46, esp. 39, left side). A follower of Maritain like Whittaker reduces St. Thomas' trichotomy to the dichotomy: material-immaterial (J. F. Whittaker, "The Position of Mathematics in the Hierarchy of Speculative

---

* In his Boethius text St. Thomas found the theologicals described as *abstracta* and *inseparabilia* (*q.* 4, *art.* 4, *lectio* 2). It is obvious that this mistake is the result of another confusion due to the ambiguity of the term χωριστόν. It is very difficult for St. Thomas to explain the term *inseparabilia*. He says: we cannot designate the theologicals as *separabilia*, because they have never been connected — scil. with matter. Therefore we call them *inseparabilia*. This is almost a *lucus-a-non-lucendo* explanation (*inseparabile* because *separatum*) —· but there was clearly no way out of this jungle of mistakes and slips of the pen.

Science", *The Thomist* 3 [1941] 467–506, esp. 471). This is simply the return to what Aristotle should have said. Centuries of interpretation of what he actually said did not succeed in proving that it made sense.

Before we conclude this chapter, we should discuss another passage in Boethius' *Introduction* to the *Isagoge* of Porphyry. Once more the tripartition of philosophy is stated. Some of the terms are unclear.

> *Erunt autem tot speculativae philosophiae species, quot sunt res in quibus iustae speculatio considerationis habetur, quotque actuum diversitates, tot species varietatesque virtutum (In Porph. Isag., CSEL v. 48, p. 8, 3–5 Brandt).*

What Boethius seems to say is that the three branches of philosophy operate with different kinds of cognitive faculties. In any case, it is only the subsequent passage which is of interest to us. The second (intermediate) branch of speculative knowledge

> *est omnium caelestium supernae divinitatis operum et quicquid sub lunari globo beatiore animo atque puriore substantia valet et postremo humanarum animarum quae omnia cum prioris illius intellectibilis substantiae fuissent, corporum tactu ab intellectibilibus ad intelligibilia degenerarunt ... Secunda [scil. branch of being] vero, merito medio collocata est, quod habeat et corporum animationem et quodammodo vivificationem et intellectibilium considerationem cognitionemque (ibid. p. 8, 21–9, 12 Brandt).*

An interesting passage. The second branch turns out to be psychology. It deals with the "fallen" souls which on the one hand give life to the bodies and on the other hand contemplate the realm of the intelligibles to which they originally belong. And, of course, this is strictly realistic; the souls subsist.

The passage must appear puzzling indeed. Baur (*op. cit.* 351 n. 3; cf. K. Bruder, *Die philosophischen Elemente in den Opuscula sacra des Boethius* [1927] 6–8) does not try to explain why mathematics should suddenly be replaced by psychology. Rather recently L. Schrade ("Die Stellung der Musik in der Philosophie des Boethius", *Archiv fuer Geschichte der Philosophie* 41 [1932] 368–400] found it so strange that he tried to prove that Boethius must have meant mathematics, after all, even though the passage speaks of psychology. But there is nothing strange in the passage for anybody who approaches it *via* Iamblichus, Proclus, and the problem of the identification of the soul with mathematicals. It was almost inevitable that somebody should have described the second branch of theoretical philosophy as psychology, instead of mathematics, since soul = mathematicals. Iamblichus had already shown the way: he insisted that mathematical and psychological "initiation" proceed *pari passu* (*Isc.* ch. IX, p. 41, 5–6 F) *. In short, we are back to the identification of soul and mathematicals.

The problem of a classification of sciences is important. A whole *Weltanschauung* can be compressed in such a classification**, as was done in modern times by Comte. But it is an almost pathetic spectacle to see Aristotelians trying to make sense out of a classification which made sense only within Platonism, to see centuries bewildered by a textual mistake in Aristotle ***. The failure to notice the conflict between the realistic and

---

* Here again it is striking that according to Wolfson ("The Classification" 278–294) psychology is often named as a sub-branch of metaphysics (theology) by Jewish medieval philosophers in their classifications of sciences (on which see also M. Stein-schneider, *Die hebraeischen Uebersetzungen des Mittelalters und die Juden als Dolmet-scher* [1893] 1–33). Wolfson is puzzled by this and tries to explain it by systematic considerations. It may be, however, that this inclusion (anticipating Wolff's in-clusion of *psychologia rationalis* in the *metaphysica specialis*) is an echo of the Boethius passage quoted above, i.e. an attempt to reconcile the ordinary tripartition meta-physics-mathematics-physics with the other, metaphysics-psychology-physics. The Ihwan-al-Safa distinguished sensible from rational mathematics (following men like Geminus; see Proclus, *In Eucl.*, Prol. I, p. 38,4 Fr; cf. J. Klein, "Die griechische Logistik und die Entstehung der Algebra", *Quellen und Studien zur Geschichte der Mathematik* ...., Abt. B: Studien 3 [1936] 18–105, esp. 23–29) and said of rational mathematics that it led "to the knowledge of the substance of the soul" (Wolfson, *op. cit.* 271; cf. F. Dieterici, *Die Philosophie der Araber im X. Jahrhundert n. Chr.*, 2 parts [1876, 1879] — corresponding to *Die Philosophie der Araber im IX. und X. Jahrhundert n. Chr.* Books 1 and 2 — v. II 132 f.; 145). Here again we seem to have an echo of Iamblichus. Another interesting tripartition of incorporeals (God and angels; the soul; mathematicals) was made by Hauréau's Anonymus in H. Willner, *Des Adelard von Bath Traktat De eodem et diverso* (1903) 105–108, esp, 105. In Ibn Khaldoun *Les Prolégomènes*, 3 vv. (1863, 1865, 1868) = *The Muqaddimah*, 3 vv. (1958) we find as three spheres of being physicals, the human souls, spirits and angels (v. II 433–435 = 419–421). It should follow that in the system of sciences psychology should take the place of mathematics; but later Ibn Khaldoun asserts of psychology that it is part of physics (v. III 161 = 111). All this points towards the equation soul = mathematicals, but as nobody would dare say explicitly that therefore psychology = mathematics, we must be prepared to meet some semi-surreptitious attempts to reconcile the claims of these two sciences.

** Cf. G. Sarton, *Introduction to the History of Science*, v. III (1947) 76–78.

*** Another textual mistake (*Met.* Λ 1,1069a30–b2) almost had equally disastrous consequences. Fortunately, it was noticed early that the Aristotle mss. disagree. See A. [J.] Festugière, "Sur les sources du commentaire de St. Thomas au livre XI des Métaphysiques", *Revue des Sciences Philosophiques et Théologiques* 28 (1929) 657–663

nonrealistic interpretation of mathematics in Aristotle himself, the failure to see that the tripartition of knowledge demanded a tripartition of being, was in the long run irreparable.

Appendix

1. I should like to add two more examples illustrative of the continuity of ancient and medieval (Arabic) interpretations of Aristotle.

In his *Physics* commentary (p. 1, 21–2, 6 Diels) Simplicius says of the third part of speculative philosophy that it deals with εἴδη which partly are partly are not, χωριστά, which part μαθηματικὴν καὶ περὶ ψυχῆς καλοῦσι. The equation (or at least the close vicinity) of mathematicals and the soul here leads to a characterization of the soul in terms usually reserved for mathematicals. It should be obvious that χωριστόν cannot mean the same when applied to the soul and to mathematicals — unless the soul is thought of as a mathematical.

The other example is taken from al-Kindi (see M. Guidi and R. Walzer, "Studi su al-Kindi. I. Uno studio introduttivo allo studio di Aristotele", *Memorie della R. Accademia nazionale dei Lincei. Classe di scienze morali, storiche e filologiche*, Ser. VI, vol. VI [1937–40], fasc. V, Rome 1940). After having relegated mathematics to a purely propedeutical status (317 f.) he divides speculative philosophy into logic, physics, psychology, metaphysics (378). Logic is, of course, added merely in its quality of an organon. Thus, to the Aristotelian tripartition corresponds the series physics — psychology — metaphysics. In other words, mathematics as an intermediate science has been replaced by psychology, which only reminds us in a strangely oblique way that the two must sometimes have been identified.

However, al-Kindi shuns the term 'intermediate', because by the inclusion of logic his theoretical philosophy has four instead of three parts. On the other hand al-Kindi says that Aristotle in *De anima* deals with objects which can exist without a body — a clear adaptation of the idea expressed by Simplicius (405–6).

2. As Aristotle in one passage of the *Metaphysics* replaced mathematics by astronomy (see above p. 60) and as on the other

hand psychology, either equated with mathematics or replacing mathematics, had established itself as intermediate science, we can also expect to find the middle branch of speculative philosophy designated as astronomy *plus* psychology. And this seems indeed often to be the case in Arabic philosophy, as can be seen from: G. Vajda, *Juda ben Missim ibn Malka* (Paris 1945) 94–101.

3. The text of Gilbertus Porreta (above, p. 79) can now be read in: J. R. O'Donnell, *Nine Medieval Thinkers* (Toronto 1955) 23–98, esp. 48, 10 and 49, 14. Perhaps what was said in the body of the book can be expanded a little. According to Gilbert Porreta physics could never adequately (*perfecte*) lay hold on its objects such as *corpus, coloratum esse, latum esse*, unless mathematics has first lead to the knowledge of the essence of these objects, i.e. of *corporeitas, color, latitudo*. We are miles from what Aristotle conceived to be the relation between physics and mathematics — but his schema is still considered to be valid.

4. I was criticized by de Strycker * for having misunderstood the terms ἀφαίρεσις and χωριστόν. No explanation is given by him. I hope that a fuller presentation of my views will cause him to do the same.

a. The best starting point for a discussion of the concept of ἀφαίρεσις is: H. Scholz and H. Schweitzer, *Die sogenannten Definitionen durch Abstraktion. Forschungen zur Logistik und zur Grundlegung der exakten Wissenschaften*. 3 (1935) 3–10. Having sharply distinguished concepts from objects Scholz quotes one of the classic passages in St. Thomas' *Summa* (*abstractio universalis* and *abstractio formae*; I q. 85, a.l., *ad primum*) and traces the doctrine of abstraction in the sense of *cogitatio collecta ex individuorum similitudine* to Boethius, to pose the question: can this doctrine of abstraction (which he calls the classical, i.e. the pre-logistic doctrine of abstraction) be traced back to Aristotle? Undoubtedly, says Scholz, Aristotle assumes a whole class of things which are reached by ἀφαίρεσις, viz. the mathematicals. And once at least, Scholz continues, Aristotle says that the objects of the first philosophy (ontology) are reached by ἀφαίρεσις. But this does not mean that Aristotle considers either the mathematicals or the 'ontologicals' to be concepts, i.e. universals. He rather considers them to be individuals (though not concrete individuals:

---

* E. de Strycker, *L'Antiquité classique* 25 (1956) 528 f.

Scholz distinguishes clearly between the individual and the universal on one hand, the concrete and the abstract on the other). This can best be seen from the passage in *De caelo* III 1, 299a15 (see above p. 67). Otherwise it would completely be inexplicable why Aristotle would as example of the results of ἀφαίρεσις always quote mathematicals and never such obvious universals as 'man', 'animal', etc. I know says Scholz, not one passage in Aristotle, where such an example could be found, unless we strain the text. Thus, Aristotle should not be considered the precursor of the classic theory of abstraction. His ἀφαίρεσις is meant to yield objects; it is not meant to yield concepts.

Now, it seems to me that the way Scholz presents the problem lends itself better to an evaluation than to an interpretation of what Aristotle actually said. It presupposes a degree of reflection which is simply absent from Aristotle's writings. If we take a passage like that in *De anima* III 8, 432a2 we read that *also* τὰ ἐξ ἀφαιρέσεως λεγόμενα have no subsistence outside of the αἰσθητά, just as the other νοητά have none. And we read in this context: πρᾶγμα οὐθέν ἐστι παρὰ τὰ μεγέθη ... τὰ αἰσθητὰ κεχωρισμένον. It is not easy to interpret the νοητά (and τὰ ἐξ ἀφαιρέσεως) as designating individuals rather than universal concepts.

In spite of these reservations it seems however that in the main Scholz is right *. It seems that it would be in vain to look in Aristotle for the 'classical' theory of abstraction (i.e. the abstracting from differences, while concentrating on similarities, of a number of things, the result being a universal concept **). This is particularly true of the passages which deal either with the concept of ἀφαίρεσις or that of χωριστόν. On the contrary, in most places Aristotle uses the concept of ἀφαίρεσις in such a way that it indeed implies what Scholz correctly characterizes as ascent, not from an individual to a universal concept but rather from an individual (object, not a concept) of a certain type of being to another individual (not a universal concept) representing a superior type of being.

But let it be repeated: we must disagree with Scholz to the

---

* *Pace* I. J. M. Van den Berg, "L'abstraction et ses degrés chez Aristote", *Proceedings of the XIth International Congress of Philosophy* (1953), v. XI 109–113. Berg unhesitatingly accepts Mansion's interpretation.

** Only a variant would be the intuitive theory of abstraction according to which it is possible to detach the universal from the individual present to us only singly.

extent that we assert the presence of at least the germs of the classical theory of abstraction. We must allow that ἀφαίρεσις in Aristotle could sometimes be understood as describing the operation of 'classical' abstraction. Whenever Aristotle asserts that something exists ἐξ ἀφαιρέσεως *only*, he is very close to the classical theory of abstraction in that he would probably assert of such a 'being' that it is not an individual and has therefore no subsistence. And 'having no subsistence' is *almost* identical with 'product of our thinking', thus with a concept rather than an object. It is of course possible to assume that τὰ ἐξ ἀφαιρέσεως are individuals, different from other individuals in that they have no subsistence (exist only in other individuals), but still individuals. In other words, no either — or interpretation seems applicable to the process of ἀφαίρεσις.

b. Our discussion of the concept of χωριστός will be much shorter. The best starting point is the *Index* of Bonitz. When not used *sensu locali*, etc., the concept χωριστόν designates *quod suapte natura et per se in re et veritate est*. In other words, χωριστόν seems to mean *only*: subsisting. Πάθη would be instances of ἀχώριστα *.

But as the term χωριστόν is by Aristotle time and again applied to Plato's ideas, who made them χωριστά, it seems to acquire the connotation of immateriality. This can with particular clarity be seen in *Met.* K 2, 1060a7–13 (cf. W. Jaeger, *Aristoteles*[2] [1955] 219; H. Cherniss, *Aristotle's Criticism of Plato and the Academy* I [1944] 318–376, esp. 368 with note 281): οὐσία χωριστὴ παρὰ τὰς αἰσθητάς obviously means both subsistent *and* non-sensible; the phrase: χωριστὸν καθ' αὐτὸ καὶ μηδενὶ τῶν αἰσθητῶν ὑπάρχον implies the same.

5. On the Thomistic doctrine of degrees of abstraction see now e.g. E. D. Simmons, "The Thomistic Doctrine of the Three Degrees of Formal Abstraction", *The Thomist* 22 (1959) 37–67 esp. his admissions on p. 57 f., note 23. Simmons never faces the problem, to what extent the concept of abstraction would be applicable to that part of metaphysics which deals with angels and disembodied souls (on purpose I omit the concept of God). The same can be said of W. Kane, "Abstraction and the Distinction of Sciences", *The Thomist* 17 (1954) 43–68.

---

* E. de Strycker, "La notion aristotélicienne de séparation dans son application aux Idées de Platon", in: *Autour d'Aristote* (1955) 119–140 arrives at the same conclusion.

IV. THE ORIGIN OF THE QUADRIVIUM

We saw that the interpretation of the *Timaeus* became combined with the problem of the division of mathematics. The meaning and importance of this latter division is well known: the quadriparted mathematics is the quadrivium. It is surprising to see how closely the quadrivium is connected with the interpretation of the *Timaeus*. It is particularly amazing to see that the inclusion of astronomy in the quadrivium made possible the equation soul = mathematicals so as to include the principle of motion in mathematicals. How, we may ask, was this combination brought about? We may also ask: what is the origin of the quadrivium idea?

The four branches of learning later to be known as quadrivium, were taught at least as early as Plato. There is no reason to believe in the authenticity of the passage in Iamblichus, *Theologoumena arithmeticae* 17, p. 21, 8–10 Falco, in which already Pythagoras is credited with having known them as a unit and in the order: arithmetic-music; geometry-astronomy. But they are enumerated in the *Protagoras* 318 E* (with the implication that it was particularly Hippias who used to teach them **); a passage in Isocrates, *Panath.* 26 proves clearly that geometry and astronomy had been added to the standard curriculum only recently. However, neither are these four brought in close connection with each other, nor do they represent a very lofty kind of learning. All are obviously elementary, without any claim to be philosophic; they are just ordinary grammar school subjects. In the *Republic* (e.g. VII 530 D) and the *Laws* the different branches of the quadrivium are mentioned rather often, but a new branch, stereometry, is often added, music sometimes (e.g. *Laws* VII 817 E) omitted. On the other hand, they are treated in the *Republic* as being much more than just grammar school subjects. They are preparatory, to be sure; but they prepare for σοφία, the highest type of knowledge. In the *Laws* (VII 809 B–D) they are to be taught on an elementary level (819 B) and for practical purposes mainly; only the study of astronomy has more important implications (821 A–822 C). But

---

* Cf. F. Marx (ed.), *A. Cornelii Celsi quae supersunt* (1915) p. VIII–XIII.
** Cf. W. Jaeger, *Paideia*, v. I² (1945) 316–318.

the decisive step is taken in the *Epinomis* 991 D–E. Here the four branches are singled out, geometry obviously including stereometry (cf. 990 D). Their unity is stressed; and far from being treated as elementary they are almost (or perhaps even completely) identified with philosophy. There seems to be no higher object of learning than these four μαθήματα. In other words, the quadrivium came into existence, if we can say so, as a very high, perhaps the highest branch of learning, equal to σοφία. Hence, after Plato and the *Epinomis*, μαθήματα could mean one of two things: the traditional grammar school subjects (with no particular reason to stress their difference from other branches of grammar school learning and without a principle of unity among them), or a highly philosophic, unified study. However, the more they are treated as philosophy, the less the μαθήματα are likely to resemble μαθήματα in the ordinary sense of the word. The terms theology or philosophy of number, of figure, of sound, and of motions of the heavenly bodies describe the subject-matter of these μαθήματα in the higher sense of the word, much better than the terms arithmetic, geometry, music, and astronomy *.

It should be noted that the unity of the four μαθήματα is postulated in the *Epinomis* rather than proved. But things were not left at that. Witness Ptolemy and, above all, Nicomachus.

Arithmetic and geometry are sisters; astronomy and music their foster-children. This we read in Ptolemy (*Harmonica* III 3, p. 94, 15–20 Duering), and this doctrine may very well go back to Archytas (cf. fr. B 1 Diels). But in Nicomachus we find more; we find a *principle* of the quadripartition of mathematics. Mathematics deals with quantity; quantity is either discontinuous, πηλίκον, or continuous, ποσόν. The πηλίκον is either per se or in relation to another πηλίκον. Arithmetic deals with the former, harmonics with the latter. The ποσόν is either unmoved or moved. Geometry deals with the former; astronomy with the latter (*Intr. arithm.* ch. I–III, p. 1–9 Hoche). In this form the quadripartition of mathematics is no longer an empirical fact, it is based on a principle. And in this form the quadripartition is accepted by Iamblichus (sometimes) and

---

* Cf. W. Jaeger, *Paideia*, v. III (1944) 257 f. on the study of mathematics in Plato.

Proclus. It is clear what this means for the quadrivium idea; the four branches of knowledge now form one solid bloc distinct from others.

The *Epinomis* had singled out the four μαθήματα. At the same time it made them the top (or near-the-top) sciences. We can always expect to find the quadrivium, hardened into one bloc, in this topmost position.

But we saw that there was still another possibility of finding a place for the μαθήματα. The solidification could be accepted, but it was possible to understand by μαθήματα the ordinary disciplines. In such a case the number of four would be kept, but the place assigned to them would be at the bottom (or close to the bottom) of the ladder of knowledge rather than at the top.

There was still one more possibility. It emerged within the frame of the interpretation of the *Timaeus*. We saw that Posidonius combined two features of Platonism. He accepted the tripartition of being into intelligibles, mathematicals, sensibles; and he identified the mathematicals with the soul. But Posidonius' mathematics had only three branches: arithmetic, geometry, harmonics. It is these tripartite mathematicals which were identified with the soul by Posidonius, and Iamblichus (sometimes) followed him.

It was different with Proclus (above, p. 21). It is the quadripartite mathematics which he identified with the soul. This means that the quadrivium was now connected with the tripartition of being and definitely made the middle branch of philosophy. The quadrivium no longer is simply philosophy (or nearly so) as it was in the *Epinomis*, but it is part of philosophy, below theology (metaphysics), above physics. We saw how the rejection of the realistic interpretation of mathematicals immediately affected the place of the μαθήματα within philosophy.

We quoted Proclus as having identified the quadripartite μαθήματα with the soul. It is interesting to compare him in this respect with Syrianus *. Incidentally, mentioning the mathematicals as intermediates, Syrianus says that these intermediate mathematicals are the ones "which the soul is supposed to encompass. Their principles, geometrical, arithmetical, and

---

* On his mathematical realism (antiabstractionism) cf. K. Praechter, art. Syrianos 47 in *RE* IVA 2 (1932) 1751; 1770; 1774.

harmonical, were implanted in the soul by the demiurgic νοῦς, as we know from the psychogony in the *Timaeus*" (*In Met.* 995b6–18, p. 4, 3 Kroll). Here once more we have the "Posidonian" interpretation. And there is one more passage clearly proving how firmly the tripartition of mathematics is established in Syrianus' mind. It is a passage which, as Festa noticed, is an excerpt from *Isc*, with only few words added by Syrianus. Iamblichus asks: What are the specific principles of the single branches of mathematics? And to interpret the word "branches" Syrianus adds: e.g., numbers, figures, harmonics (*In Met.* 1078b7, p. 101, 33 Kroll; cf. *Isc*, Table of contents, p. 3, 15 Festa). Thus, in spite of the fact that both the tripartition and the quadripartition are present in Iamblichus, it is more natural for Syrianus to assume a tripartition.

We now have what could be termed the basic elements of the quadrivium problem. This problem has three main branches:

1. What is the principle singling out and unifying the four μαθήματα? The moment this principle is forgotten, it becomes easy to substitute for one of the original μαθήματα another, or, what happens more frequently, to retain the name of a μάθημα, but to fill it with different content. One typical example: in Martianus Capella geometry comprises geography. This is possible only when the definition of geometry as a discipline dealing with continuous quantity is forgotten. It is clear that in such a case to cling to the number four is to misunderstand tradition.

2. What is the precise meaning of μαθήματα? The two possibilities are (a) to consider μαθήματα as elementary (or at least strictly non-speculative) subject matter; (b) to consider them as "philosophic", either as equivalent to philosophy, or part of philosophy.

3. With this is closely connected the question: Where in the curriculum is the appropriate place for the μαθήματα? It is clear that if they are taken to be elementary, they should be placed somewhere at the bottom of the scale of learning. If they are found higher up by someone who does not know that they may mean something more than elementary knowledge, it will be quite difficult for him to understand their being placed so high. If they are taken to be "philosophical", two possibilities

remain. One can accept the "Pythagorean" point of view and admit only two branches of theoretical knowledge: μαθή-ματα = philosophy, and physics. Or one can accept the realistic trialism of Plato and place the μαθήματα between theology (metaphysics) and physics. If one does neither, one is bound to be puzzled to find them at the top or between theology and physics. One is tempted to place them below physics rather than above.

Here we have a principle permitting us to interpret the main differences between various theories concerning the quadrivium, its content, and its place within the curriculum. Thus, the history of the quadrivium can be presented as more than an empirical enumeration of opinions. By permuting the elements we can almost *a priori* deduce all possible points of view.

Following some illustrations.

As we saw, Ammonius accepted the tripartition of philosophy, but with regard to mathematicals he was an abstractionist (*In Porph. Isag.* p. 11, 30–31; cf. 12, 6 Busse). On the other hand, he accepted the quadripartition of mathematics together with the principle of Nicomachus (*ibid.*, 14, 1–26 Busse). He was not aware at all that Nicomachus' quadripartite mathematics claims to be philosophy.

Particularly instructive and important is Boethius once more. Let us start with the passage where the word quadrivium is introduced for the first time in history. There are four branches of μαθήματα forming the quadrivium; the principle of this quadripartition is given in accordance with Iamblichus and Ammonius (*Instit. arithm.*, p. 5, 6 Friedlein; 7, 25 Fr; 9, 28 Fr; 8, 15–9, 6 Fr). Inasmuch as he terms them quadrivium we should expect them to lead to some goal beyond themselves; but we discover that Boethius describes philosophy in terms which would make it almost coincide with the μαθήματα. According to this description, philosophy is interested in

> *quae vere proprieque* (8, 13) or *vere* (9, 9) *sunt* ... [viz.] *qualitates, quantitates, formae, magnitudines, parvitates, aequalitates, habitudines, actus, dispositiones, tempora* (8, 5–7)

and, more briefly and precisely:

> *formae, magnitudines, qualitates, habitudines* ... *quae per se speculata immobilia sunt* (p. 227, 25–228, 1 Fr).

The similarity to Nicomachus *Intr.* ch. I, p. 2, 21–3, 2 Hoche is obvious; but Boethius is unaware that Nicomachus is thinking in terms of an ontic dualism (mathematicals — non-mathematicals; see ch. II, p. 4, 10 Hoche); and none of them is aware that it is impossible to describe the subject matter of philosophy as unmoved, while admitting astronomy as a branch of mathematics. It is instructive to compare the Boethius — Nicomachus passage with *Isc* ch. XXVII, p. 87, 17–88, 2 F. Here Iamblichus criticizes neo-Pythagoreans for having identified the unmoved with the mathematical, thus making mathematics the supreme wisdom, to the exclusion of philosophy. It is interesting to see Iamblichus (or his source) imagining himself to be an orthodox, old-fashioned Pythagorean, for whom mathematics and philosophy are two different branches of wisdom.

Cassiodorus, as we may mention *en passant*, took over the quadripartition of mathematics; the order in which they are treated (arithmetic, music; geometry, astronomy) is the "correct" one, i.e. based on the principle presented above (*Instit.* p. 93, 7–10 Mynors; 92, 3–5. 9f. Mynors; 130, 19–131, 8 Mynors).

It was not our intention to discuss all passages dealing with the program of education or with the character and place of the quadrivium *. But with the help of our outline established above, it is very easy to evaluate the different curricula. We see what has been selected empirically and what is based on a principle. We see that, because the quadrivium was based on a principle, it was bound to emerge as a self-contained unit, claiming a definite place within the hierarchy of knowledge.

---

* The literature on the quadrivium is very great. Its main weakness consists in treating the subject matter as a doxography. In addition to those already mentioned, I confine myself to a few items, with the help of which further references can easily be found. The comparatively large amount of musicological literature is only natural: see below p. 94f. M. Guggenheim, *Die Stellung der liberalen Kuenste oder encyklischen Wissenschaften im Altertum* (1893); C. G. [K. W.] Schmidt, *Quaestiones de musicae scriptoribus Romanis imprimis de Cassiodoro et Isidoro* (1899), esp. 2 f; 122–25 (basic); P. Abelson, *The Seven Liberal Arts* (1906); K. Praechter, "Beziehungen zur Antike in Theodoros Prodromos' Rede auf Isaak Komnenos", *Byzantinische Zeitschrift* 19 (1910) 314–329, esp. 322–325; E. Norden, *Antike Kunstprosa*, v. II (1898) 670 ff. and "Nachtraege" p. 8f. (ed. 1923); H. v. Schubert, "Bildung und Erziehung in fruehchristlicher Zeit, ..." *Festgabe ... E. Gothein* (1925) 72–105, esp. 82–84; O. Schissel von Fleschenberg, *Marinos von Neapolis und die neuplatonischen Tugendgrade* (1928), esp. n. 169; H.-I. Marrou, *Saint Augustin et la fin de la culture antique*[2] (1958), esp. 197–210 and 211–235 (cf. *idem, A History of Education in Antiquity* (1956), 406, 2); L. Schrade, "Music in the Philosophy of Boethius", *Musical Quarterly* 33 (1947) 188–200.

We see how this place was accorded or denied to it — how it was dimly felt that different interpretations of the meaning of the quadrivium were possible.

We see also how ambiguous the terms arithmetic, geometry, etc., are, according to whether they designate the "philosophy" of arithmeticals, etc., or what is termed arithmetic, etc. in the ordinary sense of the word.

We must admit, however, that though the difference between arithmetic, geometry, and astronomy as elementary branches of learning and the selfsame three sciences as "philosophic" (speculative) sciences may be great indeed, the transition from one to the other is still rather smooth. This is not the case, however, with the fourth branch of the quadrivium, music. Music as performed, music as a product of composition, music as enjoyed esthetically, music as a factor forming man's character has nothing to do with music as philosophy of acoustics. It is therefore only natural that musicologists became keenly aware of the discrepancy between music as a branch of the quadrivium and music in the ordinary sense of the word. The case of music was even more complicated because there was a great amount of theory and discussion connected with music in the ordinary sense of the word. Neither theories asserting or denying ethical (or medical) effects of music *, nor the composition or performance of music have anything to do with music as part of the quadrivium.

It was particularly H. Abert who realized the difficulties connected with treating music as part of the quadrivium (*Die Musikanschauung des Mittelalters* [1905] esp. 14–16; 29–43). He combined his criticism with his dislike for the Middle Ages. Later, therefore, more historically minded musicologists like G. Pietzsch (*Die Musik im Erziehungs- und Bildungsideal des ausgehenden Altertums und fruehen Mittelalters* [1932]), or L. Schrade ("Die Stellung der Musik in der Philosophie des Boethius", *Archiv fuer Geschichte der Philosophie* 41 [1932] 368–400) felt that they had to defend the Middle Ages. But they have excessively narrowed the basis of their whole discussion by

---

* Cf. J. Croissant, *Aristote et les Mystères* (1932); P. Boyancé, *Le Culte des Muses chez les philosophes Grecs* (1937).

paying no attention whatsoever to the problem of the quadrivium, and concentrating on music alone.

The fact is that the whole quadrivium idea, and particularly the attempt to find for the quadrivium a place between physics and theology (metaphysics), make sense only within the framework of Plato's realism and his tripartition of being *.

* Cf. also H. Klinkenberg, "Der Verfall des Quadriviums im fruehen Mittelalter"; K. G. Fellerer, "Die musica in den artes liberales", in: J. Koch (ed.), *Artes liberales* (1959) 1–32; 33–49, esp. 27; 40; 47.

V. SPEUSIPPUS IN IAMBLICHUS

In ch. III and in the last section of ch. IV of *Isc* Iamblichus had refused to identify the mathematicals with the soul. In ch. IX he insisted that the soul should be identified with all three branches of mathematics. While ch. IX is much more compatible with most of *Isc* and also with the *Timaeus*, ch. III is not completely inconsistent with some tendencies in Platonism as reported by Aristotle. While Plato, as Aristotle repeats time and again, supposed three οὐσίαι only (sensibles, mathematicals, and ideas), some Platonists assumed more. One of the examples is Speusippus, who, according to Aristotle (*Met.* Z 2, 1028b21–24; N 3, 1090b13–19; fr. 33a; 50 Lang), not only differentiated arithmeticals from geometricals, but also presumed the soul to be a separate οὐσία. It seems that the latter is precisely what the source of *Isc* ch. III did ("it is better to posit the soul in another genus of οὐσία, while assuming that mathematical principles and the mathematical οὐσία are nonmotive"; p. 13, 12–15 F). Could it be that the inspiration of this chapter is ultimately the Aristotelico-Speusippean controversy? Could it even be that there are some other traces of Speusippus in *Isc*, in addition to what amounted to a quotation from Speusippus in *Isc* ch. IX ("... idea of the all-extended")? To decide this question let us discuss Speusippus' system as criticized by Aristotle.

In *Met.* N 4 and 5, 1091a29–1092a21 (cf. Λ 7, 1072b30–34 and 10, 1075a36–37) Aristotle discusses different difficulties of the two-opposite-principles doctrine, particularly when (a) these two opposite principles are at the same time principles of good and evil, and (b) these two principles are to "engender" numbers.

I. Some of these difficulties are: 1. Everything (except the One) would be tainted with evil, because everything is a product of the two principles (one and multitude, or unequal, or great-and-small) — numbers would even be more tainted than geometricals.

2. The evil (the hyletic principle) would be the χώρα of the good, participate in it, and so [obviously] desire its own destruction or could be called potentially good (see below p. 114).

3. If the One is good and generates numbers, the result would be a great abundance of goods [— obviously because every number would be good].

II. Some tried to avoid these difficulties. They denied that the One is good: thus there was no reason for them to designate multitude as evil. As a consequence what is termed good and beautiful (and the best) would not be present in the principle [or, from the very beginning or, originally]. Good would be begotten later; it would appear only as the nature of beings proceeds. And Aristotle adds that these men remind one of tellers of fables of old concerning gods. These likewise used to start their cosmologies with chaos and let order follow later.

Now it seems that the representatives of this doctrine, according to which the principles — One and multitude — are neither good or beautiful nor evil (so that the good and the beautiful comes into existence later), felt that they had to defend their view. They did so by a simile (εἰκάζειν — a popular social game; cf. L. Radermacher, *Weinen und Lachen* [1947] 42 with n. 4; cf. Plato, *Meno* 80 C and Xenophon, *Symposion* VI 8–VII 1; a game played even in our time). Plants and animals proceed from seeds — what is more perfect springs from what is more undifferentiated and imperfect. This is always the case; therefore it is so also with the "first things". As a consequence — and it is not quite clear whether Aristotle is still reporting or whether it is his own interpretation — the One is μηδὲ ὄν τι (fr. 35 a, b, d, e; 34 a, e, f Lang).

It is generally agreed that the "evolutionist" whose views are presented sub II is Speusippus *. Only the very last words may be Aristotle's rather than Speusippus'.

Aristotle's criticism (based an the assumption that in some way the chicken precedes the egg) is well known.

Two more criticisms are of importance in the present context. One, generally admitted to be directed at Speusippus is that the latter has disjointed being; its single spheres (numbers, magnitudes, soul) become independent from one another (fr. 50 Lang). According to some, says Aristotle, magnitudes originate from numbers plus ὕλη; e.g. we could imagine that lines originate by a combination of two with matter, and so on (*Met.* N 3,1090b21–24). But with some, magnitudes are quite independent from numbers. What Aristotle seems to imply, then,

---

* There is particularly no reason to doubt that the principle which he opposed to the One was not evil according to him. This is stated by Aristotle implicitly in *Met.* N 4, 1091b34–35 and explicitly in *Met.* Λ 10,1075a37.

is that the "disjointer" had for each new sphere of being a peculiar pair of principles (one formal, corresponding to the original One, one material, corresponding to the original multitude); whereas others, according to Aristotle, used single entities belonging to the superior sphere of being (e.g. single numbers) as formal principles to constitute entities belonging to the immediately inferior sphere of being (e.g. geometricals). Thus they established, whereas the former did not, a connection between the several spheres. Still others may have used the whole preceding sphere as the formal principle for the subsequent one (*Met.* A 6,988a7–14). The "disjointing" point of view is attacked by Aristotle as polyarchy (πολυκοιρανίη; fr. 33 e Lang).

The other criticism says: It is wrong (ἄτοπον) to "generate" (ποιεῖν) place (τόπος) together with mathematical solids (or, to imitate Aristotle's pun, it is out of place to generate place). For place is peculiar to individuals [i.e. sensibles, the assumption being obviously that mathematicals are universals], whereas mathematicals have no "where" [i.e. they are not in space]; fr. 52 Lang. It is, however, not quite certain that this criticism refers to Speusippus (cf. below p. 111). If we, for the time being, presume this, then, what he said was that geometricals have place (τόπος) — obviously as their material principle.

With this presentation of Speusippus by Aristotle let us compare the content of *Isc* ch. IV, omitting what is obviously a kind of introduction (p. 14, 18–15, 5 F) and a summary (p. 18, 13–23 F).

1. Numbers have two principles: the One, which should not be called being (ὅπερ ... οὐδὲ ὄν πω δεῖ καλεῖν; p. 15, 7–8 F) and the principle of multitude [i.e. multitude as principle], responsible for division (διαίρεσις) and comparable to some moist and pliable matter. These two principles engender the first kind [sphere of being], i.e. numbers. The material principle is responsible for [their being] divided and [their being a] magnitude and [their] increase [i.e. the fact that numbers grow *in infinitum*; cf. p. 16, 17 F]; the other principle which is indifferent and undivided (ἀδιάφορον καὶ ἄτμητον) is responsible for their being a quale, a limited, a One.

2. We should not suppose that the hyletic principle (first receptacle, magnitude) is evil or ugly, even though it is re-

sponsible for magnitude, the discontinuous, and the increase.
We should not do it because:

a. sometimes the great (*magnum*) joined to a certain quality
becomes the reason for the *magnificence and liberality [which
obviously are good; so that it is proved that a thing which may
be neutral or good, becomes good or better by addition of magnitude; for an explanation see below].

b. those who assume that the One is the cause of things
beautiful in the realm of numbers, and therefore something
praiseworthy, should not say that the hyletic principle is evil
and ugly — because [obviously] this hyletic principle is "receptive" of the One [and what is receptive of something
praiseworthy should not be termed bad or ugly].

3. The One is neither beautiful nor good; it is above (ὑπεράνω)
both (p. 16, 11 F); it is only in the process of nature that the
beautiful, and later on also the good, appears.

4. There must exist more than one matter and receptacle or
everything would be number. Just as there is a monad (corresponding to the One) in numbers, so there is a point in lines. This
point is obviously one of the two principles of geometricals. The
other is position, distance of places, and place — they are the
hyletic principle of geometricals.

It is this hyletic principle which makes the geometricals more
continuous, more massive and compact, than numbers are.

The text of this section is difficult. Does it mean that we
have a change in terms: the principle of numbers is not One —
it is the monad? Shall we assume that the principle of geometricals is the point, being defined as monad having location?
Shall we assume that point plus position is line; a line plus
distance is surface; a surface plus locus is stereometrical? This
would seem the simplest explanation, though it must be admitted
that the text is not quite clear. There is no doubt, however,
that the net result is a doctrine to the effect that geometricals
do have their own receptacle different from the receptacle of
the numbers; and one of the terms applied to this "new" receptacle is τόπος.

5. The elements from which the numbers are derived are
neither beautiful nor good. The synthesis of the One with
ὕλη as the cause of multitude results in numbers. It is only in

these that being and beauty appear. Afterwards the geometrical sphere appears — out of the elements of lines [i.e., of the elements the first product of which are lines], and here we again find being and beauty, while nothing in them is ugly or evil.

Evil appears only in the fourth and the fifth spheres of being which come into existence out of the very last elements, i.e., $X_4 + Y_4$ and $X_5 + Y_5$, whereas numbers are composed of $X_1 + Y_1$, geometricals of $X_2 + Y_2$, and an unnamed entity of $X_3 + Y_3$; X and Y being the "analogies" of One and multitude respectively. The evil appears not as a result of direct action or intention (οὐ προηγουμένως); it appears as the result of some deficiency and failure to "tame" some things natural.

This is the content of the crucial section of *Isc* ch. IV. There cannot be much doubt that these ideas are Speusippean. He was the only philosopher who denied that the supreme principles were good or evil; he was the one who asserted that the good and beautiful appear only later; he was the one who posited for each sphere of being a peculiar pair of principles. The question arises, what is the source of Iamblichus?

Some will argue that he (or his source) simply culled bits of information regarding Speusippus from Aristotle's *Metaphysics* and arranged them into a coherent whole. Others will argue that some of the doctrines are distinctly Plotinian in character. The subsequent analysis of the content of *Isc* will, it is trusted, disprove both of these arguments.

First of all, in comparison with the elusive and ambiguous presentation of Aristotle, *Isc* states distinctly and univocally that the One is non-being and that it is so in the sense of being above being. Secondly, in contradiction to what Aristotle seems to imply, it makes it impossible to think of the relation between the One and the good as an evolution from worse to better or from less to more. Though it may be an evolution in a sense, it is an evolution *sui generis* — not a one-way amelioration (nor a one-way deterioration, as will be explained later). The similarity between Aristotle and *Isc* is great enough to establish that *Isc* is presenting the views of Speusippus; and the difference between *Isc* and Aristotle is great enough to establish that *Isc* is not derived from Aristotle.

Now, some will say that the difference between Aristotle and

Isc is to be explained in terms of Iamblichus' Plotinianism (we use this word rather than the too inclusive Neoplatonism). They will insist that the appearance of the doctrine of the One above being in *Isc* almost proves that Iamblichus was slanting the doctrines of Speusippus known to him from Aristotle so as to make them appear as being close to Plotinus.

The answer is that the One as presented in *Isc* is, indeed, similar in certain respects to the One of Plotinus, but in some other respects differs from it radically. The most obvious difference is that Plotinus' One is identical with the good, whereas the One of *Isc* is not. Furthermore, it is strictly un-Plotinian to assume that the beautiful appears first, the good afterwards. In Plotinus there is no doubt as to the priority of the good over the beautiful. Thus, the difference between *Isc* and Aristotle cannot be explained by the influence of Plotinus.

If the difference between Aristotle and *Isc* cannot be explained in terms of Plotinus' Neoplatonism, it can even less be explained in terms of Iamblichus' own system. According to Damascius, Iamblichus assumed as the supreme principle "the altogether ineffable", to be followed by "the absolutely One", which in turn is followed by two principles which we could call the limit and the unlimited or also One and many, it being clearly understood that the absolutely One has no opposite, whereas this latter One is one of two opposites (*Dubitationes et solutiones de primis principiis* ed. C. E. Ruelle 2vv. [1889] 50–51; v. I 101, 14–15; 103, 6–10). Nor is there any similarity between *Isc* ch. IV and the doctrine of Iamblichus in *De mysteriis* ch. VIII 2, p. 262 Parthey (cf. K. Praechter, art. Syrianos (1) in *RE* IV A 2 [1932], 1739). Where Iamblichus speaks in his own name he is a strict monist, much more so than Plotinus. When he multiplies the principles, it is precisely to make dualism begin as late as possible and to keep monism as long as possible. All this contradicts the dualism of *Isc* (see e.g. ch. III, p. 12, 25–13, 9 F).

We are so accustomed to think only of Plotinus as the originator of the theory according to which the supreme principle is above being and only of the *Parmenides* and one single passage in the *Republic* VI 509 B (cf. F. M. Cornford, *Plato and Parmenides* [1939] 131–134) as possible anticipations of that theory by Plato that it is worthwhile to point out that the step from the

Sophist to such a theory is very short indeed. In the *Sophist* Plato replaced the notion of non-being by that of otherness. This means, that all non-being is determinate non-being; in its determinateness, i.e. in its being *neither* this *nor* this, etc., consists its non-being. Now, to otherness (determinate non-being), Plato opposes sameness, to which he, however, does not pay much attention — just as he does not pay too much attention to the difficulties inherent in the concept of being. But symmetry demands that if otherness stands for determinate non-being, sameness must stand for determinate being. This term "determinate being" would indeed very well express Plato's idea that all being is permeated by non-being, just as the term "determinate nothingness" expresses that all non-being is actually only otherness, i.e. that all non-being is permeated by being.

Now, if sameness stands for determinate being, being, introduced by Plato as one of the supreme genera cannot be anything but indeterminate being. But precisely by being indeterminate it gains status above determinate being: it is being which is still un-permeated by non-being. This would exactly be the One of Plotinus. Whether we call it indeterminate being or above being makes no difference whatsover.

At the same time we can also see how what we reconstructed as a doctrine of Speusippus could easily develop out of the *Sophist*. Just as there is an indeterminate being above determinate being (sameness), so there is an indeterminate non-being above determinate non-being (otherness). It is by the interplay of indeterminate being with indeterminate non-being that determinate being and determinate non-being originate. Indeterminate being and indeterminate non-being are in every respect indifferent. Of this more will later be said (below p. 127).

We do not mean to say that Speusippus developed his system by such an interpretation of the *Sophist*. All we mean to say is that from a systematic point of view, disregarding any historic questions, the doctrine of a principle above being is close to Plato.

Thus the conclusion is: the traces of Speusippus which can be found in *Isc* ch. III and IX are not misleading. *Isc* ch. IV is a source of knowledge of Speusippus independent from Aristotle and not influenced by the doctrines of Plotinus or Iamblichus.

We should not be surprised to discover Speusippus in *Isc*. In the *Theologoumena arithmeticae* (the authenticity of the content of which we have no reason to doubt; see Zeller III/2⁵ [1923] 739 n. 1 and H. Oppermann on de Falco's edition of the *Theologoumena*, *Gnomon* 5 [1929] 545–558, esp. 558) 61–63 (p. 82, 10–85, 23 Falco; fr. 4 Lang) we find a long excerpt from Speusippus' book on *Pythagorean Numbers*. Iamblichus is the only author who preserved Speusippus' definition of the soul. Iamblichus read Aristotle's *Protrepticus*. Iamblichus knew a passage in which Aristotle used the term ἐνδελέχεια for soul (Stobaeus I 49, 32, p. 367, 1 Wachsmuth; cf. P. Merlan on Bignone, *L' Aristotele perduto e la formazione filosofica di Epicuro, Gnomon* 17 [1941] 32–41). According to Simplicius (*In Arist. categ.* ch. X, p. 407, 20 Kalbfleisch; *Aristotelis fragmenta* ed. V. Rose p. 109, 20–22) Iamblichus knew Aristotle's Περὶ ἐναντίων (ἀντικειμένων). He even read a sophist of the Fifth Century (the so called Anonymus Iamblichi). A rich library must have been at his disposal (in Apamea? see e.g. F. Cumont, *Lux perpetua* [1949] 372), a library containing at least one work by Speusippus. Thus, there is nothing particularly bold in the assumption that *Isc* contains ideas belonging to Speusippus. It could even be that the very title and topic of *Isc* (περὶ τῆς κοινῆς μαθηματικῆς ἐπιστήμης), i.e., investigation of the principles *common* to all branches of mathematics, is Speusippean in inspiration; cf. F. Solmsen, *Die Entwicklung der aristotelischen Logik und Rhetorik* (1929) 251 f.; 252 n. 3. Diogenes Laertius IV 2 quotes Diodorus (see on him [E.] Schwartz, art. Apomnemoneumata in *RE* II/1 [1895]) as having described in his Ἀπομνημονεύματα the method of Speusippus as investigating τὸ κοινόν ἐν τοῖς μαθήμασι *. This is what *Isc* professes to do: see particularly the contents (κεφάλαια) p. 3, 7. 13 F; p. 4, 1. 9. 12 F; p. 6, 7 F; p. 8, 7. 15 F; cf. ch. XXXV, p. 98, 28–99, 1 F.

Starting, then, with the assumption that *Isc* ch. IV presents doctrines of Speusippus, we are going to compare *Isc* with

---

* There is no reason to assume that the word meant anything except "branches of mathematics" (cf. F. Solmsen, *Die Entwicklung der Aristotelischen Logik und Rhetorik* [1929] 80 n. 4; 252 n. 3). Speusippus wrote a Μαθηματικός (Diog. Laert. IV 5), which can hardly mean anything except *The Mathematician*, perhaps as a counterpart to Plato's *Statesman, Sophist,* and *Philosopher* (the last of which Plato only planned and Speusippus himself wrote; see Diog. Laert. IV 5 and cf. Lang p. 42 and 48).

Aristotle in greater detail. We begin with a discussion of the formal principle.

We read in Aristotle that the theory of Speusippus results in the assertion μηδὲ ὄν τι εἶναι τὸ ἓν αὐτό. There is some doubt possible: is this Aristotle's inference or is it still a report? Doubts disappear as we read in *Isc*: the ἕν is οὐδὲ ὄν.

However, what does this mean? Οὐδέ may mean "not even" in the sense of "less than". If it means that, Speusippus described his One as *less* than being. This interpretation is, indeed, strongly suggested by Aristotle's presentation. The seed is less than the plant: the One is not even a being (anything existing). And the same would be true with regard to the relation between the One and the good or the beautiful; the One would be less than either of them. But if we check this interpretation against *Isc* we immediately notice a disagreement. According to *Isc*, the One is praiseworthy as being the cause of beauty; and it is described as being *above* the beautiful or the good. The clear implication seems to be: the One, though not a being, is above being, just as it is not beautiful or good but above them. This is the meaning of οὐδὲ ὄν in *Isc*. In other words, according to *Isc*, Speusippus said: the One is above (or previous to) being, the good, the beautiful (see above p. 98).

We have therefore to ask two questions. First, do we interpret Aristotle correctly as having reported that Speusippus' One was less than being and inferior (in some sense of the word) to what develops out of it, just as the seed is inferior to the mature organism? Secondly, if our interpretation of Aristotle is correct, did he present the views of Speusippus correctly? Did Speusippus mean to say that the One is less than being and inferior (in the sense of not being good) to what develops out of it?

The first question should be answered in the negative. The only reason why this was not seen ever since was the overconcentration of our attention on one aspect of Speusippus' doctrine of the One as presented in Aristotle, to the almost total neglect of the other aspect of this doctrine also presented by Aristotle, viz. that the material principle is not evil. If we do not forget that Speusippus was a dualist, it will be very difficult to interpret him as an evolutionist in the ordinary sense of the word. If there are two seeds in the universe of Speusippus, one for good, one for evil, the term "seed" must be taken in the metaphorical sense of the word. The words of Aristotle μηδὲ ὄν τι εἶναι τὸ ἓν αὐτό should be translated either: "so that the One itself is not any being either" or "so that we should not even say of the One itself that it is some being". In either case Aristotle, somewhat ambiguously, meant to say that according to Speusippus the One should not be designated as being. E. R. Dodds ("The Parmenides of Plato and the Origin of the Neo-Platonic One", *Classical Quarterly* 22 [1928] 129–142, esp. 140) interpreted Aristotle correctly when he said that the latter credited Speusippus with the view that the One was ὑπερούσιον or at any rate ἀνούσιον *.

But even if the traditional interpretation of Aristotle is correct, even if Aristotle meant to say that Speusippus' One is less than being, our second question should be answered in the negative. It was obviously in Aristotle's interest to present the doctrine of Speusippus in terms of his own δύναμις-ἐνέργεια concepts and so to reduce the assertion of Speusippus that the One is not to be counted among the things that are, to the assertion: the One is only potentially a being. And it was obviously in Aristotle's interest to present Speusippus' simile of the seed, as implying the inferiority of the One. It seems that Speusippus would not have admitted that the seed is inferior to the plant; it seems he would have compared their relation with the relation between the four and the ten. Full perfection appears only in the ten; but is the four inferior to the ten? Or else Speusippus would have protested against pressing his simile too far; the One may be *like* the seed — does it have to be so in every respect (cf. W. Jaeger, *Aristoteles*[2] [1955] 233)?

One additional piece of evidence will prove how cautious we should be before equating the seed with what is inferior. Having stated the principle that nature never acts in vain, Theophrastus adds: this is particularly true of what is first and most important

---

* Cf. also C. Sandulescu-Godeni, *Das Verhaeltnis von Rationalitaet und Irrationalitaet in der Philosophie Platons* (1938) 25; G. Nebel, *Plotins Kategorien der intelligiblen Welt* (1929) 32 f. For the opposite point of view see e.g. A. H. Armstrong, *The Architecture of the Intelligible Universe in the Philosophy of Plotinus* (1940) 18; 22. What is said above should suffice to disprove Armstrong's interpretation. Even so, Armstrong himself says of Speusippus that he anticipated the negative theology (*ibid.*, 18; 21 f.; 63; cf. now his *Introduction to Ancient Philosophy*[3] (1957) 67. Cf. also H. R. Schwyzer, art. Plotinos, *RE* XXI/1 (1951) 559 f.

— seed being what is the first and most important (*De causis plant.* I 1, v. II 1 Wimmer). By "first and most important" Theophrastus designates the ultimate principles — here and also in his *Metaphysics* I 3, p. 4 Ross and Fobes, where he says that some consider number to be that which is the first and most important. Clearly, Theophrastus makes a distinction between what is undeveloped and what is inferior (or imperfect in the ordinary sense of the word). While the seed is in his opinion the former, it is not the latter. Indeed, the idea that what is undifferentiated and undispersed is higher than the differentiated and spread out, so that the seed is higher than the organism, seems like a rather natural one.

Thus, we repeat: according to both *Isc* and what Aristotle either reported or should have reported Speusippus said of his One that it is not even being in precisely the same sense in which Plotinus said of his One that it is οὐδὲ ὄν (*Enn.* VI 9, 3, 38 Bréhier *).

We now proceed to present another aspect of the formal principle.

Isc discusses the question whether it is necessary to assume a plurality of material principles, to answer this question in the affirmative. We shall return to the problem of the plurality of material principles later; for the time being another detail should be stressed. While speaking of the plurality of material principles *Isc* almost casually remarks that there is such a plurality of formal principles. Just as it is necessary to posit the monad in numbers (corresponding to the One), whereas it is necessary to posit the point in lines (again corresponding to the One), so it is necessary to posit a specific receptacle in the geometricals, which would correspond to multitude or the material principle. This agrees with Aristotle: Speusippus assumed a certain One anterior to the One in numbers (*Met.* M 8, 1083a24–25; fr. 42 d Lang). And from *Isc* we learn that to distinguish the two, Speusippus applied the term monad to the formal principle in numbers, keeping the term One for the supreme formal principle.

However, it should be noted that there is a certain, obviously intentional looseness in the terminology of *Isc.* The material principle is referred to as multitude or the principle of multitude,

---

* Subsequently: Br.

the latter term leaving us the choice to interpret it either as an objective or as a subjective genitive; later, as first receptacle or magnitude "or whatever it should be called"; again, as matter which is the reason of multitude. Therefore we should not attach too much importance to the difference between the terms "monad" and "One".

We noticed that according to *Isc* beauty originates before the good does. This unusual doctrine is stated very emphatically. First comes the beautiful; second, and in greater distance from the principles (στοιχεῖα), comes the good. This seems to imply that there is no good in the sphere of mathematicals; there is in them only the beautiful. And indeed *Isc* repeats twice that there is beauty in the mathematicals (p. 16, 3 F; p. 18, 5. 8 F), while it never says it of the good, limiting itself rather to saying that there is no evil in them (p. 18, 9 F). Now, this whole doctrine immediately reminds us of a passage in Aristotle's *Metaphysics*. It is the passage M 3, 1078a31–b6, a passage strangely disconnected from anything that precedes or follows (though related to a problem raised in B 2, 996a29-bl). Mathematics, Aristotle admits, has nothing to do with the good, but it has to do with beauty. It could be that this strangely incongruent apology of mathematics is the result of Speusippus' influence on Aristotle. It should be noticed that the inclusion of beauty and the exclusion of the good from mathematics has been traced to Eudoxus by H. Karpp, *Untersuchungen zur Philosophie des Eudoxos von Knidos* (1933) 55–57, but this is purely conjectural.

But perhaps there is one more possibility of relating the *Metaphysics* passage on beauty in mathematics to some other writings of Aristotle.

The First Prologue of Proclus' commentary on Euclid contains an apology of mathematics. This apology starts on p. 25, 15 Fr and ends on p. 29, 13 Fr. It begins with a summary of objections to mathematics, these objections being of two kinds. The first criticize mathematics because it has nothing to do with the good and the beautiful; the second do it because of its entirely theoretical, impractical character (p. 25, 15–26, 9 Fr). The second section of Proclus' reply (p. 27, 17–29, 13 Fr) is mainly devoted to a defense of mathematics from the second kind of objections. It contains on p. 28, 13–22 Fr a quotation from

Aristotle, identified as being from his *Protrepticus* (see fr. 52 Rose
= *Protrepticus* fr. 5 a Walzer). The first section of Proclus'
reply (p. 26, 10–27, 16 Fr), devoted to the proof that mathematics does not lack beauty, also quotes Aristotle (p. 26, 12 Fr).
It seems to be generally agreed that this quotation refers to
Aristotle's *Metaphysics* M 3,1078a31–1078b1. But is this certain?
In the *Metaphysics* passage Aristotle proves the presence of
beauty in mathematics by saying that the main kinds of beauty
are order, symmetry, and limitation — all of which are present
in mathematical disciplines. Proclus, however, offers a different
kind of proof. His chain of thought is as follows. 1. Beauty
in body and soul is caused by order, symmetry, and limitation.
2. This can be proved by: *a.* the fact that ugliness of the body
is caused by the absence of order, form, symmetry, and limitation,
while ugliness of the soul amounts to unreasonableness, which is
full of disorder and refuses to accept limitation from reason;
b. the fact that, opposites having opposite causes, the opposite
of ugliness, i.e. beauty, must be caused by what it opposed to
disorder, etc. — precisely by order, symmetry, and limitation.
3. But these three can easily be seen in mathematics: order in
the way in which what is more complicated follows from what
is more simple; symmetry in the way in which all mathematical
proofs agree with one another and in the way in which everything
is related to the νοῦς (because νοῦς is the standard of mathematics from which mathematics receives its principles and
toward which it turns its students); limitation in the fact that
its theorems (λόγοι) are immutable. Therefore, if order, symmetry,
and limitation are the factors of beauty, mathematics contains
beauty.

One can immediately see that the passage comprizes very much
that is not contained in the few lines of the *Metaphysics* passage
which Proclus is supposed to quote. Some of this surplus may
be entirely Proclus' own (e.g. the νοερὰ εἴδη on p. 27, 10 Fr),
but must all be his? If all were, Proclus would have been very
generous indeed in crediting Aristotle with it. While this can
not be ruled out, it is not very likely. In addition, two things
are striking.

The first is that the argument, "opposites have opposite
causes", is entirely in the style of Aristotle's *Topics* (esp. III

6, 119a32–119b16; cf. also *Rhet.* II 23,1397a7–19). More specifically, the reasoning, "ugliness is caused by lack of order, etc.; therefore beauty is caused by order, etc.", reminds us of the passage in Aristotle's *Eudemus*, fr. 45 Rose = *Eudemus* fr. 7 Walzer, where sickness, weakness, and ugliness of the body are declared to be the result of ἀναρμοστία, wherefore health, strength, and beauty must be tantamount to ἁρμονία. If Proclus quoted his passage from the *Metaphysics*, he at least combined it with an idea from the *Eudemus*. But even this does not account for all the surplus. Where did Proclus find the idea that unreasonableness of the soul is ugliness of the soul and due to absence of order? Perhaps it was Aristotle himself who proved the presence of beauty in mathematics in this more circumstantial way using proofs similar to those in the *Eudemus*.

The second thing is the insistence of Proclus-Aristotle on the fact that in mathematics it is the νοῦς which is the standard. We are immediately reminded of the philosophic situation created by the theory of Protagoras and all the attempts of both Plato and Aristotle to replace his *homo mensura* maxim by some other objective and non-anthropocentric formula (see W. Jaeger, *Aristoteles*² [1955] 89f.; cf. also 249, n.l). It does not seem likely that Proclus added this argument from his own; the formula μέτρον τῆς ἐπιστήμης ὁ νοῦς sounds Aristotelian, but it does not occur in the *Metaphysics* passage.

All this sums up to saying that not only the passage p. 28, 14–22 Fr but also p. 26, 10–27, 16 Fr could be derived from an Aristotelian writing similar to or identical with his *Protrepticus*. And it would only be natural to discover some connection between it and Speusippus regarding the presence of beauty in mathematics. The full significance of the preceding discussion will become clear only in the light of the next chapter; for the time being let us return to *Isc.*

Isc calls the supreme principle not only cause of the beautiful in the mathematicals but also self-sufficient (p. 16, 3 F) and stresses that it is neither good nor beautiful itself (p. 18, 2–3 F). In other words, though neither good nor beautiful, the One or the supreme formal principle is self-sufficient. We immediately feel reminded of Aristotle's argument: the supreme principle can be called self-sufficient only if it is good — for what other reason could the supreme principle be self-sufficient (*Met.* N 4,1091b16–19)? It seems that Aristotle here criticizes precisely the doctrine of Speusippus, who on the one hand asserted that the supreme principle is self-sufficient and on the other hand denied that it is good.

The doctrine of *Isc* that the good originates only in the sphere next to the mathematicals and the complementary doctrine that evil appears only in the last spheres (of the latter doctrine we shall presently have more to say) perhaps permits us to interpret a difficult passage in Theophrastus' *Metaphysics* IX 32, p. 36 Ross and Fobes, fr. 41 Lang (on the different interpretations see H. Cherniss, *Aristotle's Criticism of Presocratic Philosophy* [1935] 394). "Speusippus makes the worthy a rare thing — he places it around the middle χώρα; all the rest are the principles (ἄκρα) and [what surrounds the middle χώρα] on both sides". Could it be that the middle χώρα does not mean the center of the spatial cosmos but the center of the spheres of being? The ἄκρα are the neutral principles; they, together with the last sphere of being, surround the center, thus forming the pattern: neutral — good — evil. And perhaps we can anticipate here what will later be elucidated: there is no difference between cosmology and ontology in the Academic system, and we should not be surprised to see these two points of view hardly distinguishable in Theophrastus' *Metaphysics*. The outermost spheres of the universe are the One (containing no good at all) and the last sphere (or spheres) of being containing evil; then the good is confined to the central sphere of being or the center of the universe — that is why it is rare.

If we assume that Speusippus' One, in spite of not being good, was not inferior to the good, we can understand why Aristotle in *Nic. Eth.* I 4, 1096b5–7 (fr. 37a Lang) could say that he placed his One in the column of goods. "The column of goods" may very well comprise the One and "the good" in the more restricted sense of the word, while the term "the goods" in the heading would be used more loosely. There cannot be much objection to the designation of the left column of the Pythagorean opposites (e.g. *Met.* A 5,986a22–26) as the column of goods, in spite of the fact that the good is one of its items (along with the One). If we, however, were to assume that the

One of Speusippus was *less* than good, it would be somewhat surprising to find it among goods.

From the formal principle we can now turn to the material one. Aristotle reports that Speusippus used to call it πλῆθος, multitude. This, indeed, is the name used for it in *Isc* (p. 15, 11. 15 F). He further reports that according to Speusippus each sphere of being had its own material principle. *Isc* elucidates this. In its longest single passage (p. 16, 18–17, 19 F) we find an explanation why a multiplicity of material principles is necessary (which corresponds to the problem posed in *Met*. B 4,1001b19–25). Without such a multiplicity everything would be number, says *Isc*. And it would not do to say that the same material principle contains differences within itself, which differences are responsible for the origin of different spheres (or kinds) of being despite the fact that it is one and the same One which pervades everything equally. Nor would it do to say that because the material principle is coarse-grained, the One does not always equally well succeed in expressing itself adequately in such a medium (just as happens when we attempt to impress some form on timber of poor quality). Why would neither of these explanations do, though they sound pretty reasonable? They contradict our ideas and experiences regarding first principles in any field by assuming a principle that contains differences within itself (is differentiated) and thus divided. Principle (element) is always that which is absolutely simple.

By this reasoning *Isc* establishes the plurality of material principles.

This material principle in the realm of geometricals is position, distance (διάστασις τόπων), and place (τόπος).

We are reminded of Aristotle's criticism (cf. above p. 98). It is wrong, says Aristotle, to generate (ποιεῖν) place (τόπος) together with mathematical solids, for place is peculiar to individuals, i.e. sensibles (and in saying that individuals are χωριστά τόπῳ Aristotle comes close to the doctrine according to which space is the principle of individuation), whereas mathematicals have no "where" (*Met*. N 5,1092a17–20; fr. 52 Lang). The whole passage is without connection with what precedes or what follows; and while it seems to refer to Speusippus (see Ross a.l.), we could not be sure of that. *Isc* eliminates any doubt; Speusippus did generate place together with geometricals, referring to its three aspects as position, spatial distance, and place. It becomes clear why Aristotle instead of speaking of geometricals *tout court*, spoke of stereometricals. As we see from *Isc*, it was only with them that Speusippus associated place, whereas points and lines had not place in general but only position and distension (spatial distance) as their material element.

Isc stresses that all three kinds of geometricals form only one sphere, or kind, of being. As Aristotle tried to prove that Speusippus was a disjointer of being because, due to the plurality of principles, his superior spheres do not contribute to the existence of the inferior and made his point clear by giving as an example the independence of geometricals from arithmeticals, we may ask whether Aristotle was fair in presenting Speusippus as a disjointer. We shall discuss this question later.

We now come to one of the most remarkable features of the doctrine of Speusippus: his assertion that the material principle is neither ugly (foul) nor evil. *Isc* fully confirms what Aristotle barely mentions (once explicitly, once by implication; see above p. 97, note). But it also brings a welcome addition in that it stresses the absence of both fairness (beauty) and evil from the material principle, whereas Aristotle concentrates entirely on the quality of evil. And *Isc* also contains an explanation as to why the supreme material principle is neither evil nor foul. True, says *Isc*, it is the material principle which is responsible for magnitude, the discontinuous, and the increase — but there are many cases where this kind of principle (i.e. a principle causing some kind of dispersion, extension in size, bulk, etc.) is not considered to be something evil. There are cases when the great, added to some other quality, can well be considered the cause of magnificence and liberality, both of which are obviously good rather than evil.

The argument is somewhat puzzling. What *Isc* means to say is obviously that the great (magnitude), i.e. the material principle or a specific representative of the material principle, when joined to some other quality sometimes improves this quality rather than impairs it. This proves that magnitude cannot be considered evil. And as an example *Isc* mentions magnificence (μεγαλοπρέπεια) or munificence along with liberality or benefi-

cence, generosity (ἐλευθεριότης). Now, an explanation seems to
be contained in a passage of the *Nicomachean Ethics*. Magnificence surpasses beneficence just by the element of magnitude
added to the latter (*Nic. Eth.* IV 4, 1122a22), and is better
than mere beneficence. And he is magnificent, says the *Eudemian
Ethics*, who selects the proper magnitude where there is a great
occasion (*Eud. Eth.* III 6, 1233a35–38). In other words, *Isc*
seems to say: in the case of magnificence and beneficence we
see that the element of greatness when coupled with a certain
quality (beneficence) turns this quality into something better,
i.e. magnificence.

   It is true that, as the words stand, a literal translation would
be: "We might say and likely to be right that the great joined
to a certain quality becomes the reason of magnificence and
beneficence". If this is precisely what *Isc* meant to say, then
not only magnificence but also beneficence would be explained
in terms of the great (magnitude) added to some anonymous
quality (in such a case the obsolete "largesse" would be an ideal
translation of ἐλευθεριότης) — perhaps "attitude towards money".
But as neither the *Nic. Eth.* nor the passage in *Rhetorics* dealing
with liberality (*Rhet.* I 9, 1366b2–16) couples it with any kind
of magnitude, it may also be that *Isc* expressed itself elliptically:
as if somebody wanted to write "the great coupled with a certain
quality becomes the reason of the difference between magnificence and liberality" but omitted the words "the difference
between".

   If the allusion is actually to the *Nicomachean Ethics* (the
parallel passages in *Eud. Eth.* and *Magna Moralia* do not have
the equation "magnificence = liberality + magnitude") and if
all of *Nicomachean Ethics* originated during Aristotle's second
sojourn in Athens, *Isc* ch. IV could not be a direct quotation from
Speusippus. But neither is certain *. It could even be that *Isc*
is indebted for its example to the wisdom of language rather
than any book.

   Isc adds still another proof that the material principle is not
evil. In spite of the fact that the supreme formal principle is
neither good nor fair, it could justly be called praiseworthy

----

* A problem similar to that posed by the fact that *Met.* A 1,981b25 seems to quote
Nic. Eth. VI 3–9, 1139b14–1142a30. See Ross, *Arist. Met.* a.l.

considering its self-sufficiency (see above p. 109) and the fact that it is the cause of some beautiful things in the realm of numbers. Now, the material principle is receptive of the formal principle, but what is receptive of something praiseworthy cannot be evil or foul.

The argument that what is receptive of something good (in any sense of the word) cannot be evil harks back to Plato's *Symposion* (203 E) and *Lysis* (217 B). In somewhat changed form it reappears in Aristotle when he insists that if the two supreme principles are opposed to each other as good and evil, this would mean that evil, when entering any combination with the good, must be desirous of its own destruction or even that evil is potentially good (*Met.* N 4, 1092a1–5). *Isc* obviously points to the fact that the assumption of a neutral hyletic principle is not open to this kind of objection.

But *Isc* insists not only that the material principle is not evil or foul; it also insists that it is not in any true sense of the word the cause of evil. First of all, neither is there anything evil or foul in the first sphere of being (numbers) nor in the second (geometricals). Only in the end, in the fourth and fifth sphere of being evil originates. And even here, evil originates not *modo recto* (προηγουμένως) but rather as the result of a certain failure to master some things natural.

This tendency of *Isc* to see in evil something negative (or relative) and a failure reminds one of Aristotle. Explaining monsters, Aristotle stresses that even what is unnatural is still, in a way, natural; namely, it takes place whenever the eidetic *nature* did not succeed in mastering the hyletic *nature*; also in the corresponding passage in *Physics* II 8, 199a30–b7 Aristotle uses the concept of failure. And Aristotle extends the concept of monsters to such an extent as to characterize all females (because of their dissimilarity with the sex of the male parent) as monsters, declaring at the same time that there must be such monsters in species with differentiated sexes (*De gen. anim.* IV 4, 770b9–17; 3, 767b5–23). In other words, there is a strong tendency in Aristotle to exclude evil in any true sense of the word from the realm of nature altogether. This also seems to be the tendency of *Isc*.

Now, all this once more reminds us of a passage in Theophras-

tus. In *Metaphysics* IX 32, p. 36 Ross and Fobes (fr. 41 Lang)
Theophrastus suggests that it is wrong (*a*) to limit the existence
of the good to few things, (*b*) to assert that there is much
evil, (*c*) to deny that evil is only indefinitness and something
hyletic *. And now Theophrastus continues: εἰ· καὶ γάρ (one
ms. has καὶ γάρ, another εἰ γὰρ καί) people like Speusippus
make that which is valuable a rare thing, etc. Now, if we read
with Ross and Fobes (cf. apparatus a.l.) εἰκῇ γάρ (eliminating
the καί), the whole passage from τὸ δ' ὅλον to ἑκατέρωθεν
would be devoted to Speusippus. As a result, Theophrastus
would class him with those who saw in evil more than mere
indefinitness. This, then, would seem to contradict *Isc.*

But it seems risky to ascribe a doctrine to Speusippus merely
on the basis of a conjecture which may be siight from the point
of view of palaeography, but is fundamental from the point
of view of content. It would appear safer to assume that Theophrastus presented two viewpoints (both of which he contradicts),
one according to which evil is something positive and which
is not the point of view of Speusippus (τὸ δ' ὅλον to ἀμαθεστάτου),
and another, that of Speusippus (εἰ· καὶ γάρ to ἑκατέρωθεν) who
limited the existence of the good to the center of being (see above
p. 100). The first point of view could very well be directed against
Philippus, if he was the author of the *Epinomis*, or any other
Zoroastrianizing Platonist (on Zoroaster in the Academy cf. e.g.
A. J. Festugière, "Platon et l'Orient", *Revue de Philologie* 73 =
21 [1947] 5–45, esp. 12–29). Thus, also Theophrastus would hold
an opinion similar to that of Speusippus as to the limited character of evil but he would object to Speusippus' limiting the good
to the "intermediate" spheres of being.

This brings to a close the discussion of the two principles
of Speusippus taken severally. Now some words on their interaction.

The first product of this interaction are numbers and it is only

---

* According to [O.] Regenbogen, art. Theophrastos in *RE* Suppl. VII (1940),
1392, Theophrastus professes (rather than opposes) this doctrine. The text is not quite
certain, to be sure, and Regenbogen's interpretation cannot be ruled out. But the
passage *De caus. plant.* IV 11,7, v. II 152 Wimmer quoted by Regenbogen himself,
ibid. 1470,' seems to indicate that Theophrastus was inclined to treat the unnatural
as becoming natural in the course of time, which he would hardly have done, had he
believed in the subsistence of evil. Thus, the interpretation of the *Metaphysics* passage
in Ross and Fobes is preferable to that of Regenbogen and was followed in the text.

in them that beauty appears and being (p. 18, 5 F). This assertion making numbers the supreme sphere of being should be sufficient to identify the doctrine as Speusippean; Aristotle repeated time and again that mathematicals are the uppermost kind of being in Speusippus, who gave up ideas and ideal numbers.

The interaction generating numbers is called πιθανὴ ἀνάγκη (p. 15, 17 F). This of course is reminiscent of the *Timaeus* (48 A), but the term (persuasible necessity) is original. Unfortunately no details are given to explain the generation of numbers or that of geometricals. Most tantalizing is the sentence saying that evil appears only in the last, i.e. in the fourth and fifth sphere of being. What is the third sphere and why is it omitted from the count? What is the fourth and fifth? If we like to guess, we could assume that arithmeticals and geometricals (and any other kinds of mathematicals: p. 17, 27–29 F) being the first and second sphere of being, soul would be the third (and it would be here that the good originates), the sensible body thus being the fourth (and only here evil would make its first appearance), just as Aristotle reported. But what would be the fifth sphere? Sensible but lifeless bodies, where indeed the good and the beautiful would be at a minimum?

In any case, the fragment is clear enough to make it desirable to discuss the problem of Speusippus' evolutionism once more. As long as Aristotle's report that Speusippus' One was not good, we said, overshadowed the other, i.e., that the material principle was not evil, it was possible to interpret Aristotle's report as asserting Speusippus' evolutionism and to accept this report as correct; but with the doctrine that one of the two supreme principles is not evil, it would be very difficult to interpret Speusippus as an evolutionist in the ordinary sense of the word. We now have additional evidence for this. If the first sphere of being are numbers and the second geometricals, does this mean that geometricals are better than arithmeticals? This makes hardly any sense; and it would make no sense either to say that what follows after mathematicals (the soul or whatever it was) is better than they. There is no good in the mathematicals, but this still does not make them worse than the subsequent sphere of being. The schema "less than good — good — best" simply does not apply to Speusippus' universe.

Aristotle of course had an interest in presenting Speusippus' views concerning the neutral character of the One in terms of δύναμις — ἐνέργεια. But is this the only way to interpret the relation between the One and the good? Is it not on the contrary likely that Speusippus would vigorously have denied that his One is *only* potentially good? Aristotle might well face Speusippus with the dilemma "either the One is identical with the good (or at least it is good) or it is less than good"; but does everybody have to accept the dictum "what is not identical with the good must be less than good"?

Furthermore, the evolutionist point of view (or the δύναμις — ἐνέργεια pair) can be applied to the hyletic principle even less. If the hyletic principle is not evil, is it possible to say that evil develops out of it? It is interesting to express this impossibility in Aristotle's own terms. Aristotle excluded the evil from the principles, reasoning as follows. If evil is a principle, then what is derived from it can only be a lesser evil, according to the maxim that what is less perfect can only come from what is more perfect. But a lesser evil is better and in this sense of the word more perfect than the greatest evil, i.e. evil as principle or evil as full actuality. And this would again contradict the fundamental assumption that the more perfect precedes the less perfect. In other words, there is something paradoxical about the nature of evil if we try to interpret it as cause and something subsisting (Arist. *Met.* θ 9, 1051a15–21). *Ens et bonum convertuntur* — not so *ens et malum*; this is the reason why it is next to impossible to interpret evil as something absolute rather than relative and also the reason why the relation between Speusippus' material principle and evil cannot be interpreted in terms of an evolution.

Thus, be it repeated, Speusippus' universe is not a one-way universe, with the good on the decrease (or increase) and the evil on the increase (or decrease). It is much more irregular, good not being present in the principles nor in the first sphere of being, being fully present only in the middle sphere, and decreasing in the last sphere (or spheres) of being.

It seems that Aristotle faced a somewhat similar problem and solved it in a somewhat similar way. In *De caelo* II 12, 291b29–292a3; 292a22–292b25 he discusses what could be called the asymmetrical aspect of his universe: there is no gradual increase in the number of the motions of the heavenly bodies as we proceed from the best (the sphere of fixed stars) to the earth. The outermost sphere performs one single movement, the spheres of the planets many movements, the earth is immobile. Aristotle explains this asymmetry by assuming that not to move (or to move only a little) may signify one of two opposite things. A thing does not move (or moves only a little) either because it is so perfect that it has already reached (or can reach with a minimum of effort) the goal of its action or because it is so imperfect that it gave up (or is satisfied with a very gross approximation) the pursuit *. Thus, one should not be surprised to see that the number of motions does not increase in direct ratio to the distance from the perfect. First comes an increase, then comes a decrease.

One more aspect of Speusippus' system remains to be discussed. It is the aspect to which Aristotle used to refer by blaming Speusippus as a disjointer. If each sphere of being, said Aristotle, has its own pair of principles, then the being or non-being of one sphere does not contribute to the being of another sphere; all are mutually independent. Now, Stenzel has noticed that Aristotle's reference to Speusippus as a disjointer seems to contradict all we know about Speusippus' tendency to find the similarities between different orders ([J.] Stenzel, art. Speusippos in RE III A 2 [1929] 1664). In what way does Isc clarify this problem?

A fair answer seems to be this. While Isc intends to present the universe as one coherent whole, the actual presentation falls short of the intention and thus to a certain extent justifies Aristotle's criticism. That intention expresses itself in two main ways. First, we find a characteristic term in Isc: the spheres of being originate as nature proceeds (προιούσης τῆς φύσεως; p. 16, 12 F). Thus, there is some kind of concatenation between the spheres; all are the product of one procession. And we see that this is, after all, confirmed by Aristotle himself. According to Speusippus, the good was "born later as nature proceeds"

---

* The ambiguous character of immobility is stressed also by Theophrastus: Met. V 16, p. 18 Ross and Fobes. Cf. the divine ἐνέργεια ἀκινησίας as opposed to ἐνέργεια κινήσεως in Arist. Met. Λ 7, 1072b16–24 and NE H 15, 1154b26–28.

(προελθούσης τῆς φύσεως), says Aristotle (*Met.* N 4, 1091a35; fr. 34 Lang). And secondly, the unity of the universe results from the strictly analogical structure of all spheres. But it seems that Speusippus neglected to discuss how that procession is effected. We can be sure that this procession (one is tempted to use the neoplatonic term and to say πρόοδος) was not meant by Speusippus to be a temporal process. He denied, as we know, the temporal interpretation of the *Timaeus* (fr. 54 a, b Lang); he denied that there were any problems in mathematics, asserting that there were only timeless theorems (fr. 46 Lang); all of which is, by the way, another proof that it is inappropriate to interpret Speusippus as an evolutionist in the modern sense of the word. But he obviously did not "derive" the monad from the One or the hyletic principle of numbers from the multitude nor did he "derive" the subsequent spheres from the preceding ones, in any explicit way. To this extent, then, Aristotle's criticism was not unfair.

However, Speusippus' stress on the analogical character of the supreme principles in each sphere seems to be also present in Aristotle. When Aristotle replaced the two-opposite-principles doctrine by his new doctrine according to which the supreme principles are neutral matter and the pair form — absence of form, he made it clear in at least one passage that these principles are abstracta. There is no one form as such (at least not in the realm of sensibles) nor one matter as such (*Met.* Λ 4, 1070a31–33; 1070b10–21). There is rather, at least within the realm of sensibles, an indefinite plurality of principles — except that by analogy they are always the same ones: matter and form or absence of form. It is only in Aristotle that the term "analogy" appears; but the underlying idea seems to belong to Speusippus*.

Nor should we be surprised to discover certain similarities between Speusippus and Aristotle in the field of metaphysics. There are undoubtedly points of contact between the two in the field of logic and the doctrine of categories (cf. E. Hambruch,

---

* On the problem of analogy cf. e.g. Zeller II/2⁴ (1921) 257; 282 n. 5; 321 n. 2; 325 n. 6; G. L. Muskens, *De vocis* ΑΝΑΛΟΓΙΑΣ *significatione ac usu apud Aristotelem* (1943), esp. 87 f.; 91 f.; H.-G. Gadamer, "Zur Vorgeschichte der Metaphysik", in: *Anteile* (1950) 1–29, esp. 13 f. See also Theophrastus, *Met.* VI 17, p. 20 Ross and Fobes; VIII 20–21, p. 24 Ross and Fobes; cf. [O.] Regenbogen, art. Theophrastos in *RE* Suppl. VII (1940) 1555; J. Stenzel, *Zahl und Gestalt*² (1933) 147–162.

120   SPEUSIPPUS IN IAMBLICHUS

Logische Regeln der platonischen Schule in der aristotelischen Topik [1904] 14; 27 f.; P. Merlan, "Beitraege zur Geschichte des antiken Platonismus", *Philologus* 89 [1934] 35–53; 197–214, esp. 47–51); and long ago it was said that Plato's and Speusippus' systems can be described as "*Identitaetssystem*" (we shall deal with this problem later) and that traces of it are still present in Aristotle (T. Gomperz, *Griechische Denker*3 and 4, v. III [1931] 10 f.; 70). That Speusippus influenced Aristotle in the field of zoology was noticed by Stenzel (art. Speusippos in *RE* III A 2 [1929] 1640), and that Aristotle was obligated to Speusippus more than is generally assumed was recently stressed by Cherniss (H. Cherniss, *The Riddle of the Early Academy* [1945] 43). All this is confirmed by the present analysis of *Isc*.

The fact that Aristotle and *Isc* can profitably be compared and elucidate each other is another strong proof in favor of the assertion: *Isc* ch. IV is a source of our knowledge of Speusippus independent from Aristotle. Some, perhaps most of it may be a literal quotation from Speusippus *.

From the stylistic point of view the chapter exhibits some pecularities which set it off from the rest of *Isc*.

In the first place, we notice its preference for understatement expressed by the optative of politeness. In the 93 Teubner lines which we claim for Speusippus, five polite optatives occur, four of them made even more urbane by a "perhaps" (p. 15, 14. 29 F; p. 17, 8. 10. 21 F). There is only one chapter in *Isc* in which we find a similar accumulation of polite optatives. It is ch. XXIII, on which see the next chapter; it contains in its 117 Teubner lines 8 such optatives. In the rest of *Isc* we find the polite optative used sparingly (some twenty times); ch. XXV which marks the use of a new source by Iamblichus marks also the virtual disappearance of the polite optative. Some striking words are εὐπλαδής (p. 15, 13 F) and συμμεμολυσμένον (p. 17, 20 F), used to describe the ὕλη. The latter term is particularly interesting. According to dictionaries, μωλυσμένον means "underdone", whereas μολυσμένον means "tainted" (modern Greek, I am informed, also adopted this spelling for "tainted"). But even the briefest check proves that the spelling of these two words varies, so that we must rely on the context rather than

* Of Iamblichus' editorial activity more will be said in the next chapter.

on spelling to decide which of the two meanings we are facing. In its meaning "underdone" it has been used by Aristotle in the *Meteorologica* IV 1–3, 378b10–381b22 rather frequently. It seems that all modern editors print the word with an omega. But at the same time they indicate that a number of manuscripts spells the word with an omicron. It is even more characteristic that all manuscripts of Alexander's commentary on the *Meteorologica*, and virtually all of Olympiodorus', spell it consistently with an o (whereas in all mss of Alexander's *Quaestiones naturales* it seems to be spelled with an omega). What, then, is the meaning of συμμεμολυσμένον in our *Isc* passage? Is it "tainted all over" or is it "entirely underdone"? The latter meaning seems to be more appropriate within our context. The whole passage is based on the assumption that matter (the material principle) should not be vilified. But "tainted" would obviously be much stronger than "underdone". The latter would simply mean "not sufficiently mastered by the formal principle", just as Aristotle describes the condition of "being underdone" as an imperfect state in which the moist, i.e. the natural matter, is not mastered by heat (see esp. *Meteorologica* IV 2, 379b33–380a10; on heat as formal principle see e.g. *Met.* Λ 4, 1070b11–12). Along with the words συνεχής and παχύς, all of which describe the hyletic principle of geometricals, it seems to express the comparative impenetrability of solids. In comparison with numbers, geometricals are "dense" and in this sense of the word, "underdone".

It is interesting that a cognate of μεμολυσμένον should occur in a text, only recently authenticated beyond doubt as being by Speusippus. In his letter to Philip (*Socr. Ep.* 30, 14, p. 12, 7 Bickermann and Sykutris), the word μωλύτερον is used to indicate some quality of recitation as the result of which the argument recited will appear to be poor. It can hardly be doubted that the word means "dull", "blunted", "lacking expression", all of which would indicate a quality of recitation similar to the condition of rawness (inconcoction or condition of being underdone) in food. It is a rare word and so is its relative in our *Isc* passage. This is another (and strong) argument in favor of deriving the latter from Speusippus *.

---

* With the above cf. the discussion of the word μωλύτερον in E. Bickermann and

The frequent use of the word ὕλη is striking. Even if we admit that it was Aristotle who started using the word in its technical meaning (which is by no means certain), there is nothing improbable in the assumption that it was also used by Speusippus who knew Aristotle for some twentyfive years. It could be that fr. 49 Lang (Arist. *Met.* M 9, 1085a32) and 35 d Lang (Arist. *Met.* Λ 10, 1075a32) preserved Speusippus' own use of this term, as Lang is obviously inclined to presume. Also Xenocrates fr. 38 Heinze (Arist. *Met.* N 3, 1090b21–24) sounds as if the term ὕλη would be Xenocrates' own. The way in which *Isc* introduces the term first (p. 15, 10–14 F) seems to suggest that it treats it as new. "Because the principle opposed to the One is able to supply discontinuity, we might designate it, portraying it adequately to the best of our ability, as being a completely moist and pliable ὕλη". This could very well be the language of a writer anxious to justify a metaphor not yet generally known.

Also the use of προηγουμένως (p. 18, 11 F) meaning "not incidentally" should be noticed.

The peculiarities of ch. IV are to a certain extent mirrored in the fact that the scholia as presented by Festa (p. 100–103) devote a considerable part (some 23 lines out of some 115, i.e. about 1/5) to a chapter which forms about 1/25 of the whole text.

This brings to an end our comparison of *Isc* with Aristotle. Now, when we said that the differences between *Isc* and Aristotle could not be explained by any Plotinian influence on Iamblichus we limited our proof to just one point: the One of Plotinus is not above good. But here again the similarities between Plotinus and Speusippus are great enough to make a comparison worthwhile, the greatest being of course the doctrine common to both that the One is above being, and in this sense of the word not even being — οὐδὲ ὄν, as also Plotinus calls his One (*Enn.* VI 9, 3, 38 Br). But, be it repeated, in their doctrines regarding this One beyond being, Speusippus and Plotinus differ in that for the former the One is not identical with the good while it is so

J. Sykutris, "Brief an Koenig Philipp", *Berichte ueber die Verhandlungen der Saechsischen Ak. der Wiss., Philos.-hist. Kl.*, v. 80 (1928) 55 f. and of the word μωλύνειν in I. Duering, "Aristotle's Chemical Treatise Meteorologica Book IV", *Goeteborgs Hoegskola Arsskrift* 50 (1944) 35 and 69. See also V. C. B. Coutant, *Alexander of Aphrodisias. Commentary of Book IV of Aristotle's Meteorologica* (1936) 88 n. 20.

for the latter. And with this difference is connected the other: Speusippus is unequivocally a dualist; Plotinus is, according to prevailing assumptions (for a dissenting opinion see e.g. F. Heinemann, *Plotin* [1921] 160 and 257 f.), a monist *. His monism (or to be more cautious: the monistic strand in Plotinus) makes the answer to the question "whence diversity at all?" next to impossible. That this question is central in both Speusippus and Plotinus becomes obvious from a comparison of some passages in Aristotle and Plotinus.

In the middle of his criticisms of the Academic attempts to derive everything from two opposite principles Aristotle explains the origin of this two-opposite-principles doctrine. Without the assumption of two opposite principles the explanation of any diversity, any plurality, seemed impossible; all being was frozen into the one being of Parmenides. To account for diversity the Academics posited two principles, being and something other-than-being, the interaction of which engendered plurality. And Aristotle makes it obvious that he interprets the two-opposite-principle doctrine as originated by Parmenides; and Plato's *Sophist* as another attempt to explain plurality by assuming the existence of non-being along with being. Thus, from Parmenides through Plato's *Sophist* to the two-opposite-principles doctrine Aristotle establishes one line of thought (*Met.* N 2, 1089a2–6; cf. B 4, 1001a29–33). In this way we see the doctrine of Speusippus as another attempt to answer the problem of plurality.

---

* Perhaps neither monism nor dualism can unqualifiedly be asserted of Plotinus. First, even if he was a metaphysical monist, he still had to find a place for ethical dualism in his system. A good example is the passage *Enn.* III 3,4 (the most dualistic in Plotinus according to W. R. Inge, *The Philosophy of Plotinus*[3], 2 vv. [1929], v. I 136 n. 2), asserting man's dual character. Secondly, even his metaphysical monism is threatened from within by the difficulty of accounting for diversity (cf. F. Billicsich, *Das Problem der Theodizee im philosophischen Denken des Abendlandes* [1936], v. I 99–103). In both respects Plotinus can profitably be compared with Spinoza. The whole embarrassment of the latter on suddenly realizing that his determinism and monism makes it impossible to blame anybody for clinging to a wrong philosophic theory reveals itself in the Introduction to the Fourth Book of his *Ethics*; cf. e.g. the discussion in H. H. Joachim, *A Study of the Ethics of Spinoza* [1901] 238–254, esp. 253 f.); and the difficulties of his metaphysical monism come to light in the permanent problem facing any interpreter of Spinoza in deciding just how real God's attributes are. The difficulty of reconciling metaphysical monism with ethical dualism originated in the Stoa; and Plotinus and Spinoza inherited it from this common source (on the indebtedness of Neoplatonism to the Stoa see E. v. Ivánka, "Die neuplatonische Synthese", *Scholastik* 20–24 [1949] 30–38).

The extent to which the same problem is present in Plotinus can be seen from a number of passages: *Enn.* III 8, 10, 15 Br; III 9, 4, 1 Br; V 1, 6, 3 Br; V 9, 14, 4 Br. All ask the same question: how to explain the origin of plurality? The answer given by Speusippus (interaction of two principles) is inacceptable to Plotinus. He has two alternatives: the "falling away" from the One, and the "overflowing" of the One. The presence of two solutions which are mutually exclusive reveals the difficulty (cf. E. Schroeder, *Plotins Abhandlung* ΠΟΘΕΝ ΤΑ ΚΑΚΑ [1916] 146–149; 161; 178 f.; 187). The passages explaining the origin of diversity by the overflowing, i.e. as involuntary and necessary (e.g. *Enn.* I 8, 7, 21 Br; other passages in Zeller III/2⁵ [1923] 550 n. 3) are numerous and well known. But the passages implying that the origin of diversity is some kind of "falling away" are perhaps not always sufficiently stressed. The very words πεσεῖν, πτῶμα (*Enn.* I 8, 14, 21–25 Br), τόλμα *, τὸ βουληθῆναι ἑαυτῶν εἶναι (*Enn.* V 1, 1, 4–5 Br), and ἀπόστασις (*Enn.* I 8, 7, 19 Br) imply voluntarism. And this voluntarism is not limited to individual souls. Even the νοῦς comes into being as the result of its τόλμα (*Enn.* VI 9, 5, 29 Br) and unfolds itself because of its will to possess all, whereas it would have been better for it not to will this (*Enn.* III 8, 8, 34–36 Br; cf. Schroeder, l.c. p. 144 n. 5; 147 n. 1; 178 n. 5). Perhaps we could say that in Plotinus we see two aspects of the problem of plurality: how plurality originates and why it originates. In Speusippus the why is absent. Indeed, as Speusippus' One is not identical with the good, the problem of why there should be anything in addition to the One can hardly interest him.

As far as the doctrine of evil is concerned, the thoughts of Speusippus and Plotinus move frequently along parallel lines: evil is not positive. In Plotinus it is the absence of good (cf. H. F. Mueller, "Das Problem der Theodicee bei Leibniz und Plotinos", *Neue Jahrbuecher fuer das klassische Altertum* 43 [1919] 199–229, esp. 228 f.), or even simply a lesser good (*Enn.* III 2, 5, 25–27 Br; II 9, 13, 28–29 Br). Sometimes Plotinus speaks of evil as being the result of the "failure" of form (*Enn.* V 9, 10, 5 Br) in a way reminding us of both Speusippus and

---

* Cf. on this term F. M. Cornford, "Mysticism and Science in the Pythagorean Tradition", *Classical Quarterly* 16 (1922) 137–150; 17 (1923) 1–12, esp. 6 n. 3.

Aristotle. But the greatest similarity between Plotinus and Speusippus can be found in the essay in which Plotinus is closer to professing a dualistic doctrine than in any other, viz. *Enn.* II 4. The indeterminate and formless, says Plotinus, should not always be vilified as there are cases in which it lends itself to the higher, to be informed by it (*Enn.* II 4, 3, 1 Br). To be sure, the whole treatise in which this passage occurs with its division of matter into two kinds (intelligible and sensible) and the ringing accusation of the latter as being ugly and evil just because it is void of beauty and the good, shows an inspiration completely different from Speusippus, at least as far as the matter of the sensible is concerned. On the other hand, the introduction (and defense) of the concept of intelligible matter, i.e. matter present in what is in Plotinus the first sphere of being (νοῦς), is a departure from the standard doctrines of Plotinus. Generally, the process of emanation (or to use a term preferred by A. Stoehr in his lectures, effulguration) is a one-track process and matter appears only at the end of it. But in *Enn.* II 4 the process is almost from the very beginning bifurcated and matter emerges immediately from the One (II 4, 5, 28–32 Br) along with otherness and motion. Monism is still preserved but in its most precarious form.

This is not the place to trace the history of the doctrine of intelligible matter from Aristotle, where we find the term and concept adopted (the former in *Met.* Z 10, 1036a9; 11, 1037a4; and H 6, 1045a34. 36; the latter in *Met.* Z 10, 1035a17; 11, 1036b35; and, perhaps, K 1, 1059b16) and also most violently opposed (*Met.* Λ 5, 1071b 19–21; N 2, 1088b14–17; *Phys.* III 6, 207a30–32) or transformed into the concept of genus (see Bonitz' *Index* 787a19–22), to Plotinus. For the time being let us quote just two passages leading up to the latter.

The one we find in Apuleius, *De dogm. Plat.* I 5,190, p. 86, 9–11 Thomas: *initia rerum tria esse arbitratur Plato; deum et materiam, rerumque formas, quas* ἰδέας *idem vocat, inabsolutas, informes, nulla specie nec qualitatis significatione distinctas.*

The passage sounds confused. To designate ideas as *formae informes* seems to make them matter *. But the other passage,

---

* Cf. the emendations suggested by Sinko in the apparatus of P. Thomas' edition (*Apulei Platonici Madaurensis de philosophia libri* [1908]).

Plutarch, *Quaestiones Platonicae* III (v. VI/1 Hubert-Drexler) *
seems to bring an elucidation.

... ἀφαιροῦντες φωνὴν μὲν τῶν κινουμένων, κίνησιν δὲ τῶν
στερεῶν, βάθος δὲ τῶν ἐπιπέδων, μέγεθος δὲ τῶν ποσῶν, ἐν
αὐταῖς γενησόμεθα ταῖς νοηταῖς ἰδέαις, οὐδεμίαν διαφορὰν
ἐχούσαις πρὸς ἀλλήλας κατὰ τὸ ἓν καὶ μόνον νοουμέν‹αις›. οὐ
γὰρ ποιεῖ μονὰς ἀριθμόν, ἂν μὴ τῆς ἀπείρου δυάδος ἅψηται
(1001 F–1002 A).

In other words, under the obvious influence of Aristotle, some
Platonists are asking the question: what is the *principium
individuationis* within the realm of the ideas themselves? And
the answer is: some kind of matter. As a result, Plotinus says:
If the ideas are many, there must be something that they have
in common and something else peculiar, by which one idea
differs from another. That something peculiar, the difference
which separates one idea from another, is the proper form.
But where there is a form, there is also that which is formed
and receives the difference. Thus, there is matter in the realm
of ideas (*Enn.* II 4, 4, 2–7 Br).

Of course, the doctrine of a matter deriving directly from the
One and present in the realm of the intelligible is hardly compatible with the rest of Plotinus' system. Plotinus is aware of
it — and in *Enn.* II 5, 3 (on Porphyry's list his twenty-fifth essay,
while *Enn.* II 4 is his twelfth) he virtually disavows it **. He
defends those who posit intelligible matter (II 5, 3, 8–13 Br),
but from the way in which he does it one hardly would assume
that he himself has ever been of this opinion ("if one would ask
those who posit matter in the realm of the intelligible"). And
it seems that this is the last time that Plotinus gives serious
consideration to the concept of intelligible matter ***.

If the presence of non-evil matter in the realm of νοῦς presents
a certain similarity between Plotinus and Speusippus, Speusippus' doctrine of the moral neutrality of the supreme principles,

---

* A passage in which the quadrivium is already presupposed but characterizing
harmonicals by sound instead of proportion (quantity = number; number + magnitude = geometrical;   geometrical + motion = astronomical;   astronomical +
voice = harmonical).
** See F. Heinemann, *Plotin* (1921) 164; 174–176; 188 f., whose interpretation
has not been refuted by A. Faust, *Der Moeglichkeitsgedanke* (1931), v. I 436–455.
*** Though the term recurs in *Enn.* III 5,6,45 Br, it is there used in a different
sense.

and particularly his description of the One as not good, is inacceptable to Plotinus. True, sometimes the latter is on the verge of denying that the One is the good, this being the result of his tendency to deny that it is good (*Enn.* VI 9, 6, 40 Br). But on the whole he clings to the identification of the One with the good (*Enn.* II 9, 1, 1–8 Br) so that he can say that things do not proceed from neutral principles (*Enn.* V 5, 13, 36–37 Br), thus reminding us that in *Isc* the supreme principle was indeed called neutral (though in *Isc* the word ἀδιάφορον means undifferentiated rather than neutral, being connected with the word ἄτμητον: *Isc* ch. IV, p. 15, 21–22 F) and almost echoing Aristotle who equally insisted that the supreme principle must be good (*Met.* N 4, 1091b16–18).

According to Speusippus, the One was above being and not good; the opposite principle of multitude was not evil. Perhaps we may go one step further and assume that Speusippus at least implicitly said that the principle of multitude, just as it was above evil, was also above non-being, though ultimately responsible for non-being. If this assumption is justified we should have a short formula comparing the systems of Speusippus and Plotinus. According to the latter, what imparts being to all beings must itself be above being. According to the former, what imparts being to all beings must itself be above being and what imparts non-being to all beings must itself be above non-being.

If this interpretation of Speusippus is correct, his system is a highly original, interesting, possibly unique system in the history of Western philosophy. Perhaps it could be compared with that of Schelling, according to whose principle of identity God originally is neither good nor evil, i.e. indifferent (*Das Wesen der menschlichen Freiheit, Saemtliche Werke*, I, v. VII [1860] 406 f.; 409 n. 1; 412 f.). If it indeed introduced the concept of what is above non-being, it anticipated some bold speculations which have their proper place in that branch of Western mysticism which harks back to Platonism and Neoplatonism (Dionysius the Areopagite, Master Eckhart, Nicholaus of Cusa). The best known passage in which this concept occurs is the distichon by Angelus Silesius:

The subtile godhead is a naught and overnaught.
Who sees it? Everyone who can see nought in aught.
(*Die zarte Gottheit ist ein Nichts und Uebernichts:*
Wer nichts in allem sieht, Mensch, glaube, dieser sichts).

As the thesis of the present book is that Neoplatonism
originated in the Academy, it would be highly remarkable if we
could trace a typically mystical doctrine directly to Speusippus.
But it must be admitted, as long as we could not find the doctrine
that the principle opposed to the One should be termed above
non-being literally expressed by Speusippus, this is only a
surmise *.

Appendix

1. My assertion that *Isc* ch. IV contains doctrines of Speusippus has been criticized by Loenen (above, p. 32). Unfortunately, Loenen seems to assume that my assertion is based on the
contradiction between *Isc* ch. III and ch. IX. I don't know how
Loenen arrived at this conclusion. My assertion is based on the
similarity of the contents of *Isc* ch. IV with what Aristotle reports
the doctrines of Speusippus have been.

2. I don't know whether I understand Santillana's criticisms
(above, p. 56) on this point. He seems to blame me for preferring
the testimony of Iamblichus as to what the doctrines of Speu-

---

* For the whole chapter E. Frank, *Plato und die sogenannten Pythagoreer* (1923),
[J.] Stenzel, art. Speusippos in *RE* III A 2 (1929), and *idem*, "Zur Theorie des
Logos bei Aristoteles", *Quellen und Studien zur Geschichte der Mathematik* ... Abt. B:
Studien 1 (1931) 34–66, esp. 46 n. 5 should be compared.
    However, Frank reconstructed Speusippus' spheres of being with greater confidence
than I should dare to do. I differ from Frank particularly in that he separates mathematicals from the soul by inserting between them perceptible bodies (physicals),
which, in spite of what Frank says (248) is hardly compatible with the report of
Aristotle in *Met.* Z 2, 1028b23 and N 3,1090b18. It may be that Speusippus contradicted himself or changed his opinion, but it may also be that he defined the soul
in such a way that some could say that he identified it with some kind of mathematical
tout court, while some others could say that he made it a mathematical specified by
some difference.
    On the attraction exercised on Greek philosophers by the concept of naught see
E. Bréhier, "L'Idée du néant et le problème de l'origine radicale dans le néoplatonisme
grec", *Revue de Métaphysique et Morale* 27 (1919) 443–476 = *Études de Philosophie
antique* (1955) 248–283.

sippus (concerning the soul) have been, to that of Aristotle when it suits my purpose, whereas, where it suits my purpose, I prove the correctness of Iamblichus' reports on Speusippus by pointing out his agreement with Aristotle. But surely Santillana does not want me to reject the testimony of Iamblichus *because* it agrees with Aristotle? If Iamblichus in his Περὶ ψυχῆς disagrees with Aristotle on the doctrines of Speusippus concerning the soul, why is it impermissible to say "the doctrines presented in *Isc* ch. IV on the supreme principles in mathematics resemble very much the doctrines ascribed to Speusippus by Aristotle, thus Iamblichus may have derived this chapter from Speusippus"?

3. However, it may be that the phrasing of my introductory paragraph (above, p. 96) was misleading. I corrected it and hope that it will cause no further misunderstanding.

4. As in this chapter of *Isc* a doctrine resembling very much that ascribed to Speusippus by Aristotle is presented, I assumed that the chapter is indeed Speusippean. But as in this doctrine the concept of a transcendent One is contained and as such a doctrine is usually considered to be characteristic of Neoplatonism, I had to discuss the question whether perhaps *Isc* ch. IV though presenting doctrines of Speusippus, adulterated them, by introducing the concept of the transcendent One into them. This question I answered in the negative, thus asserting that the doctrine of the transcendent One has already been formulated by Speusippus. But I did not feel that there was any need to ask an additional question, viz. whether in ch. IV we find doctrines of Speusippus adulterated in some other respect, in addition to the possibility of having them adulterated with regard to the doctrine of the transcendent One. Thus, after having discounted the last named possibility, I took it for granted that no other adulteration had taken place.

For this I was criticized by Rabinowitz*. Though he starts from the assumption that the ultimate authority of *Isc* ch. IV is Speusippus **, he denies that it presents his doctrines (others

---

* W. G. Rabinowitz, *Aristotle's Protrepticus and the Sources of Its Reconstruction* (Berkeley 1957), esp. 87 f.; cf. also his paper "Numbers and Magnitudes", read at the meeting of the Society for Ancient Greek Philosophy on Dec. 29, 1957.

** An assumption which I find gratifying, as it confirms my thesis, but presented in a form which is somewhat puzzling. As he kindly informed me, Rabinowitz discovered the Speusippean character of *Isc* IV independently from me. Perhaps it

than those concerning the transcendent One, of which Rabinowitz does not speak) in unadulterated form. Wherein, then, does
the adulteration consist? Whereas Speusippus assumed that the
formal principle was different in each sphere, Iamblichus (or his
source; Rabinowitz does not commit himself on this point)
according to Rabinowitz teaches that there is only one formal
principle (acting in each sphere on a different material principle).
Furthermore, whereas the numbers in Speusippus are not
composite (do not consist of units), those of Iamblichus are.
Finally, whereas the point in Iamblichus is derived from the
(unique) formal principle and a material principle (peculiar to
geometricals), the point in Speusippus is underived (a formal
principle, peculiar to geometricals).

Whether these assertions of Rabinowitz are correct depends
almost entirely on how to interpret one crucial sentence viz. p. 17,
13–19 F. Unfortunately, Rabinowitz never quotes it in extenso.
This sentence reads:

(13) λοιπὸν οὖν τινα (14) ἑτέραν μεγέθους αἰτίαν ὑποθεμένους,
  ὡς ἐν ἀριθμοῖς (15) μονάδα κατὰ τὸ ἕν,
  οὕτως στιγμὴν ἐν γραμμαῖς (16) τιθέναι,
  θέσιν δὲ καὶ διάστασιν τόπων περί τε γραμ (17) μὰς καὶ
    χωρίας καὶ στερεὰ πρῶτον (scil. ἐνταῦθα φανῆναι),
  κατὰ τὰ αὐτὰ δὲ (18) καὶ τόπον ἐνταῦθα φανῆναι,
  παρὰ τὸν τῆς ὑποδοχῆς (19) διαφορὰν ἴδιόν τι παραδιδόναι
    τῷ ἀπ’ αὐτῆς γένει.

I translate:

"After another cause [viz. that] of magnitude has been posited,
it remains to posit — just as in numbers the monad conformable
to the One, so in lines — the point. Only here [scil. in the realm of
geometricals] will appear position and spatial interval in the case
of lines, planes, and solids; but also space conformable to them,
[so as], in accordance with the difference of the receptacle, to
confer something peculiar to the genus stemming from it."

Thus, the text of Iamblichus quite clearly conceives of the
monad in numbers as *corresponding* to the One in precisely the

would have been better to state this explicitly. For he mentions my book only to
criticize it on the point mentioned in the text and so gives the reader the impression
that we both, far from being the first ones who noticed the Speusippean source of
Iamblichus, simply repeated what is common knowledge. Thus, he does not do
justice to either of us.

same way in which in geometricals the point *corresponds* to the
One. The text of Iamblichus does not derive the point from the
(unique) One plus a hyletic principle. The interpretation of
Rabinowitz compels him to assume that 'monad' in line 15 does
not mean the number one but rather the number two. Furthermore, his interpretation compels him to assume that Iamblichus
made the point correspond to the number two rather than to the
number one. The latter is difficult to accept, the former is almost
impossible. The very wording of Rabinowitz' rendering of the
passage 17, 14–15 F reveals the obstacles to his interpretation.
What is derived from the (unique) One in the realm of numbers is
called a monad (unit), though it actually is two units, viz. the
number two, says Rabinowitz. Can anybody call two a monad?

There ist still one passage left which Rabinowitz claims in
support of his position. In the realm of numbers, the text says,
the material principle is responsible for διαίρεσις and μέγεθος. But,
says Rabinowitz, neither διαίρεσις, i.e. divisibility into factors nor
μέγεθος can be predicated of the number one. Thus, Iamblichus
explicitly excludes (the number) one from numbers, whereas
Speusippus included it. However, it is by no means clear that
διαίρεσις here means 'divisibility into factors'. It may very well
mean discretness of numbers in the sense that numbers do not
form a continuum among themselves. The term 'discrete' would
thus apply to the series of numbers and not to its members. And
whether the man to whom the formula 'one plus two plus three
plus four equals ten' was as familiar as to us 'two plus two makes
four' should have denied magnitude of the number one is rather
doubtful.

With all this I do not mean to deny that the wording of *Isc*
ch. IV is not everywhere a photographic copy of the corresponding
text in Speusippus. Changes there probably are, but these
changes are hardly in the direction indicated by Rabinowitz.
Perhaps Rabinowitz will decide to analyze the texts in question
line by line, to find confirmation for his interpretation. Considering the acumen with which he proceeds this would obviously be
desirable and helpful in arriving at conclusions more certain than
his present ones.

But even if Rabinowitz is right, from the point of view of the
present book this would be secondary. The great question

remains, whether the doctrine of the transcendent One enunciated in *Isc* ch. IV should be attributed to Speusippus.

5. My book came out about July 1953. Only a few months later Klibansky published his great find, viz. the lost part of Proclus' commentary of Plato's *Parmenides*, preserved in a Latin translation*.

In this commentary a quotation from Speusippus occurs. It reads: *Quid dicit* (scil. Speusippus, *narrans tamquam placentia antiquis*)? *Le unum enim melius ente putantes et a quo le ens, et ab ea que secundum principium habitudine ipsum liberaverunt. Existimantes autem quod, si quis le unum ipsum seorsum et solum meditatum, sine aliis, secundum se ipsum ponat, nullum alterum elementum ipsi apponens, nichil utique fiet aliorum, interminabilem dualitatem entium principium induxerunt.*

Klibansky re-translated the passage into Greek. I don't think the translation could be improved but in any case it seems to me more appropriate to present his than to attempt another, as Klibansky did his translation without knowledge of my interpretation of Speusippus and was in no way prejudiced, which I as a translator might be.

Τὸ ἓν γὰρ βέλτιον τοῦ ὄντος ἡγούμενοι καὶ ἀφ' οὗ τὸ ὄν, καὶ ἀπὸ τῆς κατ' ἀρχὴν ἕξεως αὐτὸ ἐλευθέρωσαν. Νομίζοντες δὲ ὡς εἴ τις τὸ ἓν αὐτό, χωρὶς καὶ μόνον θεωρούμενον, ἄνευ τῶν ἄλλων καθ' αὑτὸ τιθείη, μηδὲν ἄλλο στοιχεῖον αὐτῷ ἐπιθείς, οὐδὲν ἂν γίγνοιτο τῶν ἄλλων, τὴν ἀόριστον δυάδα εἰσήγαγον.

To this quotation from Speusippus Klibansky observes: *Fusius de eo* (scil. *Speusippi dicto*) *agemus in dissertatiuncula quae inscribitur* "Speusippus on Pythagorean philosophy, A New Fragment Preserved by William of Moerbeke." *Ubi conicimus: 1° fragmentum pertinere ad SPEUSIPPI* Περὶ Πυθαγορείων ἀριθμῶν *2° Proclum non ipsum Speusippum legisse, sed has sententias repperisse apud Nicomachum, Neopythagoreum qui dicitur philosophum ... Nicomachum verba Speusippi more Neopythagoreorum aliqualiter variavisse veri simile est. Ad argumentum quod respicit Speusippus cf. Plato Sophistes, imprimis 252c sqq. Ad doctrinam quae attribuitur 'Pythagoreis' cf. Proclus, In Tim. 176 D. p. 86* (39 f.; 96).

---

* R. Klibansky and L. Labowsky, *Parmenides ... Procli commentarium in Parmenidem*, London 1953.

I think that Klibansky's find fully confirms my assertion that the One of which Speusippus spoke was not, as was generally believed on the basis of Aristotle's presentation of him, less than being (which would make Speusippus a kind of evolutionist) but on the contrary above being (which would prove that he anticipated a doctrine generally considered to be peculiar to Neoplatonism). In any case, the new fragment forms an entirely new basis for any discussion of Speusippus. Therefore I am not going to reply to any of the criticisms raised against my ascribing to Speusippus the doctrine of a transcendent One *, as the whole situation has now changed.

6. In comparing the concept of matter in Speusippus with that in Plotinus I said that *Enn.* II, 4 (chron. 14) with its characteristic title περὶ τῶν δύο ὑλῶν by introducing the concept of matter present in the realm of the νοῦς makes a departure from the standard doctrine of Plotinus in which usually matter appears only at the end of the emanative process. For this I was criticized by Armstrong ** and by Kristeller ***.

Now, I shall say from the outset what seems to be the weakest point in their criticism. They both remind me that in all spheres of being according to Plotinus the ἄπειρον appears. Therefore, they say, I misinterpreted Plotinus. I admit their major. But I do not admit their conclusion because it is based on a minor which is unacceptable. This minor is obviously the equation ἄπειρον = ὕλη.

Indeed, it is Armstrong himself who implicitly denies the correctness of the minor. I am referring to his paper "Plotinus'

---

* Even not to the particularly keen ones by J. Moreau, *Revue Belge de Philologie et d'Histoire* 34 (1956) 1164–1167, nor to those by Loenen (above, p. 32).

However, a few words should be devoted to one of Moreau's arguments. The One, our passage says, οὐδὲ ὄν πω δεῖ καλεῖν. Moreau translates πω by 'yet' (*encore*), not even mentioning the possibility that it could mean 'at all'. But see Schwyzer-Debrunner II (1940) 579, ⌗ 3. Even P. T. Stevens who in his article "The Meaning of οὔπω", *American Journal of Philology* 71 (1950) 290–295 comes to the conclusion that it always has the usual temporal sense, not only must emend two passages (Homer μ 208 and Sophocles *O.T.* 105) where it clearly has no such sense but also on p. 294 translates it in Euripides, *Ion* 547 by 'not at all', leaving us wondering how to reconcile this translation with the unqualified conclusion of his article. Cf. Plot. *Enn.* I 4, 2, 6 Br; 15, 11 Br.

** A. H. Armstrong, *Mind* 64 (1955) 273 f.; cf. *idem*, "Spiritual or Intelligible Matter in Plotinus and St. Augustine", *Augustinus Magister* (1954) 277–283, esp. 278, note. But see also his *The Architecture of the Intelligible Universe in the Philosophy of Plotinus* (1940) 68.

*** P. O. Kristeller, *Journal of the History of Ideas* 19 (1958) 129–133.

Doctrine of the Infinite and Christian Thought", *Downside Review* 1954/5, 47–58, esp. 49–51. From what he says there it is evident that the equation ἄπειρον = ὕλη appears only in *Enn.* II 4 *. In other places the term ἄπειρον is used by Plotinus in such a way that it can even be applied to the ἕν (ἄμορφον, ἀνείδεον: VI 9, 3; IV 3, 8: VI 9, 6) **. This clearly proves that it does not always mean ὕλη. It is worthwhile to notice that, whereas I say that the assumption of (non-evil) matter in the intelligible world in *Enn.* II 4 is an anomaly, Armstrong takes the opposite point of view. According to him the doctrine that matter (ἄπειρον) is the source of evil in the sensible world is an anomaly in Plotinus' own system. In other words, I don't see that we disagree on the *facts* regarding the treatment of ὕλη in *Enn.* II 4. We only disagree as to what the ultimate tendency of Plotinus' system actually is in this respect. Armstrong in essence says: "Plotinus should have always spoken of one matter only existing in the sensible and the intelligible world. Had he done so, he would have realized that ὕλη cannot be the source of evil. But he sees it at least faintly in *Enn.* II 4. Faintly — this is the reason why he speaks of two kinds of matter, one evil and one not, thus becoming untrue to his original insight." I say: "Because in Plotinus ὕλη is the cause of evil in the sensible world, he should never have spoken of ὕλη in the suprasensible world. By so doing, he became untrue to his original insight." Thus we both see that there is an anomaly in Plotinus' treatment of matter. Only I say that the anomaly consists in presenting us with a concept of a non-evil matter which appears in the realm of the intelligible, whereas Armstrong says that it is an anomaly to speak of evil matter in the realm of the sensible.

It should be obvious that the doctrine of a double matter in Plotinus is a reflection of the well known controversy among interpreters of Plato, viz. whether the matter (or the equivalent term) responsible for the existence of the sensible world according to the *Timaeus* is identical with the ἄπειρον in ideas (see below,

---

* It is worth while to observe that Moreau, who interprets this equation with great acumen, limits himself strictly to passages from this essay (J. Moreau, *Réalisme et idéalisme chez Platon* [1951] 119–135, esp. 131–135).

** Cf. L. Sweeney, "Infinity in Plotinus", *Gregorianum* 38 (1957) 515–535, 713–732, esp. 527–531, listing the instances where Plotinus designates the One as ἄπειρον and ἀόριστον. But is there any instance of applying the term ὕλη to it?

p. 195). It is the great merit of a paper by Miss de Vogel to have elucidated this point *. Miss de Vogel describes Plato's system by the felicitous phrase "weak dualism". She shows how easy it is to find in Plato the doctrine of a double ὕλη. On one hand, we have the χώρα in the *Timaeus*, which represents, if we may say so, the infra-sensible ὕλη, which in some way difficult to describe, contributes to the constitution of the sensible world. On the other hand, we have the ἄπειρον of the *Philebus* (and, to a certain extent, the μὴ ὄν of the *Sophistes*), responsible for the diversity in the realm of ideas and thus not only of the suprasensible but even of the supraintelligible. In this latter concept Miss de Vogel sees the origin of the concept of ὕλη νοητή as used by Plotinus. And I think to her list Miss de Vogel could have added a concept which we encounter in the *Politicus* — the σωματοειδὲς τῆς συγκράσεως αἴτιον responsible for ἀταξία (273 B).

Against this background Miss de Vogel's formula ('weak dualism') could be expanded to read somewhat like this. According to Plato, there is much disorder in the universe and disorder cannot be derived from the principle of order. It rather demands a principle of its own. Still, order prevails over disorder. Therefore the principle of disorder cannot be on a par with the principle of order. But it cannot be derived from it either. In other words, the principle of disorder is subordinated to but independent from, the principle of order **. This other principle Plato sometimes calls χώρα, sometimes ἀνάγκη, sometimes what we would call inertia (so in the *Politicus* myth), sometimes an evil soul or evil souls. The existence of this principle explains the imperfections of the universe. But the ontological status of it remains in a twilight.

When I say 'twilight', this, I trust, expresses precisely the same idea as Plato's famous phrase νόθος λογισμός. Indeed for everybody except a thoroughgoing monist and a thoroughgoing dualist there must be some not quite rational, not quite irrational surd of the universe. And 'subordinated but independent' expresses very well this paradoxical situation.

After having established the Platonic precedent Miss de Vogel

---

* C.–J. de Vogel, "La théorie de l'ἄπειρον chez Platon et dans la tradition platonicienne", *Revue Philosophique* 149, 84 (1959) 21–39.
** Cf. A. H. Armstrong, *The Architecture* ... (above p. 105), p. 66 (independent, though not co-equal).

now assembles the passages in which Plotinus uses the term ἄπειρον and she characterizes it as eternal product of ἑτερότης — this ἑτερότης itself immediately following (or emanating from) the One.

With all this I fully agree. But where I can no longer follow Miss de Vogel is when also she simply identifies the ἄπειρον of which Plotinus speaks, with his ὕλη νοητή. The hesitation with which Plotinus speaks of the latter when he undertakes to speak of it *ex professo* clearly indicates that he by no means considers the equation ὕλη = ἄπειρον a matter of course. If it is legitimate to speak of Plato as a 'weak dualist' it is also legitimate to speak of Plotinus as a 'weak monist'. Because he is a monist, matter should appear in his system only at the end of the procession from the One. But because he is a weak monist, in places his matter seems to stem directly from the One. This leaves us with the concept of some kind of matter neither completely identical with nor completely different from, the matter which appears at the end of the procession emanating from the One. In any case, in the long run monism in Plotinus prevails and therefore he very seldom speaks of ὕλη νοητή, reserving the term ὕλη for the infra-sensible ἄπειρον. The very passage which Miss de Vogel quotes (Plot. *Enn.* III 9 [chron. 13] 3, 7–16) so clearly expresses the idea that what is usually called matter in Plotinus is the product of some wrong turn on the part of the soul (πρὸς αὐτὴν βουλομένη ⟨εἶναι⟩ τὸ μετ᾽ αὐτὴν ποιεῖ εἴδωλον αὐτῆς, τὸ μὴ ὄν) that it is very difficult to see in this ὕλη the same ὕλη which must have existed 'before' the soul came into existence.

It is therefore entirely comprehensible that Himmerich asserts that the the term ὕλη should not have by Plotinus been applied to the ὕλη νοητή which comes into existence together with the νοῦς *.

If we now ask why Plotinus should have introduced the concept of ὕλη νοητή at all, I am afraid that the only answer is that in this case Plotinus the Platonist got the better of Plotinus the original thinker. As Aristotle attributed to Plato the doctrine that it is one and the same ἄπειρον which is present in ideas and in sensibles, Plotinus felt that in some way he had to incorporate this doctrine into his system. Aristotle's term ὕλη νοητή gave him his clue.

---

* W. Himmerich, *Eudaimonia* (Würzburg 1959), 199 f.

7. To prevent the reader from treating the problem of unity and multiplicity, which plays so important a role in Platonism from Plato to Plotinus, as a merely historical one, I should like to remind him that it is still one that can legitimately be posed also to-day — and that it is very far from being easily solved.

Granted that the concept of one reality as embracing all that exists is meaningful, one is immediately compelled to ask: What do we mean when we speak of *one* reality? If there is only one reality, then there must exist *some* kind of link between all parts of reality — each part of reality must have 'something to do' with all other parts of reality. Let us call each independent part or member of reality an individual. We must then postulate that all individuals must in some way be mutually connected. In other words, the annihilation of any one individual must in some way affect all other individuals — or the annihilated individual was never part of one reality. The simplest way to present the connectedness of all individuals would e.g. be to assume that they all influence each other by way of causality.

But an unexpected conclusion follows. If everything is in some way influenced by everything else then it is indeed only an aspect of all that exists. It is, if we may say so, completely open — consists only of doors and windows. It can retain no privacy at all. The area of privacy would simply no longer be part of one reality, which is against the original assumption. Even the word 'aspect' is misleading, because each individual is simply pervaded by the totality of reality. But if such is the case, what do we mean when we say that there are individuals in reality? What are the boundaries separating one from another? Either there are parts, then they must be independent from each other in some way. But precisely in gaining independence they would cut themselves loose from one reality. In fact, it would become completely incomprehensible what we actually mean when we speak of one reality. Or else all parts of reality are interconnected, but then they loose their individuality completely and there is only one individual left. In other words, the choice seems to be between absolute unity and absolute plurality.

None of these alternatives is acceptable. And the concepts of a unity which is just a little differentiated and the concept of plurality which still manages to form some kind of unity are equally self-contradictory.

Such reflections at once let us realize what was at stake when Leibniz tried to establish his system of monads. No monad has door or windows — Leibniz quite clearly perceived that if you let in even one ray of light from the outside, the monad is immediately in its totality absorbed into the totality of reality. But what does it mean, then, that there are several monads? What does it mean that they all form one reality? The existence or non-existence of one makes no difference to the other. If all monads would disappear, except one, nobody, even not the monad of monads (God) would notice anything. The plurality of monads becomes an empty concept.

It may be doubted whether Plato ever realized that it is impossible to deny the doctrine of Parmenides (there is only one reality which has no parts, even not a here or there, a now or then) without giving up unity. He became a patricide to be able to account for plurality. But in so doing he challenged his sons to become patricides in turn, so that they might account for unity.

8. It is always worthwhile to see a familiar problem in unfamiliar light. In this case we can experience this on reading the discussion of intelligible matter in Plotinus in: G. Vallin, *La perspective métaphysique* (1959) 103–111; 147 f.; 155; 163 f., etc. Vallin is an exponent of the *philosophia perennis* of the east-west style and claims Plotinus as one of its representatives. The introduction of the concept of intelligible matter Vallin interprets as expressing Plotinus' insight (one of the perennial insights, most perfectly expressed by Shankara) into the ultimate identity of Brahman and Maya, the latter being the creative aspect of the former and thus responsible for multiplicity, which Brahman completely transascends but in which he at the same time is completely immanent, thus multiplicity being Brahman in his transdescendence. Now, according to Vallin, Plotinus tends towards the assertion of the integral immanence of the One, but the tendency does not quite reach its goal. Therefore (here I am clarifying somewhat Vallin's categories) Plotinus speaks of two matters, intelligible and sensible, whereas he should have perceived that sensible matter is not different from but simply the continuation

of, intelligible matter. In other words, the way in which Plotinus speaks of intelligible matter betrays his hesitation to accept the point of view of integral immanence. It would be interesting to know, whether Armstrong, Kristeller, and Miss de Vogel * would recognize their Plotinus in Vallin's one. I think that Vallin quite correctly felt the presence of some inconsistency in Plotinus and quite correctly felt that the term ἄπειρον (ἀόριστον) hides this inconsistency. To this extent I side with him rather than with them.

Perhaps it will be permitted to ask the representatives of the 'perennial philosophy' (of whom at present A. Huxley is perhaps the most famous one) a simple question. If it can be said that ultimately Brahman and Maja are identical (though of course it can equally well be said that they are different — perennial philosophy transcends the principle of contradiction), how can we explain that Brahman is that which is always hidden, whereas Maya is that which is always manifest? Why is multiplicity that which we have always found and unity (the One) that which has always been lost? Why is of the opposites which are supposed ultimately to coincide one omnipresent, the other omniabscondite? Why is an effort (or an illumination) necessary to see the One in the many and no effort (or illumination) necessary to see the One in its dispersion? Why do we need teachers to teach us Oneness whereas we need none to teach us manyness?

9. Loenen denied that it has ever been a doctrine of the Academy that being and non-being are the ultimate opposites of which all existents are derived. It seems therefore that the texts on which my assertion was based are not as well known as they ought to be. It may be not inappropriate to quote them.

Met. N 2, 1089a1–6 (cf. above, p. 123):

ἔδοξε γὰρ αὐτοῖς πάντ' ἔσεσθαι ἓν τὰ ὄντα, αὐτὸ τὸ ὄν, εἰ μή τις λύσει καὶ ὁμόσε βαδιεῖται τῷ Παρμενίδου λόγῳ 'σὺ γὰρ μήποτε τοῦτο δαμῇ, εἶναι μὴ ἐόντα', ἀλλ' ἀνάγκη εἶναι τὸ μὴ ὂν δεῖξαι ὅτι ἔστιν· οὕτω γάρ, ἐκ τοῦ ὄντος καὶ ἄλλου τινός, τὰ ὄντα ἔσεσθαι, εἰ πολλά ἐστιν (cf. Aristotle's criticism, ibid. 9–19: ποῖον οὖν τὰ ὄντα πάντα ἕν, εἰ μὴ τὸ μὴ ὂν ἔσται; . . . . . . ἔπειτα ἐκ ποίου μὴ ὄντος καὶ ὄντος τὰ ὄντα; . . . . ἐκ ποίου

---

* Unavailable was her "Het monisme van Plotinus", *Algemeen Nederlands Tijd-schrift voor Wijsbegeerte* 49 (1956/7) 99–112.

140   SPEUSIPPUS IN IAMBLICHUS

οὖν ὄντος καὶ μὴ ὄντος πολλὰ τὰ ὄντα;) and *Met*. Γ 2, 1004b7–8:
πάντα ἀνάγεται εἰς τὸ ὂν καὶ τὸ μὴ ὄν.

10. There exists an Arabic translation of Theophrastus' *Metaphysics*. Parts of it have been edited and translated in: D. S. Margoliouth, "Remarks on the Arabic version of the Metaphysics of Theophrastus" (as part of his article "The Book of the Apple, ascribed to Aristotle"), *The Journal of the Royal Asiatic Society of Great Britain and Ireland*, 1892, 192–201. Here we find the passage which is of particular interest in the present context, viz. IX 32, p. 34, 16 — 36, 18 Ross and Fobes. It appears that the Arabic translator worked with a text different from that now extant in any of the manuscripts enumerated in the Ross-Fobes edition, which, however, itself was by no means free from corruptions. Nevertheless, two things appear worth noting.

A. The passage which according to the apparatus of Ross and Fobes reads:

ὀλίγον γάρ τι τὸ ἔμψυχον, ἄπειρον δὲ τὸ ἄψυχον καὶ αὐτῶν τῶν ἐμψύχων ἀκαριαῖον καὶ βέλτιον τὸ εἶναι seems in the translator's copy have read: .... ἄπειρον δὲ τὸ ἄψυχον καὶ αὐτῶν τῶν ἐμψύχων καὶ ⟨ὧν⟩ βέλτιον τὸ εἶναι ἀκαριαι⟨τότερ⟩ον εἰς τὸ εἶναι (i.e. what is soulless and therefore inferior to that which is ensouled and whose existence is more valuable, is greater in number and comes quicker into existence than the latter).

B. The passage which according to the Ross-Fobes edition reads in our manuscripts ει· καὶ γάρ or καὶ γάρ or ει γάρ καὶ or εἰ καὶ γάρ seems to have read ἀμαθεστάτου ⟨ἂν⟩ εἴη· καὶ γάρ so that the Ross-Fobes emendation which replaced the εἰ· καὶ by εἰκῇ finds no support in this translation.

The article by Margoliouth came to my attention only in connection with my study of the problems posed by the Latin translation of Ps. Aristoteles' *De pomo*. This study was caused by: M. Plezia, "*Aristotelis qui ferebatur liber De pomo*", *Eos* 47 (1954: published 1956) 191–217; rev. book ed. Warsaw 1960. Still later I found that R. Walzer had pointed to it in his article "New Light on the Arabic Translations of Aristotle", *Oriens* 6 (1953) 91–142.

VI. A NEW FRAGMENT OF ARISTOTLE

We are indebted to Bywater (I. Bywater, "On a Lost Dialogue of Aristotle", *Journal of Philology* 2 [1869] 55–69; *idem*, "Aristotle's Dialogue On Philosophy", *ibid.*, 7 [1877] 64–87) and Jaeger (W. Jaeger, *Aristoteles*² [1955] 60–80) for the identification of extensive passages in Iamblichus' *Protrepticus* as being excerpts from the *Protrepticus* of Aristotle. On the whole, these excerpts * present man as a being whose true destiny is the disinterested contemplation of true reality for contemplation's sake, and philosophy as the way on which man can fulfil this destiny. At the same time, two passages from ch. XXVI of Iamblichus' *Isc* have by Jaeger been identified as two additional excerpts from the same work of Aristotle: ch. XXVI, p. 79, 1–81, 7 F and p. 83, 6–22 F (fr. 52 and 53 Rose; *Protrepticus* fr. 5 b and 8, p. 31–33 and 38 f. Walzer) rather than from *On Philosophy*, as Bywater had it. These two passages contain many references to mathematical sciences. The former discusses geometry, music theory, and astronomy as examples of (purely) theoretical sciences; the latter mentions geometry and τὰς ἄλλας παιδείας as having made stupendous progress within a very short time. Thus it immediately becomes obvious that some of the matters discussed by Aristotle in his *Protrepticus* were indeed closely related to the subject matter of *Isc* **. It is therefore natural from the very outset to expect that, in addition to those quoted above, *Isc* will contain some other excerpts from Aristotle's *Protrepticus*.

If we scan *Isc* with this expectation, it is its ch. XXIII (p. 70, 1–74, 6 F) which immediately attracts our attention. This chapter contains four main ideas. The first is that the philosopher is above all a contemplator; the second that all theoretical (contemplative) knowledge is desirable for its own sake and superior to practical knowledge; the third that mathematics

---

* They are conveniently accessible in R. Walzer, *Aristotelis Dialogorum fragmenta* (1934). Here they are numbered: *Protrepticus* fr. 4; 5 a (= fr. 52 in V. Rose, *Aristotelis ... fragmenta* [1886]); fr. 6; fr. 7; fr. 9 (= fr. 55 Rose); fr. 10 a (= fr. 59 Rose); fr. 10 b (= fr. 60 Rose); fr. 10 c (= fr. 61 Rose); fr. 11; fr. 12 (= fr. 58 Rose); fr. 13–15. See now also vol. XII of the Oxford translation of Aristotle.

** Cf. [A.-J.] Festugière, *La Révélation d'Hermès Trismégiste*, 4 vv., v. II (1949) 226 f.

is a theoretical knowledge *par excellence*, belonging among the liberal sciences and eminently philosophic; the fourth that incidentally it is of great help to other branches of knowledge, both practical and theoretical. It is easy to see that these ideas, particularly the first three, are closely related to the content of the *Protrepticus* passages quoted above. How closely, can best be seen from a comparison with ch. XXVI (p. 79, 1–84, 20 F). In this chapter, containing two passages belonging to Aristotle's *Protrepticus*, Aristotle quotes at length adversaries of philosophy as a purely theoretical science and of such other branches of theoretical learning as geometry, music theory, and astronomy. These adversaries assert that the said disciplines (including "physics", i.e. philosophy of nature) are useless and contribute nothing to life, or, to be more precise, to the activities of life or to its ultimate goal which is the active fruition of good and useful things. Nay, the mastery of these theoretical sciences spoils the learner. If he happened to be an empirically skilled musician, the knowledge of music theory (the exchange of his ἐμπειρία for γνῶσις) would immediately deteriorate him *. It is the man of practical training and common sense (this is the way in which ὁ δοξάζων ὀρθῶς could be paraphrased) who is much superior to the man of theory.

To describe theoretical science the adversaries use terms like ἀπόδειξις θεωρητική, ἀπόδειξις, συλλογισμός, λόγος. They make it clear that the type of philosophy which is the target of their criticisms is a philosophy patterned after geometry.

Now, we should certainly expect that Aristotle answered these criticisms of "mathematicizing" philosophy and of theoretical mathematics. And it is precisely *Isc* ch. XXIII which meets these expectations. This will be seen even better from the analysis of ch. XXIII to be given presently; but even without such a detailed analysis it is not difficult to realize that such is the case. Indeed, it is rather difficult to see, how *Isc* ch. XXIII could not be from Aristotle's *Protrepticus* if *Isc* ch. XXVI is. And it is difficult to overlook the similarity of *Isc* ch. XXIII with ch. s VI and X of Iamblichus' *Protrepticus* — two chapters

---

* To appreciate this polemic we should think of what many creative artists like to say against the advisability of studying aesthetics, philosophy of art, sometimes even history of art, by a prospective artist.

containing excerpts from Aristotle's *Protrepticus* (fr. 5 and 13 Walzer). The main difference seems to be that in his *Protrepticus* chapters Iamblichus excerpted Aristotelian passages devoted mainly to a defense of theoretical (contemplative, mathematicizing) philosophy, while in *Isc* he utilized Aristotle's defense of branches of contemplative knowledge other than philosophy, viz. mathematics, such a defense being made necessary by the criticisms quoted by Aristotle.

But there is one more reason to assign *Isc* ch. XXIII to Aristotle. In the passage proving the high value of mathematics Aristotle explains why mathematics is a preferable science. The same reason for which one science is preferable to (better than) another, makes any science preferable. Now,

Isc ch. XXIII, p. 72,8 F

αἱρούμεθα δὲ ἑτέραν πρὸ ἑτέρας ἢ διὰ τὴν αὐτῆς ἀκρίβειαν ἢ διὰ τὸ βελτιόνων καὶ τιμιωτέρων εἶναι θεωρητικήν. ὧν τὸ μὲν [exactness] ἅπαντες συγχωρή- σειαν ⟨ἄν⟩ ἡμῖν διαφόρως ὑπάρ- χειν ταῖς μαθηματικαῖς τῶν ἐπισ- τημῶν τὸ δ᾽ [to have what is better and more valuable as its object matter] ὅσοι ταῖς μὲν ἀρχαῖς ταῖς πρώταις τὴν εἰρημένην προεδρίαν ἀπονέμουσιν, ἀριθμοῖς δὲ καὶ γραμμαῖς καὶ ταῖς τούτων πάθεσιν οἰκείαν ὑπολαμβάνουσιν εἶναι τὴν τῆς ἀρχῆς φύσιν ... [i.e. mathematics certainly deals with what is most valuable because first principles are considered to be most valuable, and numbers, lines, and their properties are related to or of the nature of, the principle]*.

Aristotle, *De anima* I 1,402a1.

Τῶν καλῶν καὶ τιμίων τὴν εἴδησιν ὑπολαμβάνοντες, μᾶλλον δ᾽ ἑτέραν ἑτέρας ἢ κατ᾽ ἀκρίβειαν ἢ τῷ βελτιόνων τε καὶ θαυμασιω- τέρων εἶναι, δι᾽ ἀμφότερα ταῦτα τὴν τῆς ψυχῆς θεωρίαν εὐλόγως ἂν ἐν πρώτοις τιθείημεν

---

* Translation: We prefer one science to another either because of its exactness or because the objects of its theory are better and more valuable. Now, everybody

Thus we discover in *Isc* a semi-quotation from Aristotle's *De anima*. This should dispel any doubts. It seems that *Isc* ch. XXIII is either a series of quotations or one quotation from Aristotle. The Aristotle quoted is a believer in the superiority of the theoretical life (on this ideal see [A. J.] Festugière, *La Révélation d'Hermès Trismégiste* v. II [1949] 168–175) and of the theoretical sciences; he is also a believer in the value of exactness (ἀκρίβεια) and therefore an admirer of mathematics *; he is a believer in the extraordinary value of the subject matter of mathematical contemplation; and for these reasons he is convinced that mathematics and philosophy are closely allied. He is convinced that mathematics has practical value, too; but it is not in this that its true value consists; mathematics is preferable because of its own intrinsic merit. Furthermore, mathematics is of tremendous help also for other more or less theoretical sciences. An outstanding example is astronomy whose subject matter is the most elevated of all objects of sensible knowledge. And the Pythagoreans are praised for having interpreted mathematics in just this manner as a truly liberal, theoretical discipline, transcending its utilitarian treatment. The outstanding quality of a liberal mind is its interest in theory for its own sake: this interest is eminently satisfied by the study of mathematics.

Who is this Aristotle? After Jaeger's investigation the answer is very easy. He is the author of the *Protrepticus*. Indeed, Jaeger's presentation of the content of the *Protrepticus* (esp. W. Jaeger, *Aristoteles*[2] [1955] 71 f; 80–83; 86–102; *Aristotle*[2] [1948] 431–440) reads like a commentary on *Isc* ch. XXIII, although he never even mentions this chapter. In fact, his statement (*ibid.* 431) that in the *Theaetetus* we find an alliance between philosophy and mathematics, reads almost like a translation of τὴν δὲ περὶ τὰ μαθήματα θεωρίαν οἰκείαν καὶ συγγενὴ φιλοσοφίᾳ [scil. εἶναι] (p. 73, 16 F). There is only one thought to add: while Jaeger stresses all passages which seem to prove that at the time of his *Protrepticus* Aristotle still

---

will admit that of these two [qualities] the former preeminently falls to the share of the mathematical among the sciences. As to the latter, those [will admit it] who grant the said place of honor to the first principles and assume the nature of the principle to be kin to numbers, lines, and their accidents.

* Ἀκρίβεια in Aristotle refers in most cases to method. But it would be strange if, when used to characterize theology or philosophical mathematics, it had not the connotation "concerning the ἄκρα", i.e. refer to both method and subject matter. One is almost tempted to translate it by "utmostness" — of precision and principles.

accepted the idea theory, also the sentence should be stressed in
which he says that every branch of mathematics has a specific
φύσις as its object matter, a clear proof that Aristotle writes
as a mathematical realist (*Isc* ch. XXIII, p. 73, 5–9 F).

But there is still another problem connected with the chapter
at hand.

It is strange that the same thought by which the superiority
of mathematics was demonstrated in the *Protrepticus* should
be used in *De anima* to demonstrate the superiority of psychology.
It is, however, even stranger that *De anima* should recommend
psychology because of its exactness *. Indeed, according to
Hicks' index (R. D. Hicks, *Aristotle De anima* [1907]) the word
ἀκρίβεια occurs in *De anima* only once. In the 117 Teubner
lines which form *Isc* ch. XXIII the words "exactness" and
"exact" occur six times; the word ἀπόδειξις, closely allied with
them another seven times. In the fragments of Aristotle's
Protrepticus preserved in Iamblichus' *Protrepticus* ch. s VI, VII,
VIII, X, XI, "exactness" and its derivatives occur seven times
(pp. 29 f., 35, 43, 54, 57 Walzer) — an additional proof, by the
way, that *Isc* ch. XXIII is also from Aristotle's *Protrepticus*.
And there is hardly any doubt possible, while the word makes
perfect sense in an apology of mathematics, it makes no sense
at all in an apology (or eulogy) of psychology, regardless of
whether it designates the greater accuracy of proof or the simplicity and abstractness of subject matter, *pace* Hicks a.l.
(p. 174 f.). Thus, it seems, the crucial words are quoted by
Iamblichus from their original context. Aristotle himself used
them in *De anima* in a purely rhetorical fashion, as an echo
from his own, earlier writing; or when he started out writing
De anima, he was still thinking of the soul as a mathematical
entity and, therefore, of psychology as a mathematical and thus
"exact" discipline (just as the passage *De anima* II 3, 414b28

---

* The inappropriateness of this recommendation makes the passage a stumbling
block in virtually all Aristotle commentaries. It is remarkable that even Pomponazzi
is still discussing the problem why psychology should be described as an "exact"
science (see L. Ferri, "Intorno alle dottrine psichologiche di Pietro Pomponazzi",
*Atti della R. Acc. dei Lincei. Memorie della Classe di Scienze Morali, Storiche e Filo-
logiche* Ser. II, vol. III [1875–76] 338–548, esp. 424 f.) while F. A. Trendelenburg,
(*Aristotelis De anima*² [1877] 155 f.) discusses it again. To cut the Gordian knot, P.
Siwek, *Aristotelis De anima libri tres*², 3 vv. (1946, 1943, 1945) translates ἀκρίβεια by
inquisitio subtilior (cf. his note a.l.).

mentioned on p. 50, could be another remnant of this psychological mathematicism), so that he repeated of psychology
what he had said about it in another writing in which the
mathematical character of the soul was fully accepted. But in
either case, it is unlikely that Iamblichus quoted from *De anima*.
To assume this would be tantamount to the assertion that he
lifted the words precisely to reset them in a most appropriate
setting. While this is not impossible, it is not very probable
either.

But once we became aware of how inappropriate these words
are in the context of *De anima*, we shall be inclined to ask:
were they actually used by Aristotle? A glance at the Biehl-
Apelt apparatus (*Aristoteles De anima*[3] ed. G. Biehl, O. Apelt
[1926]) reveals that the words from μᾶλλον to εἶναι (p. 121)
were considered spurious by Alexander Aphrodisias, according
to Philoponus (*In Arist. De an.*, p. 24, 7–13 Hayduck). We do not
know how Alexander proved his assertion that the words came
ἔξωθεν and κατὰ προσθήκην; the reasons given by Philoponus
("if Alexander had acknowledged the passage as genuine, he
would have been compelled to admit the immateriality and
immortality of the soul") are obviously not Alexander's own.
But is it too much to assume that he did not read them in his
manuscript or found some annotation in it to the effect that
though written by Aristotle they were later crossed out by him
or that they had been inserted from a margin where somebody
had quoted them from the *Protrepticus*? In any case and whichever alternative we accept, Alexander's testimony only reveals
what should be obvious: the words in question are out of place
in *De anima*.

There is still another passage in Aristotle paralleling the
De anima and *Protrepticus* passages. It is *Topics* VIII 1, 157a9.
Here we read: ἐπιστήμη ἐπιστήμης βελτίων ἢ τῷ ἀκριβεστέρα εἶναι
ἢ τῷ βελτιόνων. Furthermore τῶν ἐπιστημῶν αἱ μὲν θεωρητικαὶ
αἱ δὲ πρακτικαὶ αἱ δὲ ποιητικαί — these words being an illustration
of a διαίρεσις τῶν συγγενῶν.

Is it not rather obvious that the illustration is taken by
Aristotle from a work of his own, which is the *Protrepticus*? In this
work the superiority of theoretical over practical knowledge
was proved by pointing out that the former has the quali-

ties of both βελτιόνων εἶναι and greater ἀκρίβεια. It is interesting
to compare this with *Met.* E 1, 1026a21 and K 7, 1064b4·
Here neither the status of mathematicals nor that of mathematics is what it used to be. Accordingly, the superiority of
theology is no longer proved by its ἀκρίβεια; it is now only the
τῶν βελτιόνων εἶναι which theology claims. In *Met.* A 2 (closer
to the *Protrepticus*) on the other hand, exactness is ascribed to
theology (982a13. 25; cf. *Nic. Eth.* VI 7, 1141a16).

To what extent does this new fragment add to our knowledge
of Aristotle? What is really new in it is Aristotle's explicit high
esteem for mathematics. This should not be surprising, of
course. When he was still a full-fledged member of the Academy,
he must have shared its opinions about mathematics, too. And
his writings are full of examples taken from mathematics, to
illustrate scientific methods (cf. R. Eucken, *Die Methode der
Aristotelischen Forschung* [1872] 56–66; F. Solmsen, *Die Entwicklung der Aristotelischen Logik und Rhetorik* [1929] 80 f.).
The new fragment merely confirms what could have been guessed.
Still it is remarkable that mathematical knowledge is explicitly
described as a model of scientific knowledge; new is the assertion
that mathematics helped man to overcome many wrong beliefs
originating from [his observation of] appearances (cf. Plato,
Rep. X 602 D); new is the assertion that mathematics is the
easiest way to contemplation because mathematical knowledge
can be acquired without the background of empirical knowledge
of details, and, thus, early in life *. The latter is a remarkable
counterpart to the doctrine that political science cannot be
profitably studied by young men (*Nic. Eth.* I 1, 1095a2). Re-

---

* In his polemic against Jaeger, H.-G. Gadamer ("Der Aristotelische Protreptikos
und die entwicklungsgeschichtliche Betrachtung der Aristotelischen Ethik", *Hermes*
63 [1928] 138–164, esp. 159) tried to prove that the content of the *Protrepticus* was
on a pre-systematic level and, thus, neither specifically Aristotelian nor specifically
Platonic. The new fragment proves that Gadamer was probably wrong. Aristotle
wove into his *Protrepticus* some highly technical and specifically Academic doctrines,
though this was not necessarily apparent. An excellent example of how this can be
done is a commencement speech delivered by Bergson in 1895 (H. Bergson, *Le Bon
sens et les études classiques* [1947]). This speech contains *in nuce* Bergson's whole
system, but a layman would not even suspect it. It is highly amusing to see Bergson
describing his characteristic doctrine of intuition, while designating intuition as
"common sense". It may be that Aristotle could with similar effect use the term
φρόνησις, to hide a difficult and controversial doctrine behind an innocent and
non-technical word.

markable, too, is the way in which astronomy is brought into connection with mathematics.

Also the passage in *Nic. Eth.* VI 9, 1142a17–30 — the book so curiously reflecting Aristotle's half-hearted loyalty to the ideals of wisdom, exactness, etc.* — is significant: mathematics (based on ἀφαίρεσις) is still described as accessible to the unexperienced young man, while physics and theology are based on experience (and therefore can be studied only later in life). But obviously this is no longer meant as a compliment paid to mathematics.

Most noticeable is the assertion that "the principle" is akin to mathematicals. It is perhaps the most Academic passage in the whole fragment. Indeed, there must have been a time when Aristotle himself was on the verge of turning philosophy into mathematics (*Met.* A 9, 992a32).

Shall we assume that the whole ch. XXIII is taken *verbatim* from the *Protrepticus*? This could be so — with the possible exception of a line or two at the beginning and the end of the chapter. This is the technique used in *Isc.* ch. VI, which is a series of quotations from Plato. We must not forget that the whole *Protrepticus* of Iamblichus is simply a series of tacit excerpts from Plato, Aristotle, etc.. But this does not mean that ch. XXIII presents the words of Aristotle in their original order. In *Isc* ch. VI we find the Plato excerpts arranged as follows:

Epinom. 991 D–992 B; 991 B–C; 986 C–D. *Rep.* 537 C (5–9); 537 D (disjointed) 9–13; 536 B; 527 D–E; 521 C–D; 523 A–532 D. As we see, Iamblichus does not mind jumping back and forth.

We find an amazing example of his method on p. 21, 20 F.

In the *Epinomis* we read: Πρὸς τούτοις δὲ τὸ καθ' ἕν τῷ κατ' εἴδη προσακτέον ἐν ἑκάσταις ταῖς συνουσίαις ἐρωτῶντά τε καὶ ἐλέγχοντα τὰ μὴ καλῶς ῥηθέντα (991 C).

Iamblichus simply cuts this sentence in two. After ἐν ἑκάσταις he replaces ταῖς συνουσίαις by ταῖς τῶν μαθημάτων εἰδήσεσιν adding the words ἕως ἂν ἐξεύρωμεν τὸν ὅλον κόσμον, and now continues cutting in two a sentence in *Epinomis* 986 C and copying its last part — a triumph of the paste and scissors method, indeed.

---

* On this half-heartedness see L. H. G. Greenwood, *Aristotle. Nicomachean Ethics Book Six* (1909) 84; E. Kapp, *Das Verhaeltnis der eudemischen zur nikomachischen Ethik* (1912) 48–53.

What we find in ch. VI we may expect in ch. XXIII. The original mosaic stones composing ch. XXIII seem to be these:

1. P. 70, 1–7 F. In this section (perhaps Iamblichus' own) we find the promise to prove that Pythagoras * treated mathematics as part of liberal education, advanced it quantitatively and qualitatively, and pursued it beyond its practical aspect. But what follows does not bring the promised proof. Instead, we find

2. P. 70, 7–16 F. In this section mathematics is recommended for three reasons. It is the archetype of scientific knowledge; it reveals its power by the way it proves **; it corrects many mistaken beliefs.

3. P. 70, 16–21 F. Mathematics is the first initiation into the liberal vision befitting a philosopher. The liberal-minded man exists for his own sake; he therefore enjoys things which are for their own sake. In other words, theory is the most appropriate way of life for him. Here the text is corrupt and the transition unclear. What follows seems to take up the first idea of the present section (mathematics as first initiation).

4. P. 70, 21–26 F. [Mathematics along with other] theoretical disciplines can be taught at an early age [being in no need of induction based on acquaintance with single instances].

5. P. 70, 26–71, 15 F. This seems to hark back to 3; the philosopher is liberal minded since he desires knowledge which is valuable for its own sake (i.e. one as self-sufficient as he is himself). In any case, the utilitarian (non-liberal) interpretation of mathematics is rejected. The disciplines for the sake of which mathematics is recommended by utilitarians are inferior to mathematics, less close to truth, and much less exact.

6. P. 71, 16–24 F. Here an entirely new idea is introduced: the usefulnes of mathematics, even in practical disciplines and as a character-forming force.

---

* It should not be surprising to find Pythagoras quoted. In Iamblichus, *Protrepticus* ch. IX, p. 49, 3–52, 16 Pistelli (= *Protrepticus* fr. 11, p. 49 f. Walzer) we find Pythagoras praised as the originator of the ideal of a life of theory.

** Διὰ τῶν οἰκείων λόγων — οἰκεῖος in this connection being perhaps a favorite Academic term. In his ἐγκώμιον (fr. 673 Rose) Aristotle praised Plato for having proved the coincidence of goodness and happiness οἰκείῳ βίῳ. On the term οἰκεῖον cf. F. Dirlmeier, *Die Oikeiosis-Lehre Theophrasts* (1937), with the review by P. Merlan, *Philologische Wochenschrift* 58 (1938) 177–182, and O. Regenbogen, art. Theophrastos in *RE* Suppl. VII (1940).

7. P. 71, 24–26 F. The contribution of mathematics to excellence.

8. P. 71, 26–72, 2 F. Tying in with 5, the passage reminds us that mathematics should be enjoyed for its own sake.

9. P. 72, 2–16 F. This excerpt contains one idea: the proof that mathematics is superior to other disciplines because of its method (exactness) and subject matter (which is closely related to the first principles).

10. P. 72, 16–72, 20 F. Astronomy and mathematics.

11. P. 72, 20–73, 3 F. This section seems to be related to 3. The philosopher is interested in truth; he will therefore be interested in mathematics for its own sake, as mathematics shares in the most sublime truth and has the most exact method.

12. P. 73, 3–17 F. Mathematics has all the qualities which we demand of a knowledge desirable for its own sake, with regard to subject matter and method. We may therefore safely say that the philosophic life is an end in itself, mathematical theory is philosophy's housemate and kin.

13. P. 73, 17–74, 5 F. This portion describes the way in which the Pythagoreans practiced mathematics, culminating in their theologico-mathematical astronomy. It could be that it is already one of the customary summaries by Iamblichus himself.

The chapter exhibits many linguistic peculiarities. The frequent use of the *optativus urbanitatis* was already mentioned; as has the peculiar use of the term οἰκεῖον (13 times), ἀκρίβεια, and ἀπόδειξις (p. 120; 145). The word παράμιλλος (p. 71, 11 F) does not occur in Aristotle, according to Bonitz' *Index*; but ἅμιλλα in precisely the same meaning occurs in *Rhetoric* I 11, 1371a6. Φιλοθεάμων (p. 72, 25 F) does not occur in Aristotle, according to Bonitz' *Index*; but in *Nic. Eth.* I 9, 1099a9–10 φιλοθεάμων occurs in some manuscripts instead of φιλοθέωρος. The word πλαστός (p. 73, 1 F) does not occur in Aristotle, according to Bonitz' *Index*; but it appears (and is listed in Liddell-Scott) in *Meteorologica* IV 9, 386a27. In the last section of ch. XXIII two other words occur, not listed in the Bonitz *Index*, viz. θεολογικῶς (p. 74, 4 F) and ἀστρονομεῖν (*ibid.*). The first of these has cognates in Aristotle (on the problem involved in the term see W. Jaeger, *The Theology of the Early Greek Philosophers* [1947] 4–7; 194 n. 17; [A. J.] Festugière, *La Révélation d'Hermès*

Trismégiste, 4 vv., v. II² [1949] 598–605; V. Goldschmidt, "Théologia", *Revue des Études grecques* 63 [1950] 20–42). The second appears in Plato, but has only one cognate in Aristotle, according to Bonitz' *Index*, viz. in the *Problemata*. But it should also be noted that these two words appear in the section of the chapter which can be ascribed to Aristotle with less certainty than the rest of it.

For the sake of comparison it should also be noted that in the Iamblichus passages identified by Jaeger as having been taken from Aristotles' *Protrepticus* the words ἀνύσιμος, ἀκώλυτος, στασιώτης, ἀφύσικος (these two in Sextus Emp., *Adv. math.* X 46) are additions to Aristotles' previously known vocabulary.

If we recall the ruthless method used by Iamblichus to patch together *Isc* ch. VI we shall not claim any certainty for the analysis of ch. XXIII attempted above. But in spite of all cuts and rearrangements which Iamblichus may have permitted himself, one thing stands out clearly: the whole chapter is devoted to the interpretation and defense of philosophy as purely theoretical knowledge and to an interpretation of mathematics as a highly philosophic discipline which also has a claim to be studied for its own sake as a theoretical science. And it ought to be repeated: there can hardly be a better commentary on this chapter than what Jaeger has to say on the *Protrepticus* and the ideal of a life of theory.

To round off the interpretation of Aristotle's attitude towards mathematics it is worthwhile discussing some passages in Isocrates *. While Aristotle recommends mathematics as an early initiation to a life of theory, Isocrates is of the opinion that mathematics is a good study for young boys because it keeps them out of mischief (*Panath.* 27). While in the *Protrepticus* mathematics is treated as part of philosophy, Isocrates denies explicitly that it is a philosophic study at all (meaning by philosophy precisely what Aristotle's adversaries quoted by him in the *Protrepticus* did; see above p. 142); it has merely propaedeutic value and is on a par with the most elementary subject matters of instruction (*Antid.* 266–269). And finally, we shall appreciate Aristotle's praise of ἀκρίβεια better if we

* Cf. G. Norlin's *Introduction* to the Loeb edition of Isocrates, v. I (1928) pp. XXIII–XXVIII.

do not forget the opinion of Isocrates: It is more important to have an inexact knowledge of things useful, than an exact knowledge of things useless (*Helen* 5) *. Indeed, the new fragment of Aristotle is an excellent illustration of the well-known rivalry ** between two systems of education ***.

The reasons given by Aristotle for studying mathematics are very remarkable, particularly when they stress the liberal character of that study and the fact that in dealing with numbers, lines, and their relations mathematics is as close as possible to the supreme principle of being and thus to philosophy. Once more we are reminded of the origin of the quadrivium. Once more it becomes obvious that the (quadripartite) mathematics which is the subject of the quadrivium is originally not an elementary study but a highly philosophic science. It has the marvelous advantage that, being non-inductive, it can be taught at an early age; and from the very beginning it is a discipline closely related to philosophy and its subject matter, the ultimate principles of being. Only with the help of the newly discovered *Protrepticus* fragment can we fully appreciate Aristotle's tripartition of speculative knowledge according so high a place in the hierarchy of learning to mathematics. The pertinent *Metaphysics* passages are no longer isolated within the Aristotelian

---

* Cf. W. Jaeger, *Paideia*, v. III (1944) 68. In *Busiris* 23 Isocrates is non-committal with regard to mathematico-astronomical studies. I treated some aspects of the relations between Isocrates and Aristotle in: P. Merlan, "Isocrates, Aristotle, and Alexander the Great", *Historia* 3 (1954) 60–81.

** Cf. P. Moraux, *Les listes anciennes des ouvrages d'Aristote* (1951) 34 f.

*** Thus, I think that the presentation of A. Burk, *Die Paedagogik des Isokrates* (1923) 137–140, comparing Isocrates' attitude towards mathematics with that of Plato alone and neglecting Aristotle altogether, needs some additions. It is characteristic that, as the Platonic elements in Aristotle's ethics give way to an appreciation of the "ethical" virtues (as opposed to the dianoetic ones), the difference between Aristotle's and Isocrates' ideals becomes considerably smaller (cf. P. Shorey, art. Isocrates in Hastings' *Encyclopaedia* VII [1924]; the same seems to be true of the role of mathematics in education: E. Drerup, *Der Humanismus* [1934] 152 f.; cf. 134 f.; particularly interesting is a comparison of *Panathenaicus* 30–32, explaining Isocrates' ideal, with the ideals of the *Nicomachean Ethics*: cf. H. Gomperz, "Isokrates und die Sokratik", *Wiener Studien* 28 [1906] 1–42, esp. 20). On Isocrates' influence on Aristotle's political ideas see G. Mathieu, *Les Idées politiques d'Isocrate* (1925) 186 f. Cf. also H.-I. Marrou, *Histoire de l'éducation dans l'antiquité*[4] (1958) 136. It should also be stressed that ἀκρίβεια as a quality of *style* is approved and practiced by Isocrates (cf. H. Wersdoerfer, *Die ΦΙΛΟΣΟΦΙΑ des Isokrates im Spiegel ihrer Terminologie* [1940], esp. 96 and 138), a proof that it is not only the term "philosophy" which means different things for Isocrates and Aristotle. Could it be that the praise of mathematics as possessing true ἀκρίβεια rather than a ficticious one ἐκ λόγων (*Isc* ch. XXIII, p. 73,1 F) is directed against the ἀκρίβεια claims of Isocrates?

corpus. But at the same time it becomes clear that what Aristotle means by mathematics when he speaks of it as one of the three branches of theoretical knowledge, is Platonistic mathematics. And also the Proclus passage discussed in the previous chapter and claimed for Aristotle can more justly be estimated as expressing Aristotle's interest in mathematics and proving him to be its apologist against attacks coming from different quarters.

Appendix I

1. It is remarkable to what extent Montaigne's ideas on education (on which see e.g. E. Durkheim, *L'Évolution pédagogique en France*, 2 vv., v. II [1938] 61–67) agree with those of Isocrates. Montaigne's *Essay on the Education of Children* centers on one idea: we should educate for life. If we educate scholars and pedants, we do not educate for life. Pedantry here and so often attacked by Montaigne is simply ἀκρίβεια and knowledge for its own sake, in a modern garb; and what he attacks as futile scholarship is actually a life of contemplation. The disciplines which Montaigne dislikes strongly (mathematics, astronomy) are precisely the ones disfavored by Isocrates. Montaigne is in agreement with Isocrates in stressing that education cannot change nature so that we should not expect too much from education. The similarity between the ideals of Montaigne and Isocrates is somewhat obscured by the fact that Montaigne is an enemy of rhetoric; but there can hardly be any doubt that Montaigne is opposed to the rhetoric of his day because it has become an entirely academic affair or something to be used only for purposes of display of skill, instead of being an instrument promoting mutual understanding and thus pertinent to the business of living. The value of εὖ λέγειν Montaigne accepts unhesitatingly. Rabelais, so frequently a precursor of Montaigne's ideas, makes this very clear: one of the reasons why a person well-educated by his anti-pedantic, anti-monastic, anti-scholastic standards is superior to the poorly educated is that only the former speaks well (*Gargantua* ch. 15). In other words, Montaigne's ideal of education is precisely that of Isocrates; and what both fight is the Academy and its remote descendants together with its ideal: a life of contemplation devoted particularly to the most exact sciences *.

2. On ἄκρα see I. Duering, "Aristotle in the Protrepticus nel mezzo del cammin" in: *Autour d'Aristote* (1955) 81–97, esp. 91.

---

* Cf. W. Jaeger, *Paideia*, v. I² (1945) 311–321; E. Hoffmann, "Aristoteles' Philosophie der Freundschaft" in: *Festgabe ... Rickert*, Bühl-Baden, n.d. [1933] 8–36, esp. 16 f.

Appendix 2

1. My assertion that ch. XXIII of *Isc* is derived from the *Protrepticus* by Aristotle has fully been confirmed by Festugière*. He added proofs of his own, translated and analyzed the text of the new fragment of Aristotle and I hope that my chapter will always be read in conjunction with his paper.

As in the text in question we find ὑπέρ used as meaning περί Festugière discusses the well known problem, to what extent such use speaks against the genuineness of the fragment — a problem playing such a conspicuous role in the discussions concerning the genuineness of the *Magna Moralia* **. I should like to contribute to this discussion by repeating after Dirlmeier that in Plato's *Rep.* IV 428 C–D, within a space of 9 Teubner lines, Plato uses ὑπέρ instead of περί five times, though the principle of *variatio* would be against such use. Obviously not too much weight should be attached to this stylistic criterion.

2. My proof that ch. XXIII is derived from Aristotle does not consist as Kerferd *** seems to assume, in my pointing out that that chapter contains a sentence which is almost a literal quotation from *De anima*. This is only one of my arguments and by no means considered by me to be the strongest. I must confess that Kerferd's objections on this point made on me the impression that he read just the first four pages of my chapter and somewhat hastily at that.

3. When I assigned *Isc* ch. XXIII to Aristotle and specifically to his *Protrepticus* I did this assuming a. that there is a fairly large body of texts correctly identified as belonging to Aristotle's *Protrepticus* and b. that specifically *Isc* ch. XXVI contains two such texts, known as fr. 52 and 53 Rose (*Protepticus* fr. 5 and 8 Walzer; Ross). Even before a detailed examination of *Isc.* ch. XXIII, I said, it is difficult to see how this chapter could not be derived from the *Protrepticus*, if ch. XXVI is.

---

* A.-J. Festugière, "Un fragment nouveau du 'Protreptique' d'Aristote", *Revue Philosophique* 146, 81 (1956) 117–127.

** Cf. F. Dirlmeier (tr., comm.), *Aristoteles, Magna Moralia*, (Berlin 1958), 149–154.

*** L.c. (above, p. 56).

Now, Rabinowitz* has recently set out to prove that virtually none of the texts which for the last eighty or so years have by Rose, Bywater, Diels, Hirzel, Jaeger, Bignone and others been identified as Aristotelian (which for Rose, as is well known, meant Pseudo-Aristotelian) and, specifically, taken from his *Protrepticus*, belong to Aristotle. The whole reconstruction of the *Protrepticus*, according to him, is built on sand. There is no evidence that any of these texts belongs to Aristotle. So far, only the first part of his investigations has been published and in that part the text which concerns us most, i.e. *Isc* ch. XXIII has not yet been discussed. But as the results of this discussion can easily be anticipated, it is perhaps not inappropriate to consider Rabinowitz' thesis at least with regard to *Isc* ch. XXVI and also in general.

Of course it is common knowledge that virtually none of the texts claimed for Aristotle's *Protrepticus* are in our sources explicitly assigned to Aristotle. But somehow Rabinowitz seems never to have asked himself the question why scholars should have ever undertaken the ascription of texts which *prima facie* present themselves as written by X, to Y. Why, specifically, have portions of the *Protrepticus* by Iamblichus been assigned to Aristotle?

This is the obvious answer — which escaped Rabinowitz perhaps because he never took a look at this work of Iamblichus as a whole, but concentrated on these of its parts which were of immediate concern to him. The *Protrepticus* by Iamblichus contains c. 126 Teubner pages. Of these, p. 24, 22–27, 2 Pistelli can immediately be identified as a cento made of Plato's *Euthydemus* 278 A–289 B. It is quite true that to some 420 lines in Plato's text only some 70 in Iamblichus correspond. But to see with Rabinowitz in this a proof of Iamblichus' originality is hardly acceptable. A cento is not a photocopy. Of the 70 lines some 80% are verbatim excerpts from Plato and the changes (additions, omissions, etc.) are strictly stylistic and concern only the manner of presentation or application to the topic of Iamblichus' writing. If a student would present Rabinowitz with a paper making use of some author in Iamblichus' fashion, it is a safe guess that Rabinowitz would charge him with plagiarism

---

* See above, p. 129.

rather than give him credit for originality. But above all, Rabinowitz' defense of Iamblichus' originality is entirely beside the
point. It presupposes that Iamblichus claimed originality for his
Protrepticus. We shall presently see that this presupposition is
entirely unfounded.

The above passage from the *Protrepticus* is only a sample (the
only one, treated by Rabinowitz). But there are others.

Protrepticus, ch. V contains on p. 30, 13–31, 19 Pistelli excerpts
from *Timaeus* 89 E–90 D, among them 23 Teubner lines which
are in 99% a verbatim copy of one continuous passage (*Tim.*
90 B–D).

The same chapter on p. 31, 19–33, 27 Pistelli contains a series
of excerpts (one again of 23 Teubner lines) from Plato's *Republic*
IX 588 E–591 E, with some slight, strictly stylistic changes.

Ch. XIII, p. 61, 7–62, 29 Pistelli is a literal copy of *Phaedo*
64 A–65 D (with some phrases due to the dialogical character of
the original omitted); p. 63, 2–65, 6 Pistelli is another such copy
of *Phaedo* 65 D–67 D; and on additional 8 pages (63, 2–65, 6;
65, 7–65, 18; 65, 22–67, 16; 67, 18–70, 9; 70, 16–71, 1 Pistelli) we
have nothing but literal excerpts from *Phaedo*.

Now, all this obviously not only gives us the right but makes it
our duty to ask: from whom did Iamblichus copy the rest of his
Protrepticus, particularly the section between ch. V, p. 33, 27
Pistelli and ch. XIII, p. 61, 7 Pistelli? The question whether he
copied this section we hardly have the right to ask — it is a
question settled in advance. Only when we approach the *Protrepticus* of Iamblichus as if it was meant to be taken as his original
work in our sense of the word 'original' would such a question be
justified. But the opposite is true. Iamblichus intends to exhibit
his originality in the appropriate selection and arranging of texts
exemplifying how Pythagoreans exhorted to philosophy. From
what we should call a book of readings (with some connecting
texts and notes) it differs only in that it feels under no obligation
to state its sources. But of course it is ridiculous to assume that it
is a piece of plagiarism. Under such circumstances Rabinowitz'
defense of Iamblichus' originality is wayward.

All this is perfectly obvious to anybody who simply paged the
whole *Protrepticus* looking at the apparatus of Pistelli. With the
help of this apparatus it easy to see that of the 126 Teubner pages

about 46 are excerpts from Plato, whose name, however, never appears in the text.

There is one more fact helping us to correctly assess the claims of Iamblichus. Of its ch. XX, p. 95, 12–24; 96, 1–97, 8; 97, 16–98, 12; 98, 17–99, 15; 99, 18–99, 28; 100, 5–101, 6; 101, 11–104, 14 Pistelli are generally recognized to be excerpts from an unknown writer of the 5th century (the so called Anonymus Iamblichi) * writing in the Ionic dialect. This adds another 9 pages to the 46 mentioned above. Beyond any doubt 55 out of 126 are not the work of Iamblichus. But what makes these 9 additional pages particularly remarkable is their linguistic character. Had Iamblichus ever thought of concealing his source he certainly would have atticized it. But even where it would have been only a question of changing letters, he twice (p. 95, 14; 97, 17 Pistelli) writes εὐγλωσσία. Still he does not feel under obligation to name his author.

What is true of the *Protrepticus* is *prima facie* true of *Isc*. It contains 99 Teubner pages. Of these ch. VI, p. 20, 22–28, 14 F, i.e. about 8 Teubner pages is simply a series of excerpts from the *Epinomis* and the *Republic* with hardly a word added or changed every now and then. But Plato's name is never mentioned.

Furthermore. The same passage from the *Epinomis* which is on p. 21, 4–15 F quoted verbatim, is, a few pages later, referred to again. This time, however, it is in the form of a non-verbatim report and it explicitly names Plato (p. 31, 7–14 F).

These facts alone should be sufficient to establish that for *Isc* Iamblichus used various sources and that he did not intend to produce what we should consider a coherent and consistent whole.

As the name of Plato occurs in the text, though only once, one could perhaps say that in this way Iamblichus at least gives us a hint where to look for his sources, that we therefore can expect the rest of his text to be his own where it is not by Plato. But such a point of view cannot be defended. For, a few pages later in the book, we come in ch. XXVII to a passage, viz. p. 84, 21–85, 23 F which is a series of excerpts from Aristotle, *De part. anim.* A 1, 639a4–b5, with Iamblichus (or his source) merely changing the *examples* of Aristotle to others, more appropriate to the

---

* F. Blass, *De Antiphonte sophista Iamblichi auctore*, Progr. Kiel 1889; for additional literature see, e.g., Diels-Kranz, *Die Fragmente der Vorsokratiker*⁹ (1959) ad 89, 1.

purpose of *Isc*. But Aristotle's name does not even once occur in *Isc*.

Again these facts alone are sufficient proof that it is imperative to assume that all of *Isc* consists of excerpts and was not meant to be taken as Iamblichus' own work in our usual sense of the word. Again this is perfectly obvious from the apparatus and the index of Festa.

Now, the two passages claimed by Rose for Pseudo-Aristotle and by others for Aristotle himself, viz. his fr. 52 and 53 (ch. XXVI, p. 79, 1–83, 2 and 83, 6–22 F) immediately precede the passage quoted above, which is taken from *De part. anim*. This in itself suggests that the author from which they are derived (that they could be a work of Iamblichus himself is as unlikely as it could be) might also be Aristotle. This is confirmed by a parallel passage in Proclus, *In Eucl*. As Rabinowitz devoted considerable care to showing that the passage in Proclus proves nothing of this kind we must present the texts in question *in extenso*.

Isc. ch. XXVI, p. 83, 13–20F	Proclus, *In Eucl*. 28,13–17Fr
καίτοι τὰς μὲν ἄλλας (scil. τέχνας)	δηλοῖ δὲ τὸ δι' ἑαυτὴν εἶναι τοῖς
πάντες συνεξορμῶσι τιμῶντες	μετιοῦσιν αἱρετὴν (scil. τὴν
κοινῇ καὶ τοὺς μισθοὺς τοῖς	μαθηματικὴν ἐπιστήμην) ὁ καὶ
ἔχουσι διδόντες τοὺς δὲ ταῦτα	'Αριστοτέλης πού φησιν τὸ
(scil. μαθήματα) πραγματευομέ-	μηδενὸς μισθοῦ προκειμένου τοῖς
νους οὐ μόνον οὐ προτρέπομεν	ζητοῦσιν ὅμως ἐν ὀλίγῳ χρόνῳ
ἀλλὰ καὶ διακωλύομεν πολλάκις	τοιαύτην ἐπίδοσιν τὴν τῶν μαθη-
. . .	μάτων θεωρίαν λαβεῖν . . .

Prima facie, Proclus seems to identify the whole passage of *Isc* as belonging to Aristotle. Ὁ καὶ 'Αριστοτέλης πού φησιν refers clearly to the proof ('proof that students of mathematics chose it for its own sake is also provided by what Aristotle says some place [or: in some words like these]), viz. that it made so rapid advances in so short a time in spite of the fact that its students could expect no rewards').

This interpretation is criticized by Rabinowitz. It could be, he says, that the reference to Aristotle does not cover the proof. His translation: 'What makes clear the fact that mathematics is desirable in and of itself for those who pursue the study (which is Aristotle's assertion too, somewhere . . .)' offers an alternative interpretation. But though not impossible, this interpretation is very unlikely. The construction is δηλοῖ δὲ τό (scil. that mathematics is pursued for its own sake) ὁ καὶ ᾿Αριστοτέλης πού φησιν. The construction is not δηλοῖ δὲ τὸ (scil. that mathematics is desirable for its own sake, as also Aristotle says somewhere) τὸ μηδενὸς μισθοῦ προκειμένου etc. In other words, the construction is τό–ὅ–τό, not τό–τό. It is unlikely that Proclus should have quoted Aristotle only to buttress his assertion that mathematics is pursued for its own sake rather than for his proof of this fact.

Let us try to draw up something like a balance sheet. The minimum which Rabinowitz must concede is:

A. It is extremely unlikely that *Isc.* ch. XXVI should be the property of Iamblichus.

B. It is possible that the passage in Proclus establishes as the source of Iamblichus Aristotle.

The maximum which must be conceded to Rabinowitz is:

A. It is barely possible that ch. XXVI is Iamblichus' own property.

B. It cannot be ruled out that Proclus' reference to Aristotle covers only part of the passage in Iamblichus.

Let it be left to the reader whether this balance sheet invalidates Rose's conclusion as to the source of the whole passage in Iamblichus. To me it seems that it does no such thing.

Not that Rose's proof should amount to certainty. But it is precisely uncertainty which compels us to undertake *Quellenforschung*. Rabinowitz is so familiar with the famous dictum of Aristotle that each subject matter has different standards of certainty that he could easily have asked himself "What constitutes a proof as far as *Quellenforschung* is concerned?" And if somebody should be inclined to say "The fact that *Quellenforschung* can never yield complete certainty should discourage us from undertaking to search after hidden sources" — let him be reminded that in the case of *Isc* (as in that of the *Protrepticus*) the facts are such that they compel us to ascertain its sources. Had Rabinowitz limited himself to reminding us that none of the texts assigned by modern scholars to the *Protrepticus* of Aristotle are in our texts explicitly attributed to him it would have been a meritorious reminder to those who not participating actively in the study of Greek philosophy may form an entirely wrong opinion as to why Rose, Walzer, Ross, etc. print certain texts as belonging to that work. Unfortunately, Rabinowitz overshoots his mark by miles.

VII. *METAPHYSICA GENERALIS* IN ARISTOTLE? *

We found the tripartition of theoretical knowledge to correspond with a tripartition of being into physicals, mathematicals (= soul, world-soul), and theologicals. In this context, mathematics was a study of things subsisting and was considered to be such even by the early Aristotle. What is true for mathematics should be true *a fortiori* for first philosophy. We may expect its objects to subsist to an even higher degree than do mathematicals. And indeed, first philosophy is frequently designated by Aristotle as theology. Who could doubt that theologicals subsist?

But Aristotle changed his mind regarding the status of mathematicals (and, therefore, by implication rather than explicitly, with regard to mathematics). Is there any comparable change in Aristotle with regard to theologicals and theology (first philosophy)? **

The present chapter will be devoted to a discussion of this question. And this discussion will, at the same time, lead us back to the problem which emerged in ch. III of the present book but was left unsolved. In that chapter we saw how St. Thomas, when interpreting the tripartition of being and knowledge in Boethius, was led to what amounted to making a marked distinction between *metaphysica generalis* and *metaphysica specialis*. With the later Aristotle, St. Thomas rejected the theory of the subsistence of mathematicals — they were only objects of abstraction. But if first philosophy was located above mathematics, the assumption was close at hand that its objects, too, would be

---

* According to R. Eisler, *Woerterbuch der philosophischen Begriffe*[4] (1928), for the terms *metaphysica generalis* and *specialis*, together with their precise definition, we are indebted to Micraelius, a person otherwise little known in the history of philosophy (see on him *Allg. Deutsche Biographie*). The terms are convenient indeed and will be used to indicate the difference between metaphysics as the knowledge of the transcendental (God, disembodied souls, angels) and metaphysics as science of being as what is common to everything (so with particular clarity Petrus Fonseca: the subject matter of metaphysics is *ens quatenus est commune Deo et creaturis, Commentarii in libros Metaphysicorum*, 2 vv. [Lyon 1591], v. I 490–504).

** This question has been answered in the affirmative by W. Jaeger, (*Aristoteles*[2] [1955] 200–236). According to him, the concept of metaphysics underwent the following development. In his first (Platonic) phase metaphysics was for Aristotle identical with theology. In his second (semi-Platonic) phase it meant for him something like metaphysical logic (or dialectics), the definition of metaphysics as science of being-as-such belonging to this second stage. In his third phase, Aristotle intended to interpret it as being based on, or comprising, physics. This line of development ended in complete naturalism, with Strato as its representative.

only objects of abstraction. Such an interpretation of first philosophy was bound to result in a conception of metaphysics as
metaphysica generalis. In other words, with the status of mathematicals as subsistent gone, first philosophy, when referred to
in the context of a tripartition of knowledge, seemed to designate
metaphysica generalis. To what extent is such an interpretation
justified?

The same problem can also be stated in shorter terms.
Sometimes Aristotle refers to first philosophy as being theology;
sometimes he refers to it as being science of being-as-such. The
former reference seems to lead to *metaphysica specialis*; the latter
to *metaphysica generalis*. How are the two related?

Met. Γ and E seem to have one great difficulty in common.
Both speak of parts of being and say that some branches of
knowledge deal with such parts. Wisdom (theology) deals with
the supersensible part of being (or: with the supreme sphere
of the supersensible if there is more than just one such sphere).
On the other hand, in distinction from those partial branches
of knowledge, so we read in these two books, there is another
dealing with being-as-such, irrespective of the spheres of being.
This kind of knowledge, too, seems to be designated by Aristotle
as wisdom.

We seem to be witnessing the birth of the *metaphysica generalis*
as different from the *metaphysica specialis*.

This birth seems to be accompanied by pangs.

Thus in Γ 1 Aristotle first announces that it is his intention to
speak of being-as-such (1003a21–26) and explains that the term
"to be" is not equivocal (2, 1003a33–1003b16). This explanation
amounts to saying that in the last resort anything is only because
οὐσίαι are. "Being as such" is opposed to "some part of being".
All other branches of knowledge deal with the latter; wisdom
(metaphysics) alone deals with being-as-such in general. The
chain of thought thus started ends with the sentence: if what
originally is, is an οὐσία, the philosopher must know the principles
and causes of the οὐσίαι (2, 1003b17–19).

This ties in with 1, 1003a26–32. The concatenation of ideas
can be presented in the following manner. Metaphysics is the
knowledge of being-as-such or, as we could also say, of the elements, principles, and causes of being-as-such. "Being" ulti-

mately refers to οὐσίαι; therefore metaphysics is the quest for elements, principles, and causes of οὐσίαι. This corresponds to the opening section of *Met.* Λ 1, 1069a18–19: our quest is a quest for οὐσία, because the causes and principles which we try to ascertain, are causes of οὐσίαι. And this in turn ties in with *Met.* A 1, 981a28 where metaphysics is distinguished from subordinated kinds of knowledge by being knowledge of causes; with *Met.* A 1, 981b28–29 where metaphysics is distinguished from other branches of knowledge dealing with causes by being the knowledge of original (prime) causes and principles (cf. 982a2; A 2,982a5; 982b9–10); and with *Met.* A 2,983a8–10 explaining the "divine" character of metaphysics as knowledge of the prime causes by the reminder that divinity has always been considered an original (prime) cause and principle (and, which is beside the point in the present context, to know the prime causes).

And it is well known how Aristotle surveys the history of philosophy under the assumption that all philosophers tried to ascertain the supreme principles of all that is (*Met.* A 3, 983b3–4; the "all" appears e.g. in 983b8; A 5,985b26).

Thus, Aristotle asserts that the quest for being-as-such is essentially identical with the quest for elements, principles, and causes of all that is — οὐσία (or οὐσίαι) being what ultimately is.

The singular οὐσία and the plural οὐσίαι alternate. Now, what does the plural οὐσίαι mean? It obviously can mean one of two things: either a plurality of οὐσίαι = individuals on the same existential plane or different kinds of being. And obviously Aristotle designates by οὐσίαι, in our context not several individuals (Socrates, a plant, a stone) but rather several kinds of οὐσία. One is almost tempted to interpret: although all οὐσίαι as individuals have this in common that only to them the verb "to be" can fully and properly be applied, still "to be" does not mean precisely the same thing for different kinds (orders) of οὐσίαι. "To be" in the case of a perishable οὐσία (individual) is not the same as "to be" in the case of an imperishable οὐσία; "to be" in the case of an imperishable οὐσία which is a mathematical is not quite the same as "to be" in the case of an imperishable οὐσία which is imperishable in the way in which Plato's ideas were supposed to be imperishable.

This kind of difference between the different senses of the

term "to be" is of course different from the difference between the different senses of "to be" if applied to οὐσίαι (individuals) on one hand and their properties and relations (none of which fully and properly exist) on the other hand.

It can therefore be said: in *Met.* Γ the subject matter of metaphysics is from the very outset presented either under the designation of being-as-such or under that of οὐσία or under that of principles, causes, and elements of οὐσία, and the use of the term οὐσία from the very beginning takes it for granted that there are several *kinds* of οὐσία, only one of which will be the subject matter of metaphysics. It never occurs to Aristotle that the term being-as-such applies to all that is, in contradistinction to οὐσία which, being always just a single οὐσία, would only designate part of all that is. "Being-as-such" and "one kind of οὐσία" are not mutually exclusive terms.

Aristotle continues by proving that "being" and "One" are essentially one and the same. Therefore it is up to one and the same branch of knowledge to study such things as identity, similarity, etc. — all these being kinds of the One or of being. And, says Aristotle, all opposites (ἐναντία) can be reduced to this principle (1003b34–1004a1).

The introduction of the term "opposites" comes surprisingly. But obviously Aristotle takes it for granted that the branch of knowledge which will investigate the different kinds of being-as-such (or of what is One) will also investigate their opposites. It seems further to be understood (though not expressed clearly in this place) that these opposites are e.g. being and non-being, One and not-One (many), identity and diversity, similarity and dissimilarity, etc.

In short, Aristotle says: all that is is ultimately reducible to opposites; all opposites are ultimately reducible to the opposition: being — non-being (or One and many).

This is striking. Is this not precisely Academic and/or Pythagorean doctrine?

Immediately Aristotle introduces the distinction between three branches of philosophy as if he had forgotten that he is going to deal with general metaphysics, which leaves out of consideration the differences between beings and concentrates on what is common to all beings (1004a2–9).

But he drops this distinction to resume the discussion of the subject matter — of what? We should assume of the study of being-as-such. But what do we read? A proof that it is up to one and the same branch of knowledge (= philosophy) to investigate opposites (ἀντικείμενα): One and multitude, the same and the other, the similar and the dissimilar, the equal and the unequal. Aristotle makes it clear that the negation (not-One) may be logical or real (ἀπόφασις or στέρησις). He makes it equally clear that all these pairs of opposites ultimately go back to the One-multitude antithesis (1004a9–21).

This passage to a certain extent simply elaborates the passage 1003b34–1004a1, thus making it clear that both passages indeed describe wisdom as knowledge of the ultimate opposites (to which all other opposites can be reduced) — these opposites being explicitly designated as One and many and therefore implicitly as being and non-being. One should be inclined to restate the theme of Aristotle's metaphysics by saying that it deals with the One-as-such and therefore also with the many-as-such; or by saying that it deals with being-as-such and therefore also with non-being-as-such. But whether or not we feel entitled to this restatement, one surprising impression remains. The two passages mentioned above (1004a9–21 and 1003b34–1004a1) resemble strongly the passage *Met.* A 5,986a15–986b8 with its summary: it is the opposites, among them One and many (986a24) which are the principles of all that is (τῶν ὄντων; 986a17) or of οὐσία (986b8), according to Pythagoreans (and also Alcmaeon). And they also resemble *Met.* Λ 10, 1075a28–33 in which Aristotle presents as a universally accepted theory that all is produced out of opposites (ἐναντία), the unequal-and-the-equal and One-and-many being examples of such opposites.

Having stated that the term One is not equivocal either (1004a22–25), Aristotle goes on to say that every case ultimately refers to the original (prime) case in its own category. E.g., every case of Oneness is ultimately reducible to the original One, every case of identity and diversity is reducible to the original identity and diversity, and the same is true of all opposites. And he continues: therefore it is obvious that it is up to one and the same branch of knowledge to investigate these opposites and the οὐσία (1004a31–33).

"These opposites and the οὐσία": this implies that οὐσία has the opposites as its causes, principles, or elements. "Being-as-such" and οὐσία are used interchangeably. Nothing indicates that Aristotle feels any incompatibility between the description of the subject matter of metaphysics as οὐσία and that of being-as-such, in spite of the fact that being-as-such seems to refer to what is common to all that is, whereas the οὐσία which is the subject matter of metaphysics differs from the οὐσία of other branches of knowledge.

Only now the full importance of the passage 2, 1004a2–4 reveals itself. Here suddenly (and as an enclave between two passages proving that everything can be reduced to an original pair of opposites) we find the assertion that there are as many parts of philosophy as there are οὐσίαι. Clearly, the passage anticipates the passage *Met.* E 1, in which it turns out that there are two or three οὐσίαι (1026a23–31), one of which is unmoved and the subject matter of metaphysics — and at the same time general (cf. Γ 1, 1003a24). The fact that metaphysics deals with just one οὐσία does not prevent Aristotle from saying that it deals with being-as-such, which he said in 1003a21.

Aristotle reiterates: all opposites ultimately go back to one. They are being and non-being, One and multitude (these two pairs are obviously treated as being equivalent). All philosophers agree that everything is ultimately composed of opposites. It is therefore clear that philosophy deals with opposites and the οὐσία (1004b27–1005a18). In this section the doctrine that all things consist of opposites is repeated no less than three times (1004b27–28; 1004b29–30; 1005a3–4).

This is precisely the doctrine violently attacked by Aristotle in *Met.* A, Λ, M, N. It is a doctrine in strict opposition to his form-privation-matter theory.

Aristotle goes on to ask whether philosophy as now described includes also an inquiry into the mathematical methods of reasoning. He refers to philosophy simply as being concerned with οὐσία. But we know by now that this means also the opposites (ultimately the One-multitude antithesis) constituting the οὐσία. He answers in the affirmative, as it is the business of the philosopher to investigate being-as-such, which none of the other branches of knowledge does. Here for the first time there emerges the partition of wisdom into three branches, physics, mathematics, and philosophy proper (otherwise known as first philosophy or theology). And Aristotle quite obviously does not feel that he is changing the subject matter: theology, though having a province of being for its own, is at the same time an inquiry into being-as-such. We know already that this means: being-as-such and non-being-as-such, one-as-such and multitude-as-such, and so on (1005a19–1005b2).

Furthermore, the metaphysician is described as dealing with καθόλου and the primary (uppermost) οὐσία, i.e. with being-as-such *and* just one part of being. Thus, everywhere in *Met.* Γ οὐσία as the subject matter of metaphysics means just one kind of being. Whenever he says that metaphysics deals with οὐσία, he means it deals with one kind of οὐσία. But this does not prevent him from saying that metaphysics deals with being-as-such. Metaphysics deals with what ultimately is, i.e. with οὐσία (or, if there are different kinds, with οὐσίαι); it deals with οὐσία by ascertaining its ultimate principles (elements, causes); the ultimate principles of οὐσία are being-as-such and its opposite (or the One and the many).

It is after this that the principle of contradiction is introduced: it is impossible for the same thing to be and not to be in one and the same respect and at the same time. This, then, is the most outstanding example of an inquiry into being-as-such.

We omit all the proofs. With H. Maier (*Die Syllogistik des Aristoteles*, v. I [1896] 43–46) we stress one thing only: Aristotle states the principle of contradiction in ontic rather than epistemonic terms *. It is "for the same thing it is impossible to be and not to be" rather than "contradictory attributes may not be affirmed of the same object in the same respect and at the same time".

With this, however, we seem to have definitely left the territory of any inquiry into elements, opposites, etc., and/or into any specific οὐσία; we seem to be in the midst of *metaphysica generalis*. In fact, some would say that we are in the forefield of any philosophy, viz. in logic; most would assert that we certainly are out of theology.

---

* For what follows see G. Calogero, *I fondamenti della logica aristotelica* (1927), esp. 64–83.

But there are some passages which are noteworthy. In explaining why some accepted the Protagorean theory, Aristotle says that they did so because they paid exclusive attention to the flux of the realm of the sensible. "If a thing that was warm becomes cold, and yet nothing can come out of nothing, the thing must have been both warm and cold", was their reasoning. After having refuted this theory by the use of the δύναμις-ἐντελέχεια pair Aristotle goes on to say: "We shall have to ask them to accept the existence of another sphere of being (οὐσία of being things), totally exempt from change, passing-away, and coming-to-be" (5, 1009a36–38).

A remarkable passage. It seems to imply that the principle of contradiction, i.e. the assertion that nothing can be and not be at the same time, is more obvious when we turn to the supersensible sphere of being. One is almost tempted to say: being-as-such is present in the supersensible sphere in purer condition. In other words, Aristotle seems to say that a physical thing is never truly identical with itself. This makes no sense if identity is a universal quality applicable to any and every thing. But Aristotle is obviously not thinking in terms of formal logic.

It is not the only such passage. In addition to the Protagoreans, some others rejected the principle of contradiction. They based their rejection on the assumption that sensation is the only criterion (i.e. means of apprehension) of truth, and on the observation that the same things may cause different sensations. To refute them, Aristotle again reminds them that over and above the realm of the sensible there is still another realm, exempt from change (5, 1010a1–3; 25–35).

Once more we have the impression that this realm of the unchangeable is the true home of the principle of contradiction.

Then, as if to make sure that nobody will forget the presence of this changeless sphere, the book closes with an impressive sentence. We should not assume that there is no "always" in the universe; there is something that always moves things that are moved; and the thing that is the prime mover is [always] unmoved (8, 1012b29–31).

A strange ending, indeed, for a *metaphysica generalis*. We are back in theology. Thus, the structure of Γ reveals itself to be this: what we should be inclined to consider a piece of *metaphysica* *generalis* is sandwiched between (a) the doctrine that all being consists ultimately of two principles, and (b) the doctrine stating sharply the existence and difference of two spheres of being (sensible and supersensible); with two solemn reminders (ἀξιώσομεν ὑπολαμβάνειν — — ἄξιον ἐπιτιμῆσαι [1009a36; 1010a25]) of the latter in between *.

How about *Met.* E 1 ?

The causes and the principles, the knowledge of which would be wisdom (cf. *Met.* A 2, 982b8–10), must be the causes and principles of beings-as-such, i.e. they must not be principles of one specific province of being. This is the reason why neither physics nor mathematics is wisdom, though both are parts of speculative knowledge. Physics deals only with the changeable embedded in matter. The status of mathematics is not quite clear. Only theology, dealing with the immaterial and changeless, can claim to be truly wisdom (1025b3–1026a23).

A baffling chain of thought. It begins with the concept of being-as-such; it ends with the concept of theology. Which is the subject matter of wisdom?

To add to the confusion, Aristotle continues: does theology deal with only one province of being or with something general? After all, there is a similar problem in mathematics: single branches (geometry, astronomy) deal with single provinces of the mathematicals, but there is also a discipline of the general, common to all. How, then, about theology?

There is, answers Aristotle, a sphere of unchangeable being over and above the sphere of the changeable being; theology deals with it, and therefore [or: in this sense of the word; or: by the same token] theology is [or: deals with what is] general. And the same theology deals also with being-as-such (1026a23–32).

Here the confusion seems to reach its height. Wisdom, so we should think, should not have a specific province of being for its subject matter; it should deal with what simply is and deal with it as being. This is clearly *metaphysica generalis*. How, then, can Aristotle say that theology is wisdom, while he defines theology by its subject matter, which subject matter is only one

---

* Cf. W. Jaeger, *Aristoteles*² (1955) 220 f. There is hardly any difference between the treatment of the principle of contradiction in *Met.* Γ and *Met.* K, except in the wording. Jaeger seems implicitly to admit this.

province of being? How can we say that theology is general because it deals with the uppermost sphere of being? If we take "general" in this sense, how is it possible to say that theology deals with being-as-such? And what is the difference between the "generality" of theology in the former and in the latter senses of the word? Either general metaphysics or special metaphysics; and if the former, either because for some inscrutable reason the peculiar province of being assigned to theology is described as general or because it deals with being-as-such — but to see all these either-ors replaced by and-ands is highly bewildering.

We omit the rest of E; it has no relation to the topic of the subject matter of metaphysics.

What, then, is the way out of this whole confusion?

It is very simple. The Aristotle who wrote *Met.* Γ and E 1, and at the time when he wrote them, was not aware that his being-as-such could be interpreted as abstract or as formal; he was not aware that he was starting a general metaphysics as different from special metaphysics *. It can not be denied that it may be legitimate to interpret him in this way, if by legitimate we mean what is logically implied or what is implied in other passages dealing with the concept of being; but it can be asserted that he was not aware of it. On the contrary, he thinks of his being-as-such as an element, something indwelling in all that is. This assertion is tantamount to saying that *Met.* Γ and E 1 were written in the Academic tradition.

According to this tradition there are different spheres of being; there is at least one sphere over and above the sphere of the sensible. There is some concatenation between these spheres, so that the superior can be termed "cause" (in *some* sense of the word) of the inferior; moreover, the uppermost sphere is "composed of" (or "derived from") two opposite elements which can conveniently be called One and multitude — with the explicit understanding that they *are not abstracta* or mere predicates (in contradiction to their treatment in *Met.* I 2, 1053b11 [cf.

---

* And probably never became aware of it: cf. E. v. Ivánka, "Die Behandlung der Metaphysik in Jaegers 'Aristoteles'", *Scholastik* 7 (1932) 1–29, quoting *Met.* Z 1,1028b13–15; 11,1037a10–16; 17,1041a6–9 — all passages assumed by Jaeger to be much later than Γ, E, K, and yet all describing metaphysics as knowledge of the suprasensible, i.e. just one sphere of being.

N 1, 1087b33–1088a14] ; 1054a9–19 *). Because the superior sphere is the "cause" of the inferior, the elements of the superior must in some way be present also in the inferior (in the inferior ones, if there are many). In this sense of the word, a pair of opposite principles, being and non-being or One and multitude, are the elements of everything.

Now, it is obvious that they are more distinctly present in the superior than in the inferior sphere. If therefore wisdom is the study of the supreme principles and elements, we are philosophers by studying the supreme sphere of being, together with its elements, the One and multitude. In other words, by studying being and non-being or the One and multitude as elements we do not study them as abstracta. On the contrary, we remain within the realm of the supreme sphere of being, though obliquely we are speaking of all spheres of being, whenever we speak of being and non-being or the One and multitude. "Theology", "metaphysics", "wisdom", is therefore the study of both the supreme sphere of being *and* elements. At this stage of thought there can be no difference between a *metaphysica generalis* and a *metaphysica specialis*, because neither being and non-being nor One and multitude are considered to be abstracta.

The character of being or the One as an element can be described by stressing that we mean being-as-such and the One-as-such — i.e. not as an adjective or a quality of something else or as a predicate. It is obvious that in the Academic system the One is meant to be a thing rather than a quality (though it may be *debatable* if it ever exists outside of the things to which it imparts unity). It is therefore a legitimate task of theology to study the being-as-such.

This is precisely why *Met.* Γ and E 1 fit into the pattern of Academic speculations. If all being is one — "one" and "being" (*quodcumque ens est unum*) — the difference between an inquiry into being-as-such and one-as-such is very slight indeed. The two inquiries are ultimately branches of one and the same question. What imparts being to a thing — i.e., what makes this thing *a* thing or *one* thing? When we ask: "What imparts being to a thing?" — we do not mean: what makes the thing red or green,

* This passage explicitly speaks only of being and the One, but implicitly also of their opposites.

heavy or light. We mean precisely: what imparts existence to it? Similarly when we ask: "What imparts oneness to anything?" we mean: what makes it one being? — not one horse, or one table. In *Met.* Γ and E 1 Aristotle speaks precisely of this kind of being — being as an element equivalent to One.

With this explanation almost all difficulties of Γ and E 1 disappear. Furthermore, we can now understand perfectly why in the discussion of the being-as-such we find references to different spheres of being. Aristotle says that what can above all be said of being-as-such, is that every being (*qua* such) is identical with itself, and it is only another aspect of this self-identity which is expressed in the principle of contradiction. Now he tries to find out why some philosophers implicitly or explicitly denied this principle. One of the reasons given by him is that they saw everything around them changing, so that it was difficult for them to attain the concept of self-identity or stability. But they should have recognized the existence of another sphere of being in which stability reigns. The principle of contradiction in Aristotle is a corollary to the Academic doctrine that sensible things are permanently in flux, so that they do not exist — in the full sense of the word "to exist".

Now, to some the assertion that the principle of contradiction is applicable (or discoverable) in one sphere of being rather than in another sounds like sheer nonsense. Indeed it is — if being is taken to be an abstractum and the principle of contradiction a rule of formal logic. Not so however, if being is taken to be an element and the principle of contradiction an ontic principle. On the contrary, it is immediately clear that being, as any other element can be obfuscated in one sphere of being and appear clear in another. It is particularly clear for a Platonist that ideas and numbers are more being than sensibles. What do we mean when we say "more being"? Precisely this: being in them is more powerful, clear, undiluted. The same thing can be expressed by saying that it is less determined, less permeated by negation, and, in this sense of the word, more universal. Furthermore, the very assertion that one thing could be in a higher degree than another makes no sense whatsoever to a reader who interprets being as a formal category, an abstractum, which can be applied equally to, or abstracted equally from, every other being. But for a Platonist there are degrees of being; some things participate in being more than others. Therefore, being can be studied better with some things, less well with others. This is precisely Aristotle's viewpoint in *Met.* Γ and E 1.

Now, it is well known that in many passages outside of *Met.* Γ and E 1 Aristotle criticized the concept of being as an element, reducing it to a universal concept equally applicable to anything that exists. If we read *Met.* Γ and E 1 in the light of these passages, we could interpret *Met.* Γ and E 1 as proposing a general metaphysics. Studied within themselves, however, they do not indicate that Aristotle intended it this way. On the contrary. The introduction of the problem, the bewildering sentence in E 1 that theology deals with the unmoved οὐσία and with being-as-such, the references to a suprasensible sphere of being as justification of the principle of contradiction — all this becomes perfectly clear and coherent if we only see that in *Met.* Γ and E 1 being is not an abstractum but an element — close to or perhaps identical with the Academic (or perhaps the Platonic) One. Therefore it is one and the same branch of knowledge which studies the supreme sphere of being and being-as-such.

One more thing becomes clear immediately. On re-reading Γ and E 1 we discover throughout the fact that the theory according to which all is derived from two opposite principles is indeed taken for granted and restated. This is what we read in *Met.* Γ 2, 1003b36–1005a5 with the repeated: all things can be reduced (ἀνάγεται) to being and non-being (1004b27–28) or One and multitude (33–34); all things consist of opposites (29–30; 1005a3–5), i.e. ultimately of One and multitude. It is here that Aristotle refers to his table of opposites, with nothing to indicate that in this table the two-opposite-principles doctrine was criticized. The whole passage teaches that wisdom is the science of the opposites, and that all opposites can ultimately be traced (by ἀναγωγή) to the One-multitude antithesis, or (considering the fact that, as One and being are equivalents their opposites must be equivalents too) to the being-non-being antithesis (1004b27–31). It is really possible to overlook the fact that Aristotle here professes the two-opposite-principles doctrine, so severely criticized elsewhere? All things either are opposites or they consist of opposites, and the One and the multitude are the principles of [all] opposites (1005a3–5) — this is said by Aristotle here, not as a report on doctrines of others, but as his own conviction. It is precisely the same conviction which in *Met.* Λ 10, 1075a28–29 he dismisses with the icy: "All generate all things of opposites. But neither the concept 'all things' nor the concept 'of opposites' is correct". How is it possible to overlook this tremendous difference in Aristotle's attitudes?

But still another thing must not be overlooked. In Γ the fact that "being" and "One" have several different meanings does not prevent the assertion that there must be elements common to all beings, while elsewhere * this very fact becomes a proof that to try to find elements of *all* beings is nonsense, for how can any element be common to something that *is* a quality and to something else that *is* a quantity?

And now we can also discuss the meaning of καθόλου as used in Γ and E 1. It is not the abstract (general, universal); it is what is common to all cases as concrete. If all men have hair, it is a καθόλου quality. Because being as an element is present everywhere, it is καθόλου. It is one of the two basic constituents of the uppermost sphere of being (with non-being as the other). This uppermost sphere of being somehow "causes" all the other spheres and its elements are the elements of everything. Therefore, the true philosopher, i.e., the one dealing with first philosophy — first philosophy being the one that deals with the first (uppermost) sphere of being — deals with the elements of this uppermost sphere and thus with being. By implication, he therefore deals with being as it is present everywhere. The thesis, "first philosophy deals with the uppermost sphere of being and is *general* knowledge, because the elements of this uppermost sphere, being (and non-being), are *common* to all [this is the meaning of καθόλου] spheres of being and therefore to all beings", is perfectly consistent. Suppose everything were ultimately to consist of hydrogen and oxygen and the "first" combination of hydrogen and oxygen were water, then the study of water would imply the study of hydrogen and oxygen and thus be a

---

* E.g. *Met.* A 9,992b19; N 2,1089a7; *De an.* I 5,410a13. Perhaps it should be mentioned that according to Γ 2 the difference between πρὸς ἕν and καθ' ἕν is irrelevant for the problem at hand, which is the reducibility of all opposites to one principal pair.

study of hydrogen and oxygen in general or of these two as common to all things. Water science would be the first science, therefore general science. If, however, the "first" product of oxygen and hydrogen were oxyhydrogen gas, oxyhydrogen gas science would be the first and therefore most general science and would deal with the two above elements as such. This simile only "translates" Aristotle's assertion: if the sphere of the sensible were the only uppermost sphere of being, physics would be "first wisdom" and deal with being-as-such, because "to be" would mean "to be a physical". But as there is a higher sphere of being, it is the "first" philosopher who investigates the "general" and [therefore] first sphere of being. Here already (Γ 3, 1005a35) the καθόλου and the first οὐσία appear peacefully side by side, preparing us for the statement: general by being first (E 1, 1026a30–31). In the supreme sphere being is present as a καθόλου. In all other spheres it is present as being something. The transition from being something to being-as-such does not take place by what *we* term a process of abstraction, i.e., formalization and/or generalization, away from the truly and fully existing, the individual, the concrete, the specific, and towards the general (universal) existing only (or almost only) in our thoughts. Rather, this transition takes place by omitting some concrete i.e. limiting characters and retaining being in its pure form, unalloyed, but still concrete and non-abstract.

After all, our passages are not the only ones where καθόλου cannot be taken as meaning "universal", "general", etc. Perhaps the best known passage where such a translation would not do is *Physics* I 1 (cf. H. Cassirer, *Aristoteles' Schrift "Von der Seele"* [1932] 14–24; W. D. Ross, *Aristotle's Physics* [1936], commentary a.l.). It is obvious that the word has more than one meaning in Aristotle and it is most important to notice that it does not always mean "universal" or "general" if these words are taken in the sense of "more abstract", "more empty with regard to content and therefore more comprehensive", etc*.

---

* For a discussion of the concept καθόλου see particularly: D. Badareu, *L'Individuel chez Aristote*, n.d. [1936] 67 f.; K. v. Fritz, *Philosophie und sprachlicher Ausdruck bei Demokrit, Plato und Aristoteles*, n.d. [1938?] 39; 64 f.; cf. J. M. LeBlond, *Logique et Méthode chez Aristote* (1939), esp. 51 f.; 75–83, 214 n. 4; N. Hartmann, *Aristoteles und das Problem des Begriffs* (1940) 10 = *Kleinere Schriften*, v. II (1957) 100–129, esp. 107 f. In *An. Post.* II 19 Aristotle seems to be closest to an interpretation of

Once we read Γ and E 1 as teaching the two-opposite-principles doctrine, we have no difficulty in reading *Met.* K. All we have to do is to start with ch. 3 and read through ch. 7 (1060b31–1064b14). We see immediately that here again the two-opposite-principles doctrine is accepted by Aristotle and that he expects the hearer to accept it as having been proved elsewhere (1061a10–15, cf. 1061b12–14). A slight doubt as to whether it is possible to say of anything that it is either A or non-A is removed (1061a18–28). Without the removal of this doubt, the doctrine that in the end everything can be traced back to one of the two opposites could be impugned. Now comes a comparison of the procedure of mathematics with that branch of first philosophy which deals with being-as-such. The mathematician inquires περὶ τὰ ἐξ ἀφαιρέσεως. What does this mean? 'Αφαίρεσις *here* means a procedure opposed to πρόσθεσις — not what we usually term abstraction *. We pass from numbers to geometricals by πρόσθεσις, i.e., adding to the numerical the element of distance (distension). Or we can go back from geometricals to numbers by ἀφαίρεσις, i.e., by taking away the element of distance (distension, extension). But by so doing we always remain *within* the realm of the (relatively) individual, specific, concrete and do not pass from it to the abstract. Numbers "precede" geometricals and are general (or more general) in this sense of the word. It is only our nominalistic or semi-nominalistic bent of mind that prevents us from seeing this quite clearly. There are passages in Aristotle, the father of seminominalism, the grand-father of nominalism, in which ἀφαίρεσις does mean what we

---

καθόλου as designating the abstract universality of a concept arrived at by some kind of induction; and all passages in which Aristotle attacks Plato for having made ideas both universal and subsistent, he uses the word καθόλου to designate the abstract universal. On the other hand, in the passage where the meaning of καθόλου is discussed *ex professo*, i.e. *An. Post.* I 4,73b25–74a3, its meaning is "omnipresent" rather than "abstractly universal". In other words, it is impossible to say that the very fact that something is designated by Aristotle as καθόλου is sufficient to prove that this something could not have been meant by him to be something subsistent. In some passages καθόλου and full subsistence are mutually exclusive concepts; in some others they are not. Cf. F. Solmsen, *Die Entwicklung der aristotelischen Logik und Rhetorik* (1929) 84–90; W. D. Ross, *Aristotle's Prior and Posterior Analytics* (1949), commentary ad 73b25–32, p. 523.

* Cf. also L.-M. Régis, "La Philosophie de la nature", *Études et Recherches* ....
I. Philosophie. C. 1 (1936) 127–158, esp. 128–132; M. D. Philippe, "πρόσθεσις, ἀφαίρεσις, χωρίζειν dans la philosophie d'Aristote", *Revue Thomiste* 48 (1948) 461–479.

mean by abstraction; but in K 3 the word is used differently, and as befits a true conceptual realist. *Met.* Γ, E 1, K 3–7 is written by such a realist (with one slight qualification; see below). As long as we move in abstracts, no πρόσθεσις can fill the gap between an *infima species* and an individual in time and space. We have to jump. On the other hand, by abstracting in our sense of the word, we immediately jump from the spatio-temporal to the ideal. In K 3 ἀφαίρεσις means no jump from the "real" to the "ideal"; it is a procedure within the real. We take it for granted that by "omitting" from a sensible its qualities like weight, hardness, temperature, and retaining only quantity and continuum, we leave the realm of the real and arrive in the realm of the ideal. But this is perhaps quite untrue; it would most certainly not be granted by a Platonist and it is by no means the opinion of Aristotle in K 3. The geometricals subsist; they subsist even more than the sensibilia. The sensibilia could not exist without the geometricals, while the geometricals can exist without them. The sensibilia "originate" from the geometricals by πρόσθεσις; they need, as it were, one more quantum of the original elements plus some alloy. The ἀφαίρεσις restores the original purity of geometricals. And just as a geometrist now inquires into τὰ ἐξ ἀφαιρέσεως and by so doing inquires into sensibilia, just so the "first philosopher" inquires into a higher realm of τὰ ἐξ ἀφαιρέσεως, i.e., into objects of this realm together with their original principles, which are being and non-being and their combinations, relations, etc. (1061a28–1061b11).

It should be stressed that when Aristotle says that in addition to geometry and arithmetic there is a "first" mathematics *, he is not speaking in terms of abstraction in our sense either. The "first" mathematics has entities of its own, more real than the entities of arithmetic or geometry. In some passages he will deny this. "What is general in mathematics has no existence separate from the [geometrical] quantities and numbers" (*Met.* M 3,1077b17). But Aristotle is overshooting the mark. Quantities and numbers themselves do not subsist — if one accepts this point of view, the non-subsistence of entities of a "first" mathematics needs no proof. But if arithmetical and geometrical

---

* Cf. the discussion in T. Heath, *Mathematics in Aristotle* (1949) 223. Heath compares Aristotle's "first" (universal, general) mathematics to our algebra.

entities subsist, there is no reason to assume that pre-arithmetical entities do not subsist as well. A good commentary can be found in *Isc* ch. V, p. 19, 19–20, 18 F *.

The connection of this doctrine with another remarkable piece of Academic philosophy is obvious. It is the doctrine ascribed to Plato by Aristotle that there is no idea common to the things which stand to each other in the relation prior-posterior. As this topic has been dealt with elsewhere, one specific example in Aristotle's writings (*De an.* II 3, 414b21; 29–32) will be sufficient. The most self-sufficient plane figure is the triangle. By πρόσθεσις, from the triangle we derive the quadrilateral, etc. The quadrilateral presupposes the triangle — in other words, the triangle is contained in all later plane figures and is καθόλου in this sense of the word. From a $3 + $ x-angle we can ascend to the triangle by ἀφαίρεσις. Now, it is perfectly clear that the whole ascensus-descensus remains within the same sphere of reality; the triangle is more abstract than the quadrilateral — but not in the sense of our word abstraction; and it is the most general plane figure, but not because it is "ideal", while the quadrilateral, tenangle, etc., are "real". Therefore, the triangle science would be the "first" science of plane figures and general by being first. Should there be some elements of which the triangle consists, e.g., "three" and "extension", the first science of plane figures would study "three"- and "extension"-as-such. We could also say: the interpretation of πρόσθεσις and ἀφαίρεσις could develop in two main directions, the logical and the metaphysical. By following the first, it would arrive at specification and universalization (by abstraction), the last specifying step resulting in an *infima species*. By following the second, it would arrive at the neoplatonic concept of πρόοδος and ἐπιστροφή. In Aristotle we find indications of both directions. And precisely the same holds true for the term καθόλου — it could develop either into a logical universal, transcendental by being empty, or coinciding with the unrestricted and fully being and transcendental by being above any peculiar being.

To sum up, καθόλου should very frequently be translated by

---

* Cf. also. W. D. Ross, *Arist. Met.* (1924) ad E 1,1026a25 and M2,1077a9.

"common" rather than "general"; ἀφαίρεσις by "subtraction" rather than "abstraction" *.

Also the second part of K 7, 1064a28–36 becomes clear. There is a science of being-as-such, says Aristotle. Let us investigate whether its object matter is identical with that of physics. This cannot be, because physics deals with what is moved. But neither can its object matter be identical with that of mathematics. For mathematics deals with what is unmoved, it is true; but these unmoved objects have no subsistence (they are ἀχώριστα). Thus, metaphysics deals with a different sphere of being, which is unmoved and subsistent (ἀκίνητος, χωριστή).

The terms "being-as-such" and "unmoved and separated" are used to designate one and the same thing: the sphere of being which is the subject matter of metaphysics. There is not the slightest trace of hesitation as to the equivalency of these two terms. But if such is the case, is it not obvious that "being-as-such" cannot mean what post-Aristotelian interpreters took it to mean? Is it not obvious that it would be futile to interpret the phrase "unmoved and separated" as meaning "being-as-such" in the modern sense of the word, i.e. an abstractum? Is it not obvious that only the opposite interpretation will do, according to which "being-as-such" means the supreme, unmoved, incorporeal sphere of being?

The whole chapter ends (1064b11–14) with a summary: the subject matter of metaphysics, the unmoved and incorporeal (χωριστόν), precedes the subject matter of physics and mathematics and is in virtue of that precedence (or, by the same token), a καθόλου. No further commentary seems to be required.

It could perhaps be said that the interpretation of the phrase being-as-such as designating a logical universal would never have originated had the repated statements of Aristotle in Γ and E 1 that all things consist of opposites, ultimately of being

---

* Cf. also L. Robin, *Aristote* (1944) 106–109 who interprets the catholicity of being-as-such by saying: being as such is individual and universal at the same time; the latter by repeating itself in all spheres of being, with decreasing purity. Robin's interpretation is similar to the one by Ps. Alexander, *In Metaph.* K 7, 1064a10, p. 661, 31–39 Hayduck: καθόλου is to be taken not as a universal [predicate] but as the first [in a series] which when done away with, does away with all the subsequent terms of the series. A different explanation is given *ibid.* ad E 1,1026a16: καθόλου as applied to theology does not indicate universality, but rather the excellence of its subject matter (p. 447, 32 Hayduck).

and non-being, been taken at their face value. It would even have been sufficient to remember, on re-reading the phrase being-as-such when it occurs first, that later Aristotle will prove that knowledge that deals with being deals also with its opposites and therefore to interpret the subject matter of metaphysics from the very outset as being and non-being, but being and non-being of a special kind, viz. being-as-such and non-being-as-such. Being and non-being are present everywhere; being-as-such and non-being-as-such only in a special, the highest, sphere of being and it is this speciality which makes it, makes them most general.

The implications of this interpretation of Γ, E 1, and K 3–7 are of considerable interest. We can clearly see the Academic metaphysical system as shared by Aristotle. The basic assumption is this: over and above the realm of the sensible (changeable) there must exist *at least* one more realm — intelligible, eternally changeless. This realm must subsist. Two kinds of eternal changeless being claimed to be this realm: ideas and mathematicals. To see whether either of these could realize its claims, we must understand what their relation to the realm of the changeable was supposed to be.

First as to the ideas. It was supposed to be a *real* relation, or as we would say, a causal relation (*Met.* N 2, 1090a6). But according to Aristotle it turned out to be at best a logical relation — implication, not causation. To indicate this, we could say that the ideas turned out to be nonmotive. There was no transition from them to the realm of space and time. No matter what the amount of πρόσθεσις, there still was no way to "derive" the sensibilia from the ideas.

Whatever the specific objections to the ideas, the philosophic situation presupposed in Γ, E 1, and K 3–7 is: ideas cannot claim to be the realm of the eternal, "presiding" actually over the sensible. As to mathematicals, Γ, E 1, and K 3–7 have some doubts whether they subsist at all.

Some doubts — no more than that. This is the only point where Aristotle's conceptual realism is somewhat more restricted than the Academic one. The supersensible sphere, the existence of which is assumed in Γ, E 1, and K 3–7, is undoubtedly conceived by Aristotle as subsistent. So far the present analysis could follow Jaeger very closely.

But with this doctrine of spheres of being is connected another. The spheres (whatever they are) must be derived from one another (or there would be no unity of being). If they are not derived from each other, there must be some other link connecting them. Thus, both multiplicity and unity of the spheres are required.

But the problem of unity and multiplicity appears also within each sphere. How is unity, how is multiplicity, to be explained?

The answer given by the Academy seems to have been almost unanimous: there must ultimately be two opposite elements, one responsible for unity, the other for multiplicity. Their interaction explains the universe. What we term these elements does not matter very much. One and multitude is as good as being and non-being or as sameness and otherness. The two elements must be in some way elements of all things in all spheres of being.

In this connection it is all-important to see one thing clearly. If we apply the name "universe" to all these spheres of being (constituted ultimately by two opposite elements) we can never be sure whether we speak of the universe as something extended in time and space (real in the ordinary sense of the word), or of this universe *plus* what we should term the ideal universe, or of the universe of ideal beings. Time and again we face the question: does it make sense to "add" what we should call the ideal to what we should call the real and apply the name of the universe to this strange sum? However, if we refuse to make sense out of it, we bar ourselves from understanding some of the most basic positions of Greek metaphysics. Because the ideal belongs to the universe no less than does the real, Greek metaphysics (ontology) is often also cosmology. To say that there are spheres of being, the lowest of which is the sphere of the sensible, while the others are supersensible, seems to be a metaphysico-logical description of a non-temporal, non-spatial order. It is very difficult to see how "to be" can be applied to the sensible and the supersensible without becoming a homonym. But this description claims to be a description of the real universe. From this point of view, therefore, it makes no difference whether

(1) we say that sensible is merely one more sphere of being, "derived" from the supersensible — in other words whether we interpret the supersensible "idealistically"; or (2) we say that the supersensible "surrounds" the sensible, thus interpreting the "ideal" realistically; or (3) — most characteristic — we say that the ideal and unspatial is beyond the heavens, thus strangely combining the spatial and the non-spatial. All this is a perfectly legitimate expression of a philosophic point of view according to which there is no difference between the metaphysico-logical and any other order. There is no difference between implication and causation; or rather, causation is ultimately implication. Because the Academics are conceptual realists, the sensible must be derivable from the supersensible.

From this point of view we can appreciate much better the frequent question in Aristotle as to whether a certain process described as derivation, origin, etc., was meant by its author to have been a temporal or non-temporal process. The best-known example is the famous controversy as to whether the cosmogony in the *Timaeus* was understood by Plato to be an event in time. Another example is Aristotle's treatment of the Pythagoreans (e.g., *Met.* A 8,989b34; N 3,1090a32–35; 1091a13–20). They "generated" the physical universe from numbers, as they "generated" numbers from the even and the odd; they were clearly cosmogonists. Sometimes Aristotle describes this process as an attempt to derive magnitudes out of non-magnitudes (*Met.* A 8, 990a12; cf. Λ 10, 1075b28, see below).

It would be inappropriate to treat this as a philological problem which could have been solved by asking Plato point-blank: How did you mean your cosmogony? As a temporal event? Or was the temporal description only a literary device? Before answering such a question Plato might have asked first: Is there any real difference between implication and causation? How real is time? Only if we understand each other on this point will my answer make sense. It seems that the Academic point of view should be in favor of denying the reality of the spatio-temporal; space is next to nothing, time only an image of the eternal. In this sense of the word those Academics were correct who insisted that the *Timaeus* presented the cosmogony as a temporal event only for the sake of illustration. This does not mean that the universe existed from eternity to eternity; but rather, that it did not exist in time. No part of the universe existed in time — therefore it would be perfectly legitimate to interpret the universe as consisting of spheres of being, some of them timeless, some temporal. Temporality is only a form of timelessness *.

Thus, assuming the existence of more than one sphere of the supersensible, the universe of Academic metaphysics presents itself as follows:

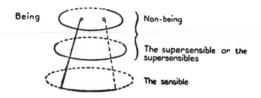

This drawing is completely adequate, *because* it presents both the supersensible and the sensible in space. In this system space cannot be anything but a particular form of otherness, diversity, etc.; diversity, etc., cannot be anything but space as existing in the supersensible. In this system one cannot insist that numbers are either extended (physical bodies) or ideal **.

All this becomes even clearer when we think of change and motion. According to a naively nominalistic point of view, change and motion are "real" events, while diversity (otherness) is a logical category. Not so in the Academic system. Change and motion are simply a particular form of otherness. From the point of view of naive nominalism the Academic universe is completely static, because naive nominalism can conceive of change only in time. But change in time is (quite literally so) but diversity in the timeless.

---

* Cf. C. Mugler, *Platon* (1948) 276 f. In his review of Mugler (*Review of Metaphysics* 4 [1951] 395–425) Cherniss says that any attempt to derive space from the realm of the unextended which would be one more aspect of the general attempt to overcome the χωρισμός between the realm of ideas and the realm of the sensible, would have been a subversion of the very motivation of Plato's philosophy. Let us admit it: can it be ruled out that Plato ultimately tried to subvert the motivation of his philosophy? It would have been an admirable undertaking. Is not Schelling's late philosophy an attempt to subvert his kind of no-χωρισμός and re-introduce the χωρισμός between essence and existence and thus a very denial of his philosophy of identity?
** Cf. A. Lautman, *Symétrie et dissymétrie* (1946) 23 f.

In other words, conceptual realism, i.e. the assertion that the supersensible subsists no less that the sensible, entails the consequence that the sensible subsists no more than the supersensible. Those who have no eyes to see the supersensible will therefore assert that in this system the sensible ultimately becomes an illusion. This is not true: we have only to understand that the relations as existing in space and time, and connected by causal links, are nothing but "logical" relations.

All this may sound very strange for a nominalist or semi-nominalist. He will insist that only what exists in space and time is real. He will insist that logical implication and causation are two completely different things; he will insist that the chain of deduction is different from the causal chain. He will insist that the *ordo idearum* is different from the *ordo rerum*. He will insist that it was one of the basic misunderstandings in most metaphysical systems to mix up the two orders. We cannot discuss the correctness of these views. This, however, we can say: to understand Greek metaphysics we have to understand the realistic way of thinking.

It is this realistic metaphysics from which Aristotle started. We have overconcentrated our attention on Aristotle's reactions to the idea theory. At the time when Aristotle wrote *Met.* Γ, E 1, and K 3–7 no more than the barest kernel of the idea theory was still accepted: that there must at least be one supersensible sphere. But the rest of the Academic system, particularly the two-opposite-principles theory including the derivation of all spheres of being, was still held in common by Academics and Aristotle. W. Jaeger (*Aristoteles*[2] [1955] 96 f.) saw this clearly with regard to the *Protrepticus*. It is strange that he did not see it clearly when he read Γ, E 1, and K 3–7. And yet let us compare. All we find in the *Protrepticus* is this single paragraph:

> Wisdom is interested first of all in causes and elements rather than in what comes after them. These latter things do not belong to the principles [ἄκρα used as in Theophrastus' *Met.* in the Speusippus passage above p. 110], and the first things did not originate from them. On the contrary, it is obviously through them that all other things come into existence and continue to be. Whatever these causes and entities prior to all others may be — air, number, or any

other things — it is impossible to know anything else as long as we do not know them. Or how could anybody read a word who does not know the syllables, or understand the syllables as long as he does not know the letters [elements]? (fr. 52, p. 61, 9–17 Rose; cf. R. Walzer *Aristotelis Dialogorum fragmenta* [1934] p. 29 with n. 2).

Jaeger is right. The man who wrote this believes that wisdom is an inquiry into the elements of which, ultimately, everything consists. Jaeger is also right when he says that precisely this point of view was later completely rejected by Aristotle. Here, however, something strange happens. It was Jaeger who liberated us from the oppression of having to interpret a book called *Metaphysics*. There has never been such a book. And yet Jaeger himself says that the elements doctrine is criticized by Aristole in "the *Metaphysics*". May we still say such a thing? Are we still unduly influenced by the bookbinder? The truth is that the doctrine is criticized in some parts of the *Metaphysics*, while in Γ, E 1, and K 3–7 it is accepted and interpreted with much more detail and rigor than in the popular *Protrepticus*.

To the extent to which Aristotle himself shared the Academic *Ableitungssystem* he started Neoplatonism together with other Academics. And the subject matter of his first philosophy, being-as-such and therefore the divine, is very much like the subject matter of the metaphysical system of Speusippus. Being-as-such, i.e., being which has not to pay the price for its existence by being something and in this sense of the word to admit non-being — just being and therefore fully indeterminate in this sense of the word; its opposite, non-being, also not having to pay the price for its existence by being only other-than-being something — these are the subject matter of Aristotle's metaphysics. From the fully indeterminate and in this sense fully and positively being and its opposite, all things are derived. As they proceed, they become more and more determinate, in the sense of being involved more and more with non-being; this non-being, in turn, becoming more and more mere otherness. On the last step of this ladder we find things fully determined and in this sense of the word, closest to non-being. In other words, determinateness and indeterminateness are polar concepts. Their polarity can be expressed in the double assertion: only what is completely indeterminate is fully real; the fully real must be fully determinate. Metaphysics is the revelation of this latent polarity and this kind of metaphysics was started in the Academy, including Aristotle. The polarity of the concepts of being and non-being left its indelible traces in Aristotle's writings. Being-as-such as the theme of Aristotle's metaphysics is richest in being, not poorest. It is the οὐσία οὐ τὶ ὄν, ἀλλ' ὂν ἁπλῶς (*Met.* Z 1, 1028a30–31). Though Aristotle applies this definition to any οὐσία, it may be said that the οὐσία which is the subject matter of supreme wisdom is being in the fully unrestricted sense of the word.

On the other hand, the thing that is fully determinate in the ordinary sense of the word, including determinateness in time and space, is one bundle of negations, whereas the fully indeterminate (being-as-such) is indeterminate not in the sense of being universal, but in the sense of being "unrestricted" and therefore absolutely positive.

For this type of thinking it is quite natural to face the problem: in what way can this "unrestricted" being become object of our knowledge? Ordinary knowledge seems to be precisely predicative knowledge, but how can anything the essence of which is to have no predicates (any predicate being the expression of determinateness) be known?

The types of answer can be classified as follows.

1. Above predicative knowledge there is another, purely intuitive, which grasps the object without the mediation of a predicate.

2. The ultimate principle (being-as-such, the One, the absolute) cannot be known in any proper sense of the word — it can be "known" only in a negative way, i.e., by first positing and then negating all possible predicates. *Agnoscendo cognoscitur* (on this principle cf. F. Cumont, *Lux perpetua* [1949] 419–421).

3. The ultimate principle can be only known by first positing and then negating all possible predicates — yet this process of positing and negating is neither subjective nor arbitrary — it is rather the repetition of the only mode in which the absolute can exist, viz. by becoming something, thus negating its own nature, its being absolute, and being forced by this contradiction to negate its negation, i.e., to posit itself. *Aliud cognoscendo se*

ipsum cognoscit. The systematic totality of all positions negated is being and knowledge of the absolute — "of the" being a *genitivus subjectivus* and *objectivus* at the same time.

Whether Plato's system culminates in the knowledge of type 1 is a well-known matter for controversy. The role of immediate knowledge by the act of θιγεῖν in Aristotle is a well-known problem. The full awareness that predicative thinking cannot be applied to what fully is (ἐνέργεια) is expressed by Aristotle in *Met.* θ 10, 1051b17–1052a5*. The "fully being" is here designated as ἀσύνθετον; and it is even said that the word being cannot be applied to these ἀσύνθετα in the same way in which it is being applied to σύνθετα (1051b23) — Aristotle's way of saying that they are above being, though the expression "above being" is not his. The method of knowing them is θιγγάνειν, completely different from predicative thinking. And just as "being" here suddenly means being-as-such, so non-being no longer means being-other-than — it is a full alternative to being-as-such (1052a1). For composites, being is being something, non-being is not being this or that (1051b34–35) — but neither of these is true of incomposites. If they still can be designated as subjects, they are subjects without positive (posited) or negative (negated) predicates. Accordingly, just as they can only exist or not exist, but can not exist *as* something or something other, they can only be known or not known, but there can be no error about them (1051b21–28).

It is well known that the whole problem appears also in Theophrastus. The ἄκρα καὶ πρῶτα (obviously corresponding to Aristotle's ἀσύνθετα) can be known to the νοῦς alone and only by a kind of θιγεῖν and ἅπτειν; as a result, there can be no deception about them (*Metaph.* VIII 25, p. 28, 13–16 Ross and Fobes; Zeller II/2⁴ [1921] 190; 195; 824).

If the above presentation of the ἀσύνθετα problem is correct the most important question here emerging will concern their

---

* An extremely difficult section, and the above interpretation is merely tentative. See on it particularly Schelling, *Einleitung in die Philosophie der Mythologie*, especially *Fuenfzehnte Vorlesung* (*Saemtliche Werke*, II, v. I 321–385, esp. 340–359). Schelling's relation to Aristotle is very interesting (cf. K. Eswein, "Schellings Verhaeltnis zu Aristoteles", *Philosophisches Jahrbuch* 47 [1934] 84–112). From it, some threads seem to lead to M. Heidegger's interpretation of Aristotle (*Platons Lehre von der Wahrheit* [1947] 44) — and also to what seems to be a voluntaristic turn in his more recent writings (*Holzwege* [1949] 215 ff; for the title cf. Schelling, *op. cit.* p. 496).

plurality. How can one ἀσύνθετον differ from another? We see immediately that this question reminds us of the problem of the plurality of unmoved movers in Aristotle's system. The assertion of such a plurality seems to be incompatible with the doctrine that matter is the only principle of individuation. Now, it is very characteristic that A. Faust, *Der Moeglichkeitsgedanke* 2 vv. (1931), v. I 216, cf. also 359, interprets the doctrines of *Met.* θ 10 as if they were related exclusively to the problem of the knowledge of God (*gen. obj.* and *subj.*). The only object of φάσις (different from both κατάφασις and ἀπόφασις) is, according to Faust, God. He who denies His existence is not committing an error, he is simply nescient. Even God knows Himself only by the non-predicative act of θιγγάνειν (*Met.* Λ 7, 1072b21). This interpretation of Faust is based on the assumption that matter being the only principle of individuation in Aristotle, there is no place in his system for more than one disembodied form, i.e. one single deity (*ibid.*, 70). Now, Faust's equating the ἀσύνθετον of *Met.* θ 10 with the divine (or the divinity) seems to be entirely correct and to this extent the above presentation is in total agreement with him. But Faust's attempt to exclude any plurality of ἀσύνθετα fails in virtue of the fact that in the whole passage *Met.* θ 10, 1051b17–1052a5 Aristotle does not use the singular ἀσύνθετον once, whereas the plural ἀσύνθετα is used time and again, and the phrase πᾶσαι μὴ συνθεταὶ οὐσίαι is used without hesitation. In other words, contrary to what Faust asserts, there is place for a plurality of disembodied forms in Aristotle's system, at least according to Aristotle's own conviction. On this whole problem (closely connected with the problem of Aristotle's monotheism) see P. Merlan, "Aristotle's Unmoved Movers", *Traditio* 4 (1946) 1–30.

The knowledge of type 2 is characteristic of Plotinus and other Neoplatonists. But it may even be that the *agnoscendo cognoscitur* was already known at the time of Theophrastus. In *Met.* VIII 23–24, p. 26 Ross and Fobes, Theophrastus says: It may be true of some things, that they are knowable by being unknowable (γνωστὰ τῷ ἄγνωστα εἶναι) — and this [ignorance[would be the proper way of their knowledge —, but some further investigation is [here] necessary and whenever possible it is more appropriate to express them by analogy rather than just by ignorance — as if one would say that things invisible [are seen] by not being seen.

From this passage a direct line leads to Albinus who in ch. X of his *Didascalicus*, p. 59–61 Louis described the ways of knowing God, the ineffable, by either ἀφαίρεσις or analogy or ascension. We need not discuss the meaning of ἀφαίρεσις in the present context. As noticed above, it may mean either abstraction in the ordinary sense or subtraction, the former leading to the emptiest the latter to the fullest concept of being-as-such and the two points of view are not clearly distinguished in Albinus (see R. E. Witt, *Albinus* [1937] 132, but also K. Praechter, art. Syrianos (1) in *RE* IV A 2 [1932]; H. A. Wolfson, "Albinus and Plotinus on Divine Attributes", *Harvard Theological Review* 45 [1952] 115–130, esp. 117–121; 129 f.); but in any case the two terms analogy and ἀφαίρεσις (some kind of negation) seem to be clearly prepared in our Theophrastus passage *.

The knowledge of type 3 seems all but unknown before the time of Hegel. But the famous theory of Speusippus that nothing can be known unless everything is known (Aristotle, *Anal. Post.* II 13, 97a6; fr. 31 a–e Lang) may very well be an anticipation of Hegel's idea of absolute knowledge as being a completely developed system. If the relation of all parts of the universe is some kind of logical relation, i.e. if knowledge has no point of reference outside itself, knowledge short of totality of knowledge would be deficient knowledge **. On the other hand, in a fully developed system of knowledge to know a thing would precisely be to know all other things, i.e. the thing would be known only by knowing everything other-than-it. The sum total of knowledge regarding all other things would be the knowledge of this thing. Full knowledge is *docta ignorantia*.

Thus, we find in Aristotle and Theophrastus, partly also in Speusippus, all problems and answers which we must expect

---

* It does not seem appropriate to refer it to Aristotle, *Rhet.* II 24, 1402a6–7, because the context shows that Theophrastus is speaking of a whole class of things, presumably above both sensibles and mathematicals, and not at all of sophisms as Aristotle does. Theophrastus takes the *cognoscitur ignorando* seriously. On the other hand, Aristotle is well aware how close philosophy, dialectics, and sophistics are when it comes to the investigation of being-as-such (*Met.* Γ 2,1004b15–26).

** The problem is formulated in a very simple way in A. N. Whitehead, *Science and the Modern World* (1927), ch. X. However, here it is restricted to conceptual knowledge, sharply distinguished from sensible "knowledge".

in a philosophy which admits the concept of being-as-such in the sense of the indeterminate and therefore most real and makes this being-as-such together with its opposite the subject matter of wisdom and concerns itself with the derivation of all existents from these two supreme principles.

We can now return to the two-opposite-principles doctrines in Aristotle. He accepted these doctrines in *Met.* Γ, E 1, and K 3–7; but it is well known that he criticized them in other parts of his writings. We are going to discuss some of the classical passages where the two-opposite-elements doctrine is criticized, to understand better the issue between Aristotle and the Academy in this respect.

1. *Met.* A 8, 989b24–990a18. It is the Pythagorean form of this doctrine which is criticized here. According to this presentation, the Pythagoreans assumed two opposite principles * to which he refers here as the "limit" and "unlimited", elsewhere (*Met.* A 5, 986a18–19) as "odd" and "even", "unlimited" and "limited". Other Pythagoreans (986a22–26) termed these two opposites one and multitude, right and left, male and female, at rest and moving, straight and curved, light and dark, good and evil, square and oblong [i.e. obviously: preserving identity, a × a, or lapsing into diversity, a × b]. At first blush, this is an extremely crude synopsis. Logical differences (or opposites) and real differences (or opposites) are enumerated side by side. But there is nothing crude in it; a metaphysical system which reduces everything to two opposite principles negates by implication any true difference between real and logical relations. Precisely the same is true for Parmenides; the relation between being and non-being is analogous to the relation between warm and cold (*Met.* A 5, 987a1).

The most incisive criticism of this two-opposite-principles doctrine is that the two principles belong to the sphere of the ideal (supersensible). Therefore they cannot account for the existence of the real, and there can be no causal link between them and the reals nor can they account for the temporal,

---

* Cf. *Met.* A 5,986a1–2. The wording is almost identical with A 6,987b19–20.

* The Pythagoreans said that the elements of numbers are the elements of *all* beings; Plato said that the elements of ideas are the elements of *all* beings. How so? It is because according to the Pythagoreans number is prior to everything else and because according to Plato ideas are the causes of everything else.

spatial, causal relations, i.e., for change and motion of real things (*Met.* A 8, 990a8–18).

A cutting criticism. But it does not seem to refute the Pythagoreans. In what follows, they will be defended and so will also be the Academic system, on some points. Such a defense should considerably clarify the point at issue.

Is it true that from ideal (supersensible) elements (principles) no real (spatio-temporal) things can be derived? Is it true that it is impossible to derive weight from number?

The problem reminds us of the polemic between Krug and Hegel. Krug challenged Hegel: Could Hegel "derive" his writing pen?

Hegel was not at all impressed. He could have answered: If Krug can explain to me what he means by "his pen", I promise I shall derive his pen.

The point is that neither Krug nor anyone else can say what "his pen" means without making this pen an ideal (supersensible) object. What is knowable at all in an object can be "derived"; because the object as object of knowledge is already an ideal object — the point where categories of thought intersect. "Pen" is an object, a thing — and object or thing are highly abstract categories; and "his" is even more so. The mistake of Aristotle in criticizing the Pythagoreans is precisely Krug's mistake: to think that "heavy" is any less abstract than "number". It is the mistake of every empiricist. In Aristotle the mistake is all the graver, because he knows very well that all knowledge is knowledge of the universal, therefore ideal and supersensible.

2. The doctrine of the two-opposite-elements is attacked by Aristotle incidentally, as he discusses Plato's theory of ideas and numbers, i.e., throughout *Met.* A 9, 990a33–993a10; but the most interesting passage is *Met.* A 9, 992b18–992b24. The very notion "all" is self-contradictory, as far as the theory of elements is concerned. How can there be an element of, say, doing? Only things seem to have elements, but things are only part of "all". Therefore, it is futile to try to find elements of "all" — of both things and relations of things.

Again a cutting criticism. But a realist would object: Of course there can be elements of things only. But everything else is only a relation of things, and, in this sense of the word, elements of all things are elements of all.

3. The next criticism (A 9, 992b24–33) is particularly weak or it overshoots the mark. Knowledge of elements is impossible, says Aristotle, because all knowledge is derived from some anterior knowledge; knowledge of elements would be ultimate knowledge because it would be knowledge of all; ultimate knowledge could not be derived from anterior knowledge. If true, this criticism would deny altogether the possibility of knowledge, or amount to the neopositivist assertion (Schlick) that all cognition is recognition (of course not Plato's anamnesis). But even those who would be ready to accept Schlick's dictum would perhaps admit that it is debatable.

4. The next two criticisms (A 9, 992b33–993a7) are of no interest in the present context. The last (A 9,993a7–10), however, is very interesting. If it is true, says Aristotle, that everything consists of the same elements, the one who knows the elements would know everything. But how about objects of sensation? This question of Aristotle means: can they be known prior to their being sensed?

Again an objection which would impress no conceptual realist. Even to be perceived by sensation, the object must be transformed into an ideal object. Let us suppose that Krug tried to meet Hegel's objection by saying: I am not going to say (to explain) what I mean by "my pen". I am going to show it to Hegel, to point at it. Here it is. Hegel's reply would be: What is it that you show me? And this question makes it clear that nothing can be "shown" but an ideal object; as long as Krug does not say what he shows (the whatness), Hegel does not know what to sense: red, long, pointed, a thing, a utensil, a thing to write with, or what? If Krug refuses to say anything, confining himself to pointing, or, what is tantamount to it, if he will say only "this", Hegel will not see a pen; he will see "this" — a most abstract category which can designate a pencil no less than a pen, or a table, etc. What can really be sensed, i.e., known by sensation, can be derived from ultimate elements. If one insists that sensation is no knowledge at all, the problem of derivation of sensations disappears. It reappears on the level of whatever will be assumed to be the most primitive knowledge*.

---

* The theories deriving knowledge from sensation by abstraction have been criticized most incisively by Hegel in his *Phenomenology* (section: *Die sinnliche Gewiszheit*

5. The violent attacks on the two-opposite-principles doctrine continue in *Met.* Λ 10, 1075a25. Some of these attacks presuppose Aristotle's three-principles doctrine (form-absence of form; neutral matter); some were already discussed in connection with Speusippus; one was quoted above on p. 173. One is particularly interesting: if there are elements of all, how shall we explain that some things are perishable, while some are not? Indeed, if we deny that there are any perishable things, we no longer have any reason to assume the existence of a second, supersensible realm of being. If we admit the existence of perishable things, we introduce time and change as real elements, different from otherness. If the conceptual realist would answer: becoming (including coming-to-be and passing-away) is only illusion, this would still leave the question of birth and death unanswered. The assertion that death is only an illusion seems hardly acceptable from any point of view. It is perhaps here that all excessively realistic systems founder. It seems preposterous to subordinate the concepts of birth and death under the concepts of coming-to-be and passing-away — contrary to what Parmenides tried to establish (fr. B 8, 26–28 Diels *).

It is important to observe that all arguments against the two-opposite-principles doctrine still take it for granted that there must exist a supersensible sphere. But neither ideas nor mathematicals can claim to be it.

6. Perhaps we should once more turn our attention to the Speusippus passage in *Met.* Λ 10, 1075b37 and its parallel in Z 2, 1028b21; also to Z 2, 1028b27, which refers to some member of the Academy. It seems that all these passages prove the great similarity between Pythagorism and the Academy in this decisive point: all tried to derive sensibles from supersensibles (mathematicals, ideas, etc.). What else could ἐπεκτείνειν (1028b24) mean? Or what could the reproach mean that Speu-

---

oder das Dieses und das Meinen, SW ed. Glockner, v. II [1927] 81–92). From a different, unmetaphysical point of view the ordinary concept of abstraction was destroyed by one single sentence of Husserl: in some respect everything is similar to everything and it would be in vain to describe concepts in terms of "abstracting" the similarities (E. Husserl, *Logische Untersuchungen* II/1³ [1922] 106–224, esp. 115–121).

* But it is more than doubtful whether birth and death can be explained by Aristotle in the semirealistic phase of his philosophy. Cf. C. Baeumker, *Das Problem der Materie in der griechischen Philosophie* (1890) 247–291.

sippus is unable to show how the sensibles depend on the preceding sphere of being (N 3, 1090b19)?

It must be admitted, however, that Aristotle says it with regard to the Pythagoreans repeatedly and with absolute clarity (*Met.* N 3, 1090a32–35; cf. *De caelo* III 1, 300a15); of Academics he says it only incidentally and sometimes by implication. Shall we assume that in the Academy the question of the derivation of the sensible from the supersensible was never the *center* of interest? The passage in the *Timaeus* 53 C–55 C (cf. A. E. Taylor, *A Commentary on Plato's Timaeus* [1928] 403–409) where Plato quite clearly derives physical bodies from geometrical extension (cf. p. 201 n.) is startling enough *; shall we assume it was an isolated attempt **? We must not forget that Xenocrates and to a certain extent, Hestiaios was praised by Theophrastus (*Metaph.* III 12 f., p. 12–14 Ross and Fobes) for doing precisely this, for deriving everything from supersensible beings — the spatial from the unspatial, the changing from the changeless. Therefore, the problem of "derivation" must have been of prime importance in the Academy. It still is of prime importance in Aristotle's *Metaphysics*; in some parts of it Aristotle still thinks in terms of a derivation system. And it is within the context of such a system that the definition of metaphysics as science of being-as-such emerges.

A synopsis of some passages will show the different attitudes of Aristotle toward two fundamental problems: (1) the two-opposite-principles doctrine; (2) being-as-such as subject matter of a separate branch of knowledge.

Γ 2,1005a3:	N 1,1087a29–1087b4:
	All ... make out the principles to be opposites. [But actually] none ... of the opposites is a principle of all things in the proper sense of the word [cf. Λ 10,1075a28, quoted on p. 173 above].
All things are opposites or consist of opposites; and the principle of opposites is the One and multitude.	

---

* But many modern physicists would have no objections. See e.g. R. Woltereck, *Ontologie des Lebendigen* (1940) 28–31. Schelling's name appears once more.

** But we must not overlook *Laws* X 894 A; cf. J. Stenzel, *Zahl und Gestalt*[2] (1933) 92–104 and F. M. Cornford, *Plato and Parmenides* (1939) 14 f. and 199.

Γ 2,1004b27–1005a3:

... all things can be reduced to being and non-being, and to One and multitude; e.g. rest belongs to the One, motion to the multitude. Now, almost all agree that beings and the οὐσία consist of opposites. Thus all say that the principles are opposite ... and also all other things are reducible to the One-and-multitude, for we take this reduction for granted ... It is clear therefrom that it is up to one and the same branch of knowledge to investigate being-as-such.

N 1,1088a27–1088b4:

No thing is great or small, much or little, and in general [there is no] relative determination, except it is [i.e. it has the quality of being] much or little, or great, or small, or a relative determination while being something else ... It is therefore odd, or rather impossible, to make something that is not an οὐσία [e.g. One and multitude] an element of an οὐσία and anterior to it.

Γ 2,1003a33–b16:

Being is predicated in more than one sense but with respect to (πρός) some one and the same φύσις ... It is clear therefore, that it is up to one [branch of knowledge] to investigate all beings-as-such.

N 2,1089a7:

As "being" has many meanings ..., it is odd, or rather impossible, that any one φύσις in existence should be the cause of this being here to be a thing, of that being there to be a quality ...

Met. K 3,1060b35 (cf. 1061b14–15):

If [being] is predicated according to (κατά) something common, it would belong to *one* branch of knowledge.

Eud. Eth. I 7,1217b34–35 *:

There is no one branch of knowledge dealing with being nor with the good.

It is possible to deny that the two columns represent different attitudes toward the same two problems?

---

* The problem of the authenticity of *EE* cannot here be discussed. See on it J. Geffcken, *Griechische Literaturgeschichte*, v. II (1934), *Anmerkungen*, pp. 220–222.

If the Academics, and to a certain extent Aristotle, professed an *Ableitungssystem*, should we assume that Plato's own system (if he had one) could without hesitation be called an *Ableitungssystem* as was recently done by H. Gomperz, "Platons philosophisches System", *Proceedings of the Seventh International Congress of Philosophy* (1931) 426–431 and after all by Stenzel (*Studien zur Entwicklung der Platonischen Dialektik von Sokrates zu Aristoteles²* [1931] 54–62; 83 f.; 118; *Zahl und Gestalt²* [1933] 71; 77–79; 110; 119–125)?

The reasons for and against such an interpretation are most judiciously discussed in Zeller (II/1⁵ [1922] 744–765). The crux of the problem is this: Is the non-being, i.e. otherness present in the ideas according to the *Sophist* identical with the non-being in the realm of the sensible? Is the matter present in ideas according to Aristotle's report identical with the matter underlying the realm of the sensible? Zeller answers both questions in the negative only to conclude: I have to admit, however, that Plato did not distinguish with sufficient clarity the element of multiplicity and otherness in the ideas from the reason of the divisibility and changeableness of the sensible (754). And as Zeller finally denies the Platonic character of these identifications, he condemns not only Aristotle as having misunderstood Plato but also Plato's pupils as having abandoned genuine Platonism in favor of Pythagorism. Now, it should be obvious that any interpretation of Plato resulting in the assertion that he was misunderstood by Aristotle and "betrayed" by Speusippus, Xenocrates, etc., will forever have to remain on the defensive *.

Zeller's discussion is remarkable in one more respect. While denying that Plato's is an *Ableitungssystem*, he at the same time

---

* Cf. also A. Levi, *Sulle interpretazioni immanentistiche della Filosofia di Platone* (1919) 159–140; E. Hoffmann, "Platonismus und Mittelalter", *Vortraege der Bibliothek Warburg 1923–1924* (1926) 72–74; 80 note ad p. 35 (but cf. also 73 on Aristotle, Xenocrates, and Speusippus); P. Shorey, "Platonism and the History of Science", *American Philosophical Society, Proceedings* 66 (1927) 159–182, esp. 170 f.; E. Hoffmann, "Platonismus und Mystik im Altertum", *SB der Heidelberger Ak. der Wiss., Philos.-hist. Kl.* 25, 1934/5, esp. 8–22; 44; C. Sandulescu-Godeni, *Das Verhaeltnis von Rationalitaet und Irrationalitaet in der Philosophie Platons* (1938) 60–62; 101–135; H. Cherniss, *The Riddle of the Early Academy* (1945), lecture II. On the other hand cf. particularly A. Rivaud in the introduction to his *Timaeus* and *Critias* edition (Budé, 1925), who compares what he takes to be Plato's attempts to pass from the ideal to the sensible order with Leibniz (68).

stresses the fact that Plato's system is in the last resort unsatisfactory precisely because the relation between reality (realm of ideas) and the realm of becoming remains unexplained (II/1 [5] 760–765). He insists that it is the duty of the historian of philosophy to understand the basic contradiction vitiating Platonic philosophy (whereas on one hand ideas claim to be the only reality, yet the realm of sensibles, although not derived from the realm of ideas, acquires some kind of reality of its own). But if it can be shown that Aristotle and other direct students of Plato interpreted him as having attempted to remove this contradiction, it should not be denied that this attempt exists in Plato's thought at least potentially. And is it not a legitimate task of a historian of philosophy to present a system of philosophy together with its inherent possibilities, only leaving it at that? What is wrong with the assumption that only two mutually exclusive interpretations of a philosophic system taken together, are the adequate interpretation of it?

Some of the most succinct pages written on the relation between the two realms corresponding to Plato's ideas and sensibles are to be found in Schelling's writing quoted already: *Religion and Philosophy* (1804), *Saemtliche Werke* I, v. VI (1860) 11–70. In this writing Schelling discusses the following possibilities.

Either matter is made responsible for there being a realm of the real, different from the realm of the ideal, and this matter is either interpreted as a second principle, co-eval with the principle of the ideas, or as mere negativity. Schelling rejects the first possibility, because that would make evil a first principle. He rejects the second, because it leaves unexplained how something non-being can lend any kind of being different from the being of the ideal, to anything.

If it is not matter, Schelling continues ,then the realm of the real can come into existence seemingly only by emanation. But emanation from the ideal can never produce anything but another ideal — extenuated, if we may say so, but no amount of extenuation will turn the ideal into the real. Thus we are left with only one possibility: the real is the product of an act of apostasy, a fall, a leap. And Schelling asserts that this is the true meaning of Plato, rejecting the doctrines in *Timaeus* as expressing Plato's relapse into more primitive modes of thinking. It seems indeed, that Schelling enumerated all possibilities explaining the relation between the ideal and the real that are open to a philosopher for whom the ideal is not only the product of abstraction (cf. *ibid.* 35–39).

However, for the present purpose the question whether Plato's system was misunderstood or interpreted correctly as essentially an *Ableitungssystem* is not very important. What seems to be incontestable and important is that such was the system of Speusippus and Xenocrates (or their interpretation of Plato) and that it was a development of tendencies present in Plato's philosophy *. Aristotle, for a while at least, shared this system with the Academy. In his later polemic against Plato and the Academy the theory of ideas is only one aspect of the more comprehensive doctrine which he really attacks: an excessively realistic system in which implication is the only type of causation. But what has for centuries been interpreted as general metaphysics (the doctrine of being-as-such) originated in Aristotle as another presentation of this excessively realistic Platonico-Academic *Ableitungssystem*. To see this clearly let us first review some passages implying that, according to Aristotle, Plato and/or the Academics thought that *all* things, i.e. sensibles and non-sensibles alike, consist of the same elements.

Met. A 6, 987b18–20 (cf. 988a11):

As the ideas are causes of [all] other things, Plato thought that the elements of the ideas are elements of *all* beings.

Ibid., 9, 992b18–24 (cf. 993a8):

There is no answer to the question: of what elements do *all* things consist?

Met. B 4, 1000a5–1001a3:

A long passage implying that all philosophers asserted that

---

* Hoffmann's objections (Zeller II/1⁵ [1922] 1089–1098) do not carry conviction (in spite of Cherniss, *Aristotle's Criticism of Plato and the Academy*, v. I 475 n. 426). Hoffmann narrows the basis of his discussion unduly by limiting the whole problem to the relation between ideas and the realm of senses, without ever taking a look at the "genesis" problem within the realm of the ideas themselves. Hoffmann succeeds only in proving that ideas should not be interpreted as forces (which, however, they do not have to be to become causes, just as Hegel's spirit is not a force). As a result Hoffmann says: Aristotle was right in objecting to Plato that the idea (representing the One) and matter (representing the many) could never engender an actual thing; but this objection of Aristotle expects the ideas to be dynamic, which nobody should do who wants to remain true to the original motives of the theory of ideas (1096). By this Hoffmann obviously means: what Plato should have thought to remain true to the spirit of Platonism as conceived by Hoffmann.

all things, perishable [sensibles] and imperishable, have the same principles.

Met. Γ 2, 1004b27–1005a5:

The passage presupposes that *all* things can be traced back (ἀνάγεται) to two opposite principles. Principles like "warm-cold" and like "limit-unlimited" appear side by side. The obvious implication is that according to some philosophers even sensibles can be derived from such principles as limit-unlimited.

Met. Z 2, 1028b18–27:

The whole passage presupposes that there is a continuous transition from ideas and/or mathematicals to sensibles according to Plato, Speusippus, and Xenocrates (cf. Theophrastus *Met.* III 12–13, p. 12 f. Ross and Fobes; the word γεννᾶν is used, the implication being that sensibles are "generated" from non-sensibles).

Met. K 3, 1061a10–17 (cf. Γ 2, 1004a1):

This passage presupposes that the task of metaphysics is the tracing back (ἀναγωγή) of *all* beings to the original principles (oneness and manyness, or similarity and dissimilarity).

Met. Λ 4, 1070b4–10:

This passage contains a polemic of Aristotle against the theory that *all* things consist of the same elements. It is difficult to assume that Aristotle does not think here of the Academy.

Ibid., 5, 1071a24–35:

This passage contains Aristotle's own version of the "identity" of elements of which all things consist. This identity is interpreted by him as analogy. Sensibles are included: 1071b1.

Ibid., 10, 1075a25–33:

Aristotle criticizes all other philosophers for having attempted to reduce *all* things to one pair (or pairs) of opposites. The Academics are obviously included. It is they who introduced the pairs "equal-unequal" or "one-many".

Ibid., 1075b11–13:

Aristotle reproaches those assuming the opposite-principles doctrine with not having made proper use of these opposites. This reproach seems to be identical with that of Theophrastus, *Met.* III 11–12, p. 12 Ross and Fobes: Those who introduce the One and the indefinite dyad as principles frequently fail to generate *all* things from them as they should. "All" includes sensibles (cf. Arist. *Met.* Λ 10, 1075b14).

Met. M 9, 1086a26–29:

There are philosophers who say that the elements of ideas and numbers are elements and principles of beings. The reference to the Academy is obvious. "Beings" clearly means "*all* beings".

Met. N 2, 1088b35–1089b14:

The whole discussion presupposes a system in which *all* things are derived from two opposite principles, e.g. being and non-being.

Ibid., 1090a1–7:

Aristotle speaks of a theory according to which the ideas (and/or numbers) are the causes of [all] other things. Obviously the ideas are taken to be the only "causes" of sensibles, i.e. efficient causality is ruled out.

Ibid., 3, 1090b13–19:

Here Aristotle objects to Speusippus. His prior spheres, says Aristotle, do not contribute anything to [the being of] posterior spheres. Even if we do away with mathematicals, soul and sensibles would still continue to exist. This criticism implies that Speusippus intended to "derive" *all* posterior spheres, including sensibles, from prior ones. It makes no difference whether or not Aristotle's criticism was entirely fair. He takes it for granted that anybody establishing mathematicals, soul, sensibles, as spheres of being would do so in order to show how *all* things are derived from the supreme sphere of being (or its elements).

Ibid., 4, 1091b35–37:

If evil is one of the elements, *all* things will participate in it.

Met. N 5, 1092a21–22:

Aristotle speaks of philosophers who assert that [*all*] things consist of [the same] elements.

Ibid., 6, 1093b8–9:

Aristotle blames philosophers according to whom mathematicals are causes of φύσις.

To this list we should add some passages on Pythagoreans.

Met. A 5, 986a1–2:

The Pythagoreans assumed that the elements of numbers are elements of *all* beings.

Ibid., 8, 989b29–990a32:

A long passage the gist of which is that it is impossible to

derive or generate sensible qualities from non-sensible principles.
Met. M 6, 1080b16–19:
The Pythagoreans construct the whole universe from numbers.
Met. N 3, 1091a18–22:
Pythagoreans derive the sensible universe from [non-sensible] elements.

This list omitted passages where Aristotle speaks of magnitudes but does not make it perfectly clear whether he is thinking of geometrical magnitudes or of sensible bodies. Let us consider *Met.* Λ 10, 1075b28–30: πῶς ... ἐξ ἀμεγεθῶν μέγεθος ∼ A 8, 990a12–18: ἔτι δὲ εἴ τε δοίη τις αὐτοῖς ἐκ τούτων (scil. πέρατος καὶ ἀπείρου or περιττοῦ καὶ ἀρτίου) εἶναι μέγεθος εἴτε δειχθείη τοῦτο, ὅμως τίνα τρόπον ἔσται τὰ μὲν κοῦφα τὰ δὲ βάρος ἔχοντα τῶν σωμάτων;

Here μεγέθη could mean either (physical) σώματα or geometrical magnitudes. However, *Met.* M 6, 1080b16–21 seems to bring the decision. The Pythagoreans, says Aristotle, assert that sensibles consist of numbers. They construct the whole universe of numbers and these numbers they take to have magnitude. How a number could have (or perhaps rather: could have come to have) magnitude, they are at loss to explain. Here magnitude obviously means a sensible body, or Aristotle could not say that all Pythagoreans construct the universe of numbers which have magnitude. Any doubts still left disappear as we read in *Met.* N 3, 1090a30–35: the Pythagoreans produce bodies out of numbers, i.e. weight out of what is weightless. And Aristotle adds: it is impossible to assume that they speak of ordinary sensibles. The irony of Aristotle proves that this was precisely what the Pythagoreans did: to "derive" what we call real from what we call ideal.

The same holds true for Plato as interpreted by the Academics and Aristotle, and for the Academics themselves: universals engender particulars.

This fact has still another aspect. It is well known that Aristotle asserts that Plato constructed sensible bodies out of geometrical planes (*De caelo* III 1, 299a6–11; *De gen. et corr.* I 2, 315b30; I 8, 325b24–33; II 1, 329a23). In *De caelo* III 1, 299a2–300a19 (cf. III 7, 306a7–17) we find a long discussion placing this problem in the proper perspective. Throughout this discussion

Aristotle tries to establish the thesis that it is impossible to derive physical properties from mathematical entities. And the end of the discussion (300a14–19) makes it clear that Aristotle considers the Pythagoreans to have committed precisely the same error with which he charges Plato and the Academics, viz. the derivation of physicals from mathematicals *.

The construction of the universe out of two elements and the derivation of bodies from planes are, to a certain extent, two independent problems. But what is common to them is that in both cases there is no gap between the realm of the ideal and the realm of the real.

It is only against the background of all these passages that we can adequately appreciate Aristotle's well-known criticism of the presentation of causality in Plato's *Phaedo* (*De gen. et corr.* II 9,335b9–16; *Met.* A 9, 991b3–4; M 5, 1080a1–2). Aristotle asserts that Plato makes ideas "causes" of being and becoming. But ideas do not cause anything, says Aristotle. Plato simply is blind to the necessity of an efficient cause.

We must ask ourselves two questions with regard to this criticism by Aristotle. First, did Plato do in the *Phaedo*, what Aristotle asserts, viz. did he ascribe causality to ideas alone, excluding any other kind of causality? This question should unhesitatingly be answered in the affirmative. Ideas are not only the reason that a thing is *called* something (e.g. great) **, they

---

* See F. M. Cornford, *Plato and Parmenides* (1939) 13 f. Cf. C. Mugler, *Platon* (1948) 120–122 for a discussion of this problem in terms of contemporary physics. See also A. Goerland, *Aristoteles und die Mathematik* (1899) 22–25; 207. It should also be noted that the doctrine of mathematical atomism is another shock to our ways of thinking, perhaps not much more lenient than the derivation of body from geometrical figures. See S. Luria, "Die Infinitesimaltheorie der antiken Atomisten", *Quellen und Studien zur Geschichte der Mathematik* ... Abt. B: Studien 2 (1933) 106–185, esp. 120–160; A. Schmekel, *Die positive Philosophie in ihrer geschichtlichen Entwicklung*, v. I (1938) 15–17; 59; for a modern defense cf. P. Bernays, "Die Erneuerung der rationalen Aufgabe", *Proceedings of the Tenth International Congress of Philosophy* (1949) 42–50, esp. 47. The whole problem of deriving existence from essence is treated in a very stimulating way in A. Lautman, *Essai sur les notions de structure et d'existence en mathématique*, 2 vv. (1938), esp. 126 and 150–156; and *Nouvelles recherches sur la Structure dialectique des mathématiques* (1939), esp. 31.
** This is the interpretation of F. M. Cornford, *Plato and Parmenides* (1939) 1–27, and 76–80. Cf., however, e.g. S. Marck, *Die Platonische Ideenlehre in ihren Motiven* (1912) 57. The problem of the efficient causality by the demiurge is beyond the scope of the present inquiry; there is certainly not the slightest trace of him in the *Phaedo*. The almost complete absence of any efficient causality in Plato has recently been asserted e.g. by M. D. Philippe, "La Participation dans la philosophie d'Aristote", *Revue Thomiste* 49 (1949) 254–277, esp. 254–257. He even considers it possible that

are — somehow — the reason that the thing *is* or *becomes* great. *How* the idea manages to be a cause is not explained by Plato, but he insists on the fact *that* it is the only cause. Secondly, we have to ask ourselves, is Aristotle's criticism fair when we take into consideration other Platonic dialogues in addition to the *Phaedo*? The majority of critics of Aristotle reproaches him with unfairness. He never mentions, they say, that there is a soul in the system of Plato, which soul is the efficient cause of a thing's participating in an idea and being, thus, either produced or altered. But it seems that Aristotle is not unfair to Plato, because (or, to be cautious: if) Plato's soul equals mathematicals. If such is the case, the soul cannot be more of an efficient cause than the ideas. With or without soul, the Academic system, i.e. perhaps Plato's own system and certainly that of his pupils, is a system of "derivation" in which there is no room left for Aristotle's efficient causality. Aristotle insisted that it is the concrete thing (in space and time) that can cause or alter another concrete thing, while it is impossible for an ideal (universal, general thing, exempt from time and space) to cause or alter a concrete thing. If we accept this assertion as valid, we shall have to say that Plato's world-soul does not meet Aristotle's requirements for a cause either, because Plato's world-soul is only the totality of mathematical relations underlying the universe. These relations have neither less nor more efficient causality in themselves than have the ideas. If Aristotle rejected the ideas because they lacked efficient causality, there was no reason for him to accept Plato's world-soul instead.

In this connection one philosophic text deserves particular attention as showing the survival of the idea of derivation. It is the text of Sextus Empiricus, *Adv. mathem.* X 248–284 *. According to Sextus, the Pythagoreans analyze all things into ultimate elements. These elements are not only ἄδηλοι and ἀφανεῖς (νοητὰ σώματα as the atoms), they are incorporeal.

Plato's incipient admission of some kind of causality different from the causality of ideas is the result of Aristotle's influence on Plato.

    * Cf. on it C. Baeumker, *Das Problem der Materie in der griechischen Philosophie* (1890) 391–399; A. Schmekel, *Die Philosophie der mittleren Stoa* (1892) 403–439; *idem, Die positive Philosophie in ihrer geschichtlichen Entwicklung,* v. I (1938) 79–81; F. M. Cornford, *Plato and Parmenides* (1939) 16–18; C. J. de Vogel, "Problems Concerning Later Platonism", *Mnemosyne* 1949, p. 197–216; 299–318, esp. 209–216.

And not all incorporeals which are prior to the bodies, are already elements and first principles. For example, ideas, which according to Plato are prior to the bodies, are not elements. Prior to them are numbers. And if we say that geometricals, i.e. incorporeal stereometrical forms, precede the bodies, we do not mean to say that they are elements. They themselves go back to numbers. And numbers fall under the One. Therefore Pythagoras said that the monad is the principle of beings. This monad, if thought in-and-by-itself (κατ' αὐτότητα ἑαυτῆς νοουμένη), is simply the monad; if thought as being one-with-itself-in-otherness (ἐπισυν-θετεῖσα ἑαυτῇ καθ' ἑτερότητα), it creates the indefinite dyad.

Thus, there are two principles, the first monad and the indefinite dyad.

This fact the Pythagoreans prove in different ways (263–268).

How to derive body (σῶμα) is controversial among the Pythagoreans. Some derive the point from the One, the line from the two, etc.; others derive body from the flux of the point. In any case: after the geometricals have been derived (constructed) in this way, they derive (construct) from them the sensibles (αἰσθητά or, according to some mss, στερεά, but inspite of the difference in the text the meaning is made perfectly obvious by the examples), earth, water, air, fire, and generally the universe.

There can hardly be any doubt: Sextus reports that his Pythagoreans derived sensibles from non-sensibles *.

Now, who are these Pythagoreans? Most recently the text has been scrutinized by Wilpert, who tried to prove that it is derived directly from Plato's Περὶ τἀγαθοῦ (P. Wilpert, Zwei aristotelische Fruehschriften ueber die Ideenlehre [1949] 125 ff.; cf. the review of Wilpert's book by W. Jaeger, Gnomon 23 [1951] 246–252, esp. 250 f.) This is utterly improbable. The main reasons against Wilpert's assumption are: (1) it would imply that Plato's lecture contained not only a mention of, but a long report on, Pythagorean doctrines, because, if Sextus' excerpts are derived from Plato's lecture, he would have ascribed these doctrines to the Pythagoreans instead to Plato himself, only if Plato himself

---

* Just as does the famous report of Alexander Polyhistor (Diog. Laert., VIII 24–33), on which cf. A.-J. Festugière, "Les 'Mémoires Pythagoriques' cités par Alexandre Polyhistor", Revue des Etudes grecques 58 (1945) 1–65.

had done it. (2) The excerpt in one passage quotes Plato himself (258), thus making it clear that the rest is not Plato's doctrine. (3) The excerpt in one passage contains an interpretation of Epicurus (257) — a strange one, to be sure, extorting from his words the admission that atoms consist of incorporeals.

All this sums up to the assertion that the doctrine presented by Sextus is not an excerpt from Plato's lecture. But this does not mean that it does not contain Academic doctrines or Pythagorean doctrines as presented by Academics *. In fact, it contains a section (263–277) ** which has always been known to be closely related to Hermodorus' presentation of Plato's lecture *On the Good*. What was proved for that section, viz. that it is Academico-Pythagorean doctrine, can safely be assumed for the rest also; and it is possible that the whole presentation was written after Plato's delivery of his lecture and contains some ideas which were expressed in it; but it seems to be going much too far to claim virtually the whole for that lecture.

But within the present context the problem of the source of Sextus' excerpt is immaterial anyhow. What is interesting is to see that the derivation of the sensible from the non-sensible (One and the dyad) is presented as a matter of course and was taken to be such in a period preceding Neoplatonism.

To sum up. Aristotle always presented Plato's system as a system attempting to derive all things (sensibilia and intelligibilia) from two supreme, opposite principles. Sometimes he criticized this idea of derivation; sometimes he shared it. His definition of metaphysics as knowledge of being-as-such is consistent with this latter phase of his thought. We can see this particularly well if we remember two things: first, the knowledge of being would imply also the knowledge of its opposite, non-being. Second, being and One are convertible and therefore we could define the subject matter of Aristotle's first philosophy

---

* A. Schmekel, *Die positive Philosophie*, v. I (1938) 84–86 traces parts of the Sextus passage to Eratosthenes, who, however, according to Schmekel admitted the (generic?) difference between mathematical solids and physical bodies.

** On which see K. Janáček, "Novopythagorský text u Sexta Empirika x 263–277", *Československa akademia Věd, Sekce jazyka a literatury. Sbornik filologický III, I = Studia antiqua Antonio Salač .... oblata*, Prague 1955, 96–101.

also as the One-as-such (this term in *Met.* Γ 2, 1004b5) and
therefore the many-as-such. Neither of these terms (being-non-
being; one-many) means what we would call a universal. Lacking
all determination they are what is most real, i.e. present in all
other reality. Lacking all determination they are prior to all
other reality. Because they are prior they are — in this sense
of the word — most universal.

But let us go back to our attempt to isolate *Met.* Γ, E 1, K 3–7
from the rest of the context of *Metaphysics,* as based on the
conviction that being-as-such is not a universal in the ordinary
sense of the word, and on the acceptance of the two-opposite-
principles doctrine.

A possible objection to this interpretation could be this:
Met. Γ refers back to *Met.* B; B is referred to in A; therefore we
must take A B Γ as forming one unit (cf. W. D. Ross, *Aristotle's
Metaphysics,* v. I, p. XVII). But the two-principles theory is
severely criticized in A; therefore it is impossible to assume that
it is accepted in Γ. Furthermore, K 6, 1062b31 and, by implication Γ 3, 1009a32 refer to *Physics* I (cf. W. D. Ross, *Aristotle's
Metaphysics,* v. II 319) in which the two-principles theory is
criticized and replaced by the form-(neutral) matter concept.
Thus, we cannot imagine that E 1 und K 3–7 still profess this
very doctrine.

It is easy to dispose of the first objection. The reference to
Met. B in *Met.* A 10,993a24 (if it is a reference to B at all; see the
discussion in Ross, *Aristotle's Metaphysics,* v. I 211 f.) is obviously
a later insertion; thus the unity A B Γ is highly precarious.
Furthermore, it is quite obvious that *Met.* A contains different
layers of thought (see e.g. H. Cherniss, *Aristotle's Criticism of
Plato and the Academy,* v. I 192); and it is impossible to be sure
to what form of *Met.* A *Met.* B would be related.

As to the second objection, it proves only that when writing
Met. Γ and K 3–7, Aristotle was not aware that his criticism of
the two-principles doctrine in the field of physics destroyed every
basis for a metaphysics based on such an assumption.

In addition, it is well known that Aristotle is careful to state
in *Physics* that his discussion at hand deals exclusively with the

sphere of the sensible und excludes metaphysical considerations. Accordingly, his criticisms of the two-opposite-principles doctrine and its replacement by his own matter-form-privation doctrine are limited to the explanation of becoming and change *.

Furthermore, it is immediately obvious that what we read as *Physics* I cannot have been written by Aristotle *uno ductu*: 185a9–12 is literally repeated in 186a7–10. To explain this by a gratuitous gloss of a copyist (Ross a.l.) seems somewhat strained. On the other hand, if it was written *uno ductu*, it contained a reference to the *Metaphysics* in 8, 191b29 (if we eliminate this reference with Ross as a later addition, we have another proof that *Physics* I, in its present form, is not an original whole). In other words, it remains dubious what form of *Physics* I preceded *Metaphysics* Γ, E 1, K 3–7.

On p. 173 the question was asked how it could ever have been overlooked that Γ, E 1 (and, by implication, K 3–7) was based on the two-opposite-principles doctrine, so violently attacked by Aristotle elsewhere. The question exaggerated rhetorically; the contradiction was not overlooked. Some examples will suffice to show this. St. Thomas says: *Sciendum tamen est quod hoc, quod dixit omnia entia contraria esse vel ex contrariis, non posuit secundum suam opinionem, sed accepit quasi opinionem philosophorum antiquorum (In Met. Arist. comm.,* # 585, p. 196 Cathala[3]). And Ps. Duns Scotus repeats after him: *Notandum quod cum ait philosophus omnia entia vel esse contraria vel esse ex contrariis, loquitur modo antiquorum (Opera,* v. V 663 Vivès). The insertion of the single word *"recentiorem"* after *"opinionem"* in the Thomas passage and, therefore the omission of the word *"quasi"* is all that is necessary to state the "developmental" position in terms of St. Thomas. We say "change" where St. Thomas says "contradiction" — or we accept frankly the ex-

---

* And there is perhaps no other passage in Aristotle which so clearly proves the origin of his notion of matter from Plato's *Sophist*. Aristotle describes his matter in terms equivalent to saying: matter is not non-being; it is rather determinate non-being, i.e. non-being this or that. From here only one step leads to the further insight: by being always determinate non-being, matter is potentially — not everything but — this or that, precisely the potentiality of that of which it was the determinate negation.

istence of a contradiction, even if it cannot be explained in terms of Aristotle's development.

On the other hand, it was not always overlooked either that being-as-such as occurring in the definition of metaphysics could not mean a mere concept. The passage quoted from Robin on p. 178 above, together with the two passages from Ps. Alexander show this clearly. We can also mention F. A. Trendelenburg (*Historische Beitraege zur Philosophie. I. Geschichte der Kategorienlehre* [1846] 68 f.), who contrasts the concepts of being as a category and as a metaphysical entity. In recent times particularly G. L. Muskens, "De ente qua ens Metaphysicae Aristoteleae obiecto", *Mnemosyne* III/13 (1947) 130–140 stressed that in *Met.* K *ens qua ens* designates the incorporeal and that καθόλου in *Met.* E does not mean logical universality — what should be added to the results of Muskens is only that the former part of his assertion is true also of *Met.* Γ and E 1. If, however, being-as-such was interpreted as a logical universal, the difficulty in explaining the contradiction within the definition of metaphysics became paramount.

This difficulty was of great importance in the development of Western thought. The *status controversiae* in the Middle Ages was described by Duns Scotus in his *Quaestiones subtilissimae super ll. Met. Arist.* (*Opera*, v. VII 11–40 Vivès) *. According to this passage Avicenna asserted that it is the *ens* which is the subject matter of metaphysics while Averroes asserted that it is God and the *intelligentiae separatae* **. The classic definition of St. Thomas (metaphysics deals with the *ens commune* and also with the *ens primum a materia separatum*) attempts a bold synthesis by subordinating the Aristotelian God (and in general God as the subject matter of metaphysics) to the concept of

---

* Cf. E. Gilson, "Avicenne et le point de départ de Duns Scot", *Archives d'histoire doctrinale et littéraire du Moyen Age* 2 (1927) 89–149, esp. 93 f.

** Cf. also Avicenna in Gundissalinus, *De divisione philos.* p. 268 f. Baur. Avicenna's reasoning is as follows. No science proves the existence of its subject matter; metaphysics proves the existence of God; therefore God is not the proper subject matter of metaphysics. Furthermore, metaphysics, being the first science, can have no other science above itself which could prove the existence of the subject matter of metaphysics. Therefore, the subject matter of metaphysics must be something the existence (being) of which needs no proof. This is being, since the being of being needs no proof. The completely un-Aristotelian, quasi-Anselmian character of this chain of thought (un-Aristotelian, that is, from the historical point of view) reveals the difficulty in question.

an *ens primum* and *ens commune*. There are other passages in which the unity of the two metaphysics is achieved in a somewhat different way. But the question whether such a unity actually existed was never considered as settled beyond dispute. A recent book, M. Wundt's *Die deutsche Schulmetaphysik des 17. Jahrhunderts* (1939) showed the consequences with great clarity (161–227, esp. 170) *. It would be highly desirable to have similar investigations for Italian, French, English, and other philosophy. It is remarkable to what extent the question of the dual character of metaphysics was a stock-topic of philosophic discussion.

In the 19th century the clearest expression of doubts concerning the whole problem was voiced by P. Natorp, "Thema und Disposition der Aristotelischen Metaphysik", *Philosophische Monatshefte* 24 (1888) 37–65; 540–574, esp. 51 n. 23; 550; 542 **. We may disagree with his solution, just as Jaeger did; we must disagree with his assertion that actually Aristotle meant by metaphysics only the investigation of being-as-such, while "theology" (science of one particular sphere of being) could not have been what Aristotle meant by metaphysics. Just as Jaeger disagreed with Natorp, we must, however, disagree with Jaeger's solution, according to which the definition of metaphysics as *metaphysica specialis* and *metaphysica generalis* at the same time was the result of an ill-reconciled contradiction in Aristotle's thought as he was developing away from his Platonic, "theological" stage. But here again, we must agree with Jaeger that the two points of view (the special and the general) are irreconcilable. In a way, the solution presented here is simply the opposite of Natorp's (*op. cit.* 545). There never was any *metaphysica generalis* in Aristotle.

Nor should it be forgotten that neither Eudemus nor Theophrastus deals with metaphysics in terms of a *metaphysica generalis*.

All branches of knowledge, says Eudemus, investigate their

---

* Cf. also E. Lewalter, *Spanisch-jesuitische und deutsch-lutherische Metaphysik des 17. Jahrhunderts* (1935), esp. 44–76. Some pertinent material can be found in P. Petersen, *Geschichte der Aristotelischen Philosophie im protestantischen Deutschland* (1921) 298–338.

** But cf. E. v. Ivánka, "Die Behandlung der Metaphysik in Jaegers 'Aristoteles'", *Scholastik* 7 (1932) 1–29, esp. 17 and 20.

specific objects, but not the principles of these objects (fr. 34 Wehrli). This is an Aristotelian passage restated: the mathematician takes his subject matter for granted (*Met.* E 1, 1025b11–18; cf. *Anal. Post.* I 1, 71a1–17). Its essence is assumed hypothetically, its existence is not proved. Now Eudemus continues: Therefore there will ultimately be a branch of knowledge which will investigate both its specific objects and their principles. This is Aristotle's metaphysics; the principles of the uppermost sphere of being will be on the same existential plane with the entities of this sphere.

As to Theophrastus, the whole bent of his so-called metaphysical fragment is unmistakably towards theology and special metaphysics.

Thus, while the metaphysical systems of Theophrastus and Eudemus are frequently criticized as one-sided or even illegitimate interpretations of Aristotle, we consider them to be perfectly legitimate.

In spite of the disagreement with Jaeger's interpretation of the key sentence in *Met.* E 1, it must be stressed once more: if the usual interpretation of the phrase "being-as-such" is correct, the sentence does contain an unacceptable contradiction. Only by interpreting it in the way suggested above is the contradiction removed. Aristotle never intended to start a general metaphysics and therefore his science of being-as-such would be neoplatonic in character *.

But if this interpretation avoids any contradiction within the

---

* To a large extent these results agree with the ones reached by J. Owens, *The Doctrine of Being in the Aristotelian Metaphysics* (1951). The disagreement starts when it comes to the problem as to how the causality of the supreme sphere of being is to be explained. Owens unhesitatingly assumes that it can only be the kind of causality ascribed by Aristotle to the unmoved movers in *Met.* Λ. But it can safely be said, that in *Met.* E 1 and K 3–7 the causality of the supreme sphere of being is of an entirely different character. This sphere is a cause by containing the elements out of which everything else consists, particularly being-as-such and non-being-as-such. Owens pays no attention to the presence of the two-opposite-principles doctrine in the aforementioned parts of the *Metaphysics*. The present book was completed before the one by Owens was published so that the agreement is all the more significant. There is only apparent disagreement in that Owens insists that Aristotle's concept of being is not Platonic, because for him "Platonic" means "as found in the dialogues by Plato", whereas in the present book it means "as presented and interpreted by Aristotle".

definition of metaphysics, is not its net result to originate another, even more glaring one? If *Met.* Γ, E 1, and K 3–7 are all based on the conviction that being-as-such is not an ordinary universal, do they not contradict the bulk of other metaphysical writings of Aristotle? If these three complexes profess the two-opposite-principles doctrine, do they not differ radically from the rest of Aristotle's writings?

These two questions ought to be answered in the affirmative. There is a rift in Aristotle's metaphysical writings, analogous to the rift in his logical writings, stressed by Calogero. The description of the subject matter of metaphysics as being-as-such is incompatible with the assertion that being-as-such is a purely logical category. But it does not seem that we have the right to interpret Aristotle's definition of metaphysics given *ex professo* in *Met.* Γ, E 1, and K 3–7 in the light of what he says about the concept of being (esp. in *Met.* I) nor do we have a right to assume that he cannot subscribe to the doctrine of two-opposite-principles in *Met.* Γ, E 1, and K 3–7, because he criticized it in other parts of his metaphysical writings (esp. in *Met.* Λ and N).

How shall we explain this rift?

There are obviously four possibilities. The first would be the return to the traditional interpretation of Aristotle. According to it, Aristotle professes one entirely consistent system of philosophy, this consistency, coherence, and non-contradictoriness being entirely that of an ordinary mathematical system. Apparent contradictions must be only apparent; by appropriate distinctions they can be removed and shown to be only verbal. At present, this kind of interpretation is decidedly on the defensive.

The second is connected with the name of Jaeger. His developmental method achieved two effects at the same time. First, it made us eager rather than afraid of finding contradictions in Aristotle; second, it gave an explanation of them. Aristotle started as a Platonist, but changed slowly towards a more naturalistic and empirical type of philosophy. What first looked as contradictions reveals itself as layers of Aristotle's thoughts.

This second possibility, when developed by Jaeger, was likely to meet resistance from those who believed that it was possible to establish something like a coherent Aristotelian system. This kind of resistance was natural. It must be said, however, that its spokesmen did not succeed too well in eliminating the contradictions from Aristotle's writings and thus had no real alternative to Jaeger's solution. A particular obstacle in their path was the discovery of new, and a proper appreciation of old, fragments of Aristotle which incontrovertibly proved that many of Aristotle's writings were indeed Platonic in character — including even the acceptance of the theory of ideas.

But still another kind of protest was raised against the results of Jaeger, a protest establishing a third possibility. The existence of all the contradictions spotted by Jaeger was admitted, but it was denied that they could be explained with the help of Jaeger's development method. The opponents were quick to point out that in passages which according to Jaeger were late, transcendentalism and Platonism were still present and that in passages which were early according to Jaeger the whole empirical interest of Aristotle was already present. And they also pointed out that the contradictions between the transcendentalist and the empiricist existed in one and the same passage and were repeated indiscriminately in writings belonging by Jaeger's count to early, middle, and late periods of Aristotle. Among the spokesmen of this view was Shorey, though he expressed it only in short papers (see e.g. "Note on the 'Evolution of Aristotle' and Calogero's I fondamenti della Logica Aristotelica", *Classical Philology* 22 [1927] 420–423) and had no time to present his fully elaborate opinions on this point. How, then, did he explain the existence of these contradictions? He did it by assuming a radical lack of clarity in Aristotle's own mind which he was never able to overcome (cf. also A. Brémond, "Le Dilemme aristotélicien", *Archives Philosophiques* 10 [1933], c. 2). The transcendentalist and the naturalist, the rationalist and the empiricist in Aristotle, said Shorey, do not present different phases in Aristotle's development. They existed in Aristotle all his life long *.

Now, it is to be noticed that Shorey was not without prede-

---

* But Shorey also tried to establish his own developmental theory, according to which Aristotle passed through three stages: the Platonic, the anti-Platonic, return to Platonism. See P. Shorey, "Les Idées de Platon et l'évolution d'Aristote", *Mélanges P. Thomas* (1930) 633–649. Cf. J. Burnet, "Aristotle", *Proceedings of the British Academy* 11 (1924/5) 109–124, esp. 121 f.

cessors. It is sufficient to look up Zeller's evaluation of Aristotle's logic to become aware of it. Side by side in Aristotle, says Zeller, we find elements of Platonic logic and of logic based on experience. This contradiction is revealed best in the tendency of Aristotle to base all knowledge on syllogism, i.e. to confine the apprehension of truth to discursive thinking and at the same time to insist on the necessity of an immediate, intuitive insight as the basis for all discursive thinking. What is particularly interesting about Shorey's approach is just that it is already a reaction to Jaeger's developmental view. Due to this view, it was possible to see in Aristotle a much greater mass of contradictions, whereas earlier generations of scholars were reluctant to admit any except by way of last resort.

The fourth possibility is more in the character of a prospect. It is perhaps possible to interpret the two aspects of Aristotle's philosophy as rooted in one and the same attempt of not to become dogmatic, i.e. neither to remain a Platonist nor to settle down into an anti-Platonic system. Perhaps Aristotle did not belong among the philosophers who were interested mainly in erecting a coherent system of philosophy. Perhaps behind Aristotle the Platonist and Aristotle the anti-Platonist is Aristotle who is neither, an Aristotle interested in philosophizing more than in philosophy.

With the enumeration of these four possibilities of explaining the rift in Aristotle's metaphysical writings the present investigation comes to a close. Which of the four possibilities will be accepted is immaterial in the present context. For the purpose of this chapter was exclusively to establish the notion of an *Aristoteles Neoplatonicus.* He is not the whole Aristotle, to be sure. But the traditional Aristotle is not the whole Aristotle either.

Appendix

1. My assertion that ὄν ᾗ ὄν means the most real being, most real by not being something and, in this sense of the word, most real by being fully indeterminate, was criticized by Mansion. As I answered Mansion's criticisms elsewhere, I must here limit

myself to listing two papers of mine, in which further bibliography
will be found. They are: "Metaphysik — Name und Gegenstand",
Journal of Hellenic Studies 77 (1957) 87–92; ὄν ᾗ ὄν und πρώτη
οὐσία: Postskript zu einer Besprechung", *Philosophische Rundschau* 9 (1957) 148–153.

2. It was also criticized by Theiler *. Recognizing that a strong
(he even says: incontrovertible) argument in favor of my position
are the words that the subject matter of metaphysics is τὸ ὄν ᾗ ὄν
καὶ χωριστόν in *Met.* K 7, 1064a29 he declared that these words
are simply the results of a scribe's mistake, thus have never been
actually written by a philosophically responsible author. This
solution is partly more radical than that of Mansion, partly less so.
The latter, because it permits Theiler to retain the rest of *Met.*
K as a work of Aristotle, whereas Mansion is compelled to declare
the whole book as spurious, viz. as written by a pupil of Aristotle
who misunderstood his master on most fundamental matters.
The former, because it presupposes that the text is disfigured by
what we should call a misprint. I think Theiler has been adequately answered by Wagner **, who pointed at the context, esp.
1064a33–35.

3. I should like to point out that important as the objections of
Mansion and Theiler are, they are inconclusive with regard to an
important part of my thesis. Even if *Met.* K or parts of it are
spurious there can be no doubt that they were not in antiquity
considered to be so. It is therefore more likely that the Aristotle
who influenced subsequent philosophic thought was more similar
to my Aristotle than to that of Mansion or Theiler.

4. It is always worthwhile to take into account Zeller's
opinions. Now, the paper by Natorp (see above, p. 208) was
immediately criticized by him***. The subject matter of Aristotle's
metaphysics, says Zeller, are the ὄντα ᾗ ὄντα i.e. οὐσίαι. But in the
full sense of the word only those οὐσίαι = ὄντα ᾗ ὄντα are (exist)
which are suprasensible. Thus, as the subject matter of meta-

---

* W. Theiler, "Die Entstehung der Metaphysik des Aristoteles ...", *Museum
Helveticum* 15 (1958) 85–105, esp. 88.
** "Zum Problem des aristotelischen Metaphysikbegriffes", *Philosophische Rundschau* 9 (1957) 129–148, esp. 146.
*** E. Zeller, "Bericht ueber die deutsche Litteratur der sokratischen, platonischen
und aristotelischen Philosophie 1886, 1887", *Archiv fuer Geschichte der Philosophie* 2
(1889) 259–299, esp. 264–271.

physics ὂν ᾗ ὄν (or ὄντα ᾗ ὄντα) designates the divine. Zeller is neither in sympathy with such a view nor of the opinion that it is consistent with other fundamental tenets of Aristotle. His interpretation is all the more remarkable.

5. I noticed repeatedly the similarity of my interpretation of the subject matter of metaphysics to that of Owens, whose book I read only after my own manuscript was completed. I therefore should like to turn the attention of my readers to Gewirth's review of Owen's book*, because some of Gewirth's objections can equally well be applied to mine. But I trust that the defense of my position in the papers quoted above at the same time answers these objections. But of course I cannot presume to speak in Owens' name.

6. From a completely different point of view my interpretation of the ὂν ᾗ ὄν concept has been criticized by Loenen (*op. cit.*, above p. 32). Pointing at the concluding sentence of *Met*. Γ 8 (ἔστι γάρ τι ὃ ἀεὶ κινεῖ τὰ κινούμενα, καὶ τὸ πρῶτον κινοῦν ἀκίνητον αὐτό) Loenen says that here Aristotle obviously equates τὸ ὂν ᾗ ὄν with τὸ πρῶτον κινοῦν ἀκίνητον, i.e. with the subject matter of metaphysics as defined in *Met*. Λ. Therefore, Loenen says, it is impossible to interpret ὂν ᾗ ὄν the way I do, viz. as indeterminate being.

It is interesting to observe that this objection of Loenen already presupposes what I tried to prove (and for which I was criticized by Mansion and Theiler), viz. that there is no *metaphysica generalis* in Aristotle, ὂν ᾗ ὄν designating nothing else but the supreme being, in other words the divine. He, I take it, unhesitatingly assumes that also in *Met*. Γ Aristotle when talking of ὂν ᾗ ὄν actually means τὸ πρῶτον κινοῦν ἀκίνητον. Loenen's disagreement with me begins only when it comes to the problem: why does Aristotle use the phrase ὂν ᾗ ὄν to characterize the divine? Now, Loenen does not notice that his objection cuts both ways. If we must interpret ὂν ᾗ ὄν as simply another designation of the changeless source of change, what prevents us to see in the phrase τὸ πρῶτον κινοῦν ἀκίνητον another designation for ὂν ᾗ ὄν? In other words, how shall we decide which of the two phrases of the equation (assumed as a matter of course by Loenen)

---

* A. Gewirth, "Aristotle's Doctrine of Being", *The Philosophical Review* 62 (1953) 577–589.

ὂν ᾗ ὄν = τὸ πρῶτον κινοῦν ἀκίνητον is, if we may says so, the leading phrase, ultimately determining the sense of the other?

Therefore, my answer to Loenen is this. Whoever wrote the concluding passage of *Met.* Γ indeed indicated that τὸ πρῶτον κινοῦν ἀκίνητον is closely related to the ὂν ᾗ ὄν. He took the two designations to be only two aspects of one and the same subject — the divine. That he should use two designations apparently so different will seem strange only when we forget that the concept of τὸ πρῶτον κινοῦν ἀκίνητον is no less paradoxical than the concept of indeterminate being, because in the framework of Aristotle's philosophy it designates a form which is not form of anything.

In my book I referred only briefly to the concluding sentence of *Met.* Γ as another proof that even in this book Aristotle did not think of his metaphysics as being anything like general metaphysics (see above p. 167). The recent edition of the *Metaphysics* by Jaeger brings the problem into focus. For Jaeger double bracketed the whole concluding section of *Met.* Γ thus indicating that he considers it to be a later addition, either by Aristotle himself or by an editor who made use of a marginal note of Aristotle himself *. This assumption of Jaeger's is supported by the fact that the whole section Γ 8, 1012b22–31 was absent in some manuscripts and is thus independent from his developmental theories. But it has a bearing on them. For, whoever added the last words clearly indicated that he was not of the opinion that there is any difference between the subject matter of metaphysics as stated in Γ from that stated in Λ.

7. Kohnke ** (followed by Doerrie ***) asserts that the 'Neoplatonism' of Aristotle in *Met.* Γ and E is directed against the 'Neoplatonism' of Speusippus, whereas I assumed that we in both cases have instances of the same 'Neoplatonism'. For, says Kohnke, there can be no one supreme science according to Speusippus, because Speusippus did not notice that all opposites (one pair of which constitutes the several spheres of reality) ultimately hark back to one substrate, identified by Kohnke with τὸ πρῶτον,

---

* W. Jaeger (ed.), *Aristotelis Metaphysica*, Oxford 1957; cf. *Aristoteles²* (1955) 221 (with a somewhat different explanation: written by Aristotle as it now stands; crossed out by him when he revised *Met.* K; restituted to its original place by the editor).

** *Op. cit.* (above, p. 33).

*** H. Doerrie, *Philosophische Rundschau* 3 (1955) 14–25.

which has no opposite. In that Aristotle teaches that there is only one supreme science, he criticizes the two-opposite-principles doctrine of Speusippus for its failure to account for the unity of metaphysics. In other words, Kohnke asserts that *Met.* Γ E are later than *Met.* Λ whose well-known criticism of the two-opposite-principles doctrine together with the attendant doctrine of a neutral substrate in which the opposites appear they presuppose. *Die reine Gegensatzlehre* (the stress in on *reine*) *wird als Lehre anderer Philosophen eingeführt.* I don't see that Kohnke's interpretation is tenable. In *Met.* Γ 2, 1004b27–28 we read: πάντα ἀνάγεται εἰς τὸ ὂν καὶ τὸ μὴ ὂν καὶ εἰς ἓν καὶ πλῆθος. This is confirmed in 1004b33–34: πάντα δὲ καὶ τἆλλα ἀναγόμενα φαίνεται εἰς τὸ ἓν καὶ πλῆθος. And now comes the conclusion in 1005a2–3: φανερὸν οὖν καὶ ἐκ τούτων ὅτι μιᾶς ἐπιστήμης τὸ ὂν ᾗ ὂν θεωρῆσαι, πάντα γὰρ ἢ ἐναντία ἢ ἐξ ἐναντίων, ἀρχαὶ δὲ τῶν ἐναντίων τὸ ἓν καὶ πλῆθος. There is not the slightest hint in this text that Aristotle criticizes the two-opposite-principles-doctrine. The conclusion that there is only one supreme science is not based, as Kohnke has it, on the doctrine that all opposites have a common substrate. It is on the contrary based on the assumption that all opposites are ultimately reducible to one *pair* of opposites and nothing is said to the effect that this pair of opposites must have as its third a substrate different from them.

8. Using his own criteria I. M. Bochenski (*Ancient Formal Logic*, 1951) comes to the conclusion that *Met.* Γ belongs with the *Topics* (incl. the *Soph. El.*) to the same period. Using a different criterion one immediately could reply that this is impossible. For, the *Topics* quite obviously operate with the concept of being as an abstractum (in our sense of the word: IV 1, 121a16–18; 6, 127a26–31). Unfortunately, it is infinitely easier to reject any of the developmental theories so far suggested than to replace them by something better. Perhaps it is appropriate to have a list of all passages in Zeller, pointing at some unresolved dilemma in Aristotle. They are: *Philosophie der Griechen* II/2[5] 192–196; 236; 309–313; 345–348; 801–805.

9. I am afraid that in my presentation of Avicenna's doctrines on p. 207 I simplified them to the point of distortion. Actually, the definition of the subject matter of metaphysics by Avicenna is rather complex and complex to the point of unclarity. We see

this best when we simply follow the outline of his *Danesh-name* now available in a French translation *.

Here we first find the subject matter of metaphysics designated as *science de tout qui est au-delà de la nature* (p. 90). At the same time, its subject matter are said to be *choses* whose *être ne se rattache nullement à la matière sensible, non plus qu'à la combinaison ou au mouvement, de sorte, qu'on peut les concevoir comme détachés de la matière et du mouvement (ainsi l'intelligence, l'être, l'unité, la causalité et la causéité, et autres analogues) car il est possible de concevoir ces états en dehors des choses sensibles (ibid.).*

Having become acquainted with all the problems connected with the definition of the subject matter of metaphysics in ontic terms or else in epistemonic ones, one immediately sees that Avicenna is unable to escape the confusion resulting from the combination of two different points of view. The examples given by Avicenna are partly illustrative of beings *existing* without matter (*intelligence*) and partly of *états* which we can *conceive* independently from matter in which they are embodied (unity, causality, etc.). But this is not the end. These things which we can conceive as existing without matter are said by Avicenna to be of two kinds. Either they *ne soient jamais susceptibles d'attachement à la matière (ainsi les intelligences et Dieu ...).* Or they *se rattachent à la matière et au mouvement, sans toutefois que cela soit nécessaire par leur nature — comme la causalité ...* (p. 91).

This division is of course nothing but a division of metaphysics into a special and a general branch. But to this comparatively simple determination of the subject matter of metaphysics Avicenna adds another. This subject matter *est non pas une chose particulière, mais l'être absolu en tant qu'absolu* and *les états* of this *être absolu* (p. 92). As such *états* Avicenna among others enumerates the universal and the particular, potency and act, the necessary (*nota bene!*) and the contingent, substance and accident, unity and plurality (p. 93).

Here, we should think, we have restated the subject matter of general metaphysics and are left wondering how it relates to the subject matter of metaphysics in terms of the immateriality of its subject matter, this immateriality being, as we have seen, of a double kind. In other words, we suddenly have in addition to the

---

* *Avicenne. Le Livre de Science.* I. (tr. by M. Achena and H. Massé, Paris 1955).

two branches of metaphysics described on p. 90 f. still another, described on p. 92, which, however, looks like a duplication of one of the former branches. If we combine both descriptions, we have something like a special metaphysics (dealing with God and the intelligences), another branch dealing with such concepts (or should we say states, qualities, etc.?) as being, unity, causality, and a third dealing with absolute being and its *états* (obviously πάθη), among them the necessary.

The confusion does not end here. Part of metaphysics, Avicenna continues, is the knowledge of God, the creator of all things (p. 93). This part is called 'divine science'. Here we have the origin of all the interminable discussions concerning the relation of metaphysics, particularly of special metaphysics, to theology. Quite obviously the different interpretations of one and the same text of Aristotle are mechanically added one on top of another till in the end the concept of theology is superimposed on a bipartite (or tripartite) metaphysics, one (or two) of whose parts, in the language of Aristotle, is already theology.

So far we had before us the introductory part of Avicenna's metaphysics. If we now follow the execution of it, a surprise awaits us. Avicenna discusses the concepts of οὐσία and σῶμα (p. 94–108), accidens and other categories (p. 108–116), the universal and the particular (p. 116–121), the one and the multiple, the anterior and the posterior, cause and effect, potency and act (p. 121–136). Thereupon he investigates the concept of the necessary, but by no means as an *état* as we should expect from the preceding. Rather 'the necessary' here suddenly means 'necessary being', i.e. being from which multiplicity, change, etc. must be excluded (p. 143–146). To this necessary (or as we should say, absolute) being neither the concept of οὐσία nor that of accidens applies. It is uncreated and eternal. It is not only *connaissant et connu de lui-même, mais encore le savoir même* (p. 152) and by its self-knowledge causes and knows everything that exists (p. 152–160). In the union with it consists man's happiness (p. 167–173). All things emanate from it (p. 173–177).

Quite obviously *l'Être nécessaire* is Avicenna's designation of God. But whether the home of this necessary being is that branch of metaphysics which deals with things that actually exist without matter, or the other which deals with things which can but don't have to, exist in matter, or the third which deals with being-as-such and its πάθη, among them the necessary, or finally the one which deals with the creator of all things, remains unclear. Avicenna imperceptibly, one could almost say surreptitiously by singling out the concept of the necessary from among the πάθη of absolute being (p. 93) introduces the concept of necessary being, thus overcoming in a peculiar way the division of metaphysics into a special and general branch, a division in favor of which nothing can be said, except that it originated in a mistaken interpretation of Aristotle, this mistake itself due to the peculiarity of Aristotle's way of philosophizing.

10. On the concept of immediate (intuitive) knowledge in Aristotle now see Plutarch, *De Is. et Osir.* 77, 382 D–E recently included among fragments of Aristotle's *Eudemus* by W. D. Ross, *Aristotelis fragmenta selecta* (1955), p. 23. If Ross is right, before us we have a veritable egg of Columbus. Though Plutarch explicitly quotes the doctrine as that of Plato *and* of Aristotle, the passage has simply been overlooked. The reason is obvious but hardly good. We can immediately see that the doctrine can indeed easily be derived from Plato, therefore we don't take seriously the fact that Plutarch ascribes it also to Aristotle — just as the sun blinds us so that we don't see the stars shining by day. But it seems entirely inappropriate to treat the passage as erroneous and to assume that Plutarch arbitrarily credited Aristotle with a doctrine peculiar only to Plato. After all, Plutarch is obviously very familiar with Aristotle's writings, both those which have been preserved and others now lost. A glance at the Index of Bernardakis and another at Rose's Index of authors are sufficient to prove this. And we must not forget that among Plutarch's writings not preserved is a study of Aristotle's *Topics* and another of his *Categories*. It is furthermore well known that Plutarch severely rebuked Colotes for having treated Aristotle simply as another representative of the Platonic theory of ideas; and finally that he explicitly told us that Aristotle changed his philosophical opinions. Thus, all evidence is in favor of Ross. Strangely enough, no reviewer of his book seems to have noticed that he without further ado presented us with a new and extremely important fragment of the platonizing Aristotle. At the same

time it once more becomes obvious to what extent his philosophy actually considered itself to be τελέτη:

ἡ δὲ τοῦ νοητοῦ καὶ εἰλικρινοῦς καὶ ἁπλοῦ νόησις ὥσπερ ἀστραπὴ διαλάμψασα τῆς ψυχῆς ἅπαξ ποτὲ θιγεῖν καὶ προσιδεῖν παρέσχε. διὸ καὶ Πλάτων καὶ Ἀριστοτέλης ἐποπτικὸν τοῦτο τὸ μέρος τῆς φιλοσοφίας καλοῦσιν, ὡς οἱ τὰ δοξαστὰ καὶ μεικτὰ καὶ παντοδαπὰ ταῦτα παραμειψάμενοι τῷ λόγῳ πρὸς τὸ πρῶτον ἐκεῖνο καὶ ἁπλοῦν καὶ ἄυλον ἐξάλλονται καὶ θιγόντες ἀμωσγέπως τῆς περὶ αὐτὸ καθαρᾶς ἀληθείας οἷον ἐν τελετῇ τέλος ἔχειν φιλοσοφίαν νομίζουσι *.

---

* The text is that of F. C. Babbitt (*Plutarch's Moralia*, Loeb Library, vol. 5, 1936, repr. 1957); but in the one but least line I followed Sieveking's text in the Teubneriana (ἐν τελετῇ instead of Babbitt's ἐντελῆ).

On Plutarch in this context see K. Ziegler, art. Plutarchos (2), *RE* XXI/1 (1951), esp. No. 56 and 192 of the Lamprias catalogue; W. Jaeger, *Aristoteles*[2] (1955) 35f.; 435 f.

It is hardly necessary to remind the reader of the terms used by Plotinus in the classic passages describing the *unio mystica*: ἐφάψασθαι καὶ θιγεῖν (VI 9, 4, 27Br), θιγεῖν (VI 9, 7, 5 Br), ἔλλαμψις (16 Br), θέα (21 Br; cf. VI 9, 11, 30–46 Br), ἐπαφή (25 Br), θίξις καὶ οἷον ἐπαφή (V 3, 10, 42 Br), ἐφάψασθαι (V 3, 17, 25 Br), ἐξαίφνης φῶς λαμβάνειν (29 Br), ἐφάψασθαι φωτός (34 Br), etc. (see Zeller III/2[5] [1923], 613–615).

CONCLUSION

The division of being into three spheres of being (οὐσίαι), viz. ideas (theologicals), mathematicals, and physicals, was reported by Aristotle as Platonic. It is immaterial in the present context whether Aristotle was correct in his report. He himself was not only of the opinion that he was; he even adapted this division to his own purposes. If he misunderstood Plato, in this case at least he cannot be charged with having maliciously done it. The adaption mentioned before was Aristotle's division of theoretical philosophy into theology (metaphysics), mathematics, and physics. More will be said about that presently.

Posidonius, in interpreting Plato's *Timaeus*, took over this division. In connection with it, he established a characteristic equation. On one side, he had the tripartition into ideas, world-soul, and sensibles, derived from the *Timaeus*. On the other side, he had the Aristotelian tripartition into ideas, mathematicals, and physicals. He now equated the middle terms of the two tripartitions, viz. the world-soul and the mathematicals.

In Iamblichus and Proclus, the tripartition and the equation (soul = mathematicals) reappear to be discussed, accepted, or rejected. In them and originally, in this division not only ideas (theologicals or whatever we choose to call the entities contained in the supreme sphere of being) but also mathematicals subsist. Mathematicals are not the product of abstraction in the ordinary sense of the word. The fact that Aristotle on one hand kept the Platonic tripartition and on the other hand had doubts as to the subsistence of mathematicals (doubts, that is, in some places in his writings, while in other places such a subsistence is explicitly denied) involved him and his interpreters and followers in endless difficulties. The adaptation of the Platonic tripartition mentioned above resulted in Aristotle in a tripartition of theoretical philosophy into metaphysics (theology), mathematics, and physics. But it is obvious that the value of this latter tripartition becomes more than dubious, if the objects of metaphysics and physics are taken to subsist, whereas mathematicals are supposed to be only objects of abstraction in the ordinary sense of the word.

With this tripartition of being (and of philosophy) are connected three particularly interesting problems.

1. One is the relation between mathematicals and the soul. The identification of the soul with some kind of mathematical (which Plato's *Timaeus* is on the verge of asserting) was explicitly stated by Xenocrates (soul = a self-changing or motive number) and probably also by Speusippus (soul = form of the all-extended), so that in equating the soul with mathematicals, Posidonius only continued and developed an Academic tradition. Even in Aristotle we can still find some traces of this identification which he himself was ready to accept. Just as there was a time when he designated the soul as an idea rather than an immanent form of a living body, so there must have been a time when he described it as a transcendent, subsistent mathematical form.

This identification is connected with another problem: that of the origin of change (motion) in a universe consisting of the three aforesaid spheres. The identification of the soul with mathematicals was connected with the further assumption that the mathematicals were, in some way, the source of change. This was most clearly stated by Xenocrates, but the assumption reappears in Proclus and Iamblichus. Such an assumption was bound to cause much discussion. The rejection of the idea of making mathematicals the source of change, frequently led to splitting up the sphere of mathematicals so as to make only part of them motive (source of change or motion) and thus identical with the soul. Of course, the whole discussion can be appreciated only if we decide to give up the idea that the only thinkable type of causality is some action of one thing on another thing, a process in space and time. But after all, whatever causality the soul seems to have according to the doctrines of Plato, he certainly does not conceive of it in terms of spatio-temporal causality.

One of the most characteristic reinterpretations of the tripartition was that of Aristotle himself. While generally adopting the tripartition theologicals — mathematicals — physicals, he sometimes adopted a different tripartition: theologicals — astronomicals — physicals. The astronomicals took the place of mathematicals as a secondary source of motion. Their own motion was caused by the existence of the entities constituting the theological sphere of being (the unmoved movers).

The divine character of Aristotle's astronomicals is obvious

and stressed by him. This is an implicit proof that the mathematicals also, as long as they were considered to be subsistent,
were taken to be divine. Mathematics, within this framework,
was indeed closely allied with theology. The clearest expression
of the theological character of mathematicals we find in Xenocrates. The theological interpretation of mathematicals will
find its full expression also in all the *Theologoumena arithmetices.*
Astral theology and mathematical theology are two sisters,
though the former could ally itself to astral religions and so
survive to the present day in the form of astrology. Mathematical
theology remained always limited to professional circles. But
this whole complex of mathematical theology must be dealt
with separately.

It is in this context that the new fragment of Aristotle is of
particular interest. There was a time when mathematics was for
Aristotle closely related to philosophy — not as a means to turn
away our eyes from the sensible and to train our mind to perceive
the immaterial as it is in Plato's *Republic,* and not only because
of the exactness of its method — but rather as a study of a
reality closer to the ultimate reality of theologicals.

The problem whether Aristotle's astronomicals are living beings
having a soul is a matter of controversy. Some passages clearly
indicate that sometimes they are so interpreted by Aristotle.
In this way the connection between mathematicals and the soul
is still preserved in Aristotle. In him, stars are animated and
moving mathematicals. Astronomy is psychology — or at least
that branch of psychology which deals with souls embodied in
stars.

Again, an appreciation of all these speculations is possible
only when we are ready to grant that soul does not mean necessarily something like consciousness; further if we are ready
to grant that mathematicals are *in rerum natura* and not only
in our thoughts. And once we grant that the universe contains
mathematicals, it is only natural to assume that in some way
these mathematicals are causes. Furthermore, the equation soul
= mathematicals is not at all fantastic if we grant that the idea
of self-thinking (and, in this sense of the word, self-moving or
self-changing) mathematicals is not an absurdity. And is it not
true that after all what has been called Aristotle's νοῦς ποιητικός

may be interpreted precisely as the system of all immutable truths thinking themselves and, thus, changelessly self-changing?

The problem as to whether all, some, or none of the mathematicals are the source of change; the further question whether all, some, or none are changeable; and the connected question whether all, some, or none of them are identical with the soul led to the problem as to how many branches the study of mathematics contained. The two main divisions known to us are a tripartition without astronomy and a quadripartition with astronomy included, the other three branches being arithmetic, geometry, and harmonics (acoustics).

The branches of the quadripartite mathematics are identical with the four branches of the quadrivum. In the very idea of the quadrivium the problem of the identification of the soul with mathematicals, the problem of the motive character (changeability and cause of change) of mathematicals, the problem as to the ultimate meaning of mathematics, survived.

The history of the quadrivium idea is not very edifying. The quadripartition of mathematics in Nicomachus is the product of a philosophically sterile mind, interested in divisions for its own sake. That it should have become universally accepted as curriculum is a strange event. From the way the meaning of the quadrivium was formulated and reformulated it is clear however that nobody felt too sure how meaningful the quadrivium was.

A further element of confusion was added by the fact that this quadripartite mathematics as conceived by Nicomachus and accepted by men like Iamblichus or Proclus, meant a branch of science close to or identical with first philosophy — which in turn, made sense only within an excessively realistic interpretation of mathematicals. Whenever the notion of the quadrivium became detached from this excessively realistic background the status of the quadrivium became immediately uncertain and its four branches were likely to be treated as artes pueriles *.

The tripartition of being into theologicals, mathematicals, and physicals continued to be accepted also after Iamblichus. A good example is Proclus. The tripartition of theoretical philoso-

---

* Cf. W. Gerhaeuszer, Der Protreptikos des Poseidonios (1912) 45–47.

phy into metaphysics (theology), mathematics, and physics also continued to be adopted, but it was almost from the very beginning adopted also by philosophers who refused to accept the tripartition of being. The result were numberless attempts to reconcile what amounted to a tripartition of knowledge with what amounted to a bipartition of being. Aristotle himself did not succeed in doing this; nor did any of his successors. The impossibility of this reconciliation and the initial problem of this reconciliation are the result of the contradiction between Aristotle the Platonist and Aristotle the moderate realist.

The most famous attempt to reinterpret the tripartition of theoretical knowledge so as to make it consistent was that of St. Thomas. Physicals, mathematicals, and metaphysicals were interpreted by him in terms of degrees of abstraction. In other words, St. Thomas replaced the faulty tripartition of theoretical knowledge in Aristotle (faulty, because based on the *ratio essendi* and the *ratio cognoscendi* at the same time) by one based entirely on the *ratio cognoscendi*. But this new tripartition would have presupposed that the objects of metaphysics are "abstractible" in the same sense in which the objects of physics or mathematics were supposed to be. This was a consequence which St. Thomas could not accept and which cannot be accepted by anybody who (implicitly or explicitly) interprets metaphysics as being exclusively or even also special metaphysics, i.e. a branch of knowledge dealing with immaterial beings like God, angels, disembodied souls. These immaterial beings cannot be made objects of abstraction in the same sense in which this is possible for physicals and mathematicals. Being immaterial, they cannot be disengaged from matter in the same way in which embodied forms or universals can; the approach to them is not by way of abstraction. This means that the consistency of the tripartition of theoretical knowledge (based on the principle of abstraction) is achieved by St. Thomas at the price of exclusion of special metaphysics from this tripartition. The name of metaphysics for the uppermost of the three branches of theoretical knowledge is kept; but it now designates what was later named general metaphysics. In other words, metaphysics is clearly divided into two branches, general or formal metaphysics and metaphysics as knowledge of immaterial beings, only the former of which is included in the tripartition of theoretical knowledge. This net result once more proves the impossibility of Aristotle's tripartition of theoretical knowledge, once the tripartition of being is dropped.

The identification of mathematicals with the soul resulted in a division of being in theologicals, soul, and physicals. This division is virtually identical with that presupposed and elaborated by Plotinus. The similarity is somewhat obscured by the fact that Plotinus concentrates his attention on the νοῦς, i.e. the first sphere of being, corresponding to theologicals, and the soul, whereas he neglects the physicals; furthermore by the fact that he treats these two spheres of being (νοῦς and soul) in close connection with the highest principle (which is above being). It is also true that in most places in his writings Plotinus is a monist, i.e. he does not recognize a principle opposed to the One and coordinated with it. But it is not quite sure either, whether such a strict coordination was generally assumed by Plato and all his disciples. In any case, in spite of differences there is a fundamental similarity between Plotinus and the Academy.

Both tripartitions of being (into theologicals, mathematicals, physicals; or into theologicals, the soul, physicals) survived the vicissitudes of the history of philosophy with an amazing vitality. It is beyond the scope of the present book to investigate this topic; besides the book of Strong (above p. 59) gives an adequate picture. We limit ourselves to one example. The tripartition mathematics — physics — metaphysics furnishes the outline for Kant's *Prolegomena*. Their three fundamental questions (cf. also Preface to the Second Edition of the *Critique of Pure Reason*) are: how is mathematics possible? how is physics possible? how is metaphysics possible? But certainly Kant succeeded in giving this Aristotelian tripartition a completely new meaning.

2. The second great problem emerging in the context of the tripartition of being was that of the concatenation of the three spheres of being. This concatenation was supposed to be established by some kind of derivation. Derivation is a process that is understandable and at the same time fully real. It is a logical process — but the word "logical" has to be taken in its most comprehensive sense. Logos, spirit, mind, meaning — any of these words conveys this sense. The universe is an organized

totality, and the principle of this organization, no less than the terms of the organized whole, is such that mind even when conversing with itself alone (and being in this way dialectical), exhibits the structure of reality. The reality itself is dialectical or, to use a less committal word, dialogical. Its parts are related to each other precisely in the same way in which single steps of a dialogue are.

The most striking feature of this derivation system was the derivation of physicals, i.e. sensibles, from the anterior, non-sensible, unextended, timeless spheres. As presented by Aristotle and as confirmed by what we know about Speusippus and Xenocrates, the derivation of physicals from nonphysicals was a principle accepted by Plato and his disciples.

It is this principle which is the clearest anticipation of some tenets which we are wont to term Neoplatonic.

In Plato's published writings the problem of the transition from the so called ideal to the so called real appears mainly in the form of two questions. The first question is: "In what way are ideas causes of sensibles?"; the second: "What is the origin of sensibles?". The answer to the first question seems to terminate in the assumption that the ideas are causes *only* by being originals which are mirrored in some kind of mirror. The nature of the mirror itself remains largely undisclosed. On the whole we are left with the impression that the ideas are in no way responsible for the existence of the mirror and that their own existence is in no way dependent on the mirror; furthermore, that ideas and the mirror together are *conditiones sine quibus non* for the existence of sensibles, while it is at least controversial whether they are also *conditiones per quas* of this existence. Once they have come into existence, sensibles may also be said to imitate ideas; but this kind of causality of ideas is irrelevant in the present context. Now, if we keep the term "mirror", we shall have to say that according to Aristotle this mirror is present already in the first sphere of being (ideas), so that there is something like a continuous transition from the ideas to the sensibles. The same assumption underlay the systems of Speusippus and Xenocrates, though instead of the identity of the mirror in the different spheres of being the concept of analogy or similarity may appear.

The answer to the second question implied indeed that from the purely geometrical to the sensible a transition takes place, excluding any radical difference between physicals and mathematicals. There are traces of such an assumption in Plato, though they are not clear enough to warrant the assertion that his system was one of derivation. The possibility cannot be excluded that the radical difference between ideas and sensibles was a fundamental assumption in Plato, never seriously doubted by him.

This latter interpretation of Plato will however remain unsatisfactory for two reasons. First, there will always be readers of Plato who will feel that he could not have left this kind of gap in his system. We may say that as historians of philosophy we should pay no attention to this feeling — that we should concentrate on what Plato said, not on what he should have said. Indeed, much of the content of the present book is entirely in favor of such an attitude. But on the other hand we should admit that this feeling has its legitimate function in stimulating ever renewed attempts to interpret Plato.

The second reason is that such an interpretation results in the assertion that Plato was misunderstood by all his first generation students whose philosophic ideas we know, as all of them either professed or attributed to Plato a derivation system. Such a misunderstanding cannot certainly be ruled out, because every great philosopher is likely to be misunderstood by his students. But it would still remain striking that they all misunderstood him in the same way. For few will deny that the systems of Speusippus and Xenocrates were systems of derivation, few will deny that such a system was ascribed to Plato by Aristotle.

3. The third great problem emerging in the context of the tripartition of being is the constitution of the several spheres. As testified to by Aristotle, the prevailing tendency in the Academy was to assume ultimately a pair of opposite principles. They are in some sense of the word the constituents of the uppermost sphere of being and, as an effect of the concatenation of all spheres, constituents of all reality (in our ordinary language, ideal and non-ideal) alike.

Whether these two principles are always and strictly coordinated is not quite clear.

When it comes to the description of these two principles, it

becomes necessary to use a language elevating them above
other existents and describing them as being a source of being
of existing entities rather than existent themselves. The language
varies; "above being" is as good a phrase as "being-as-such".
In other words, by ascending from what common sense calls
beings we arrive at something which is void of any determination
and therefore by only being (not being something determinate),
being in the fullest sense of the word.

It is in this context that the newly discovered fragment of
Speusippus becomes important. It turns out that the description
of one of his two supreme principles, known to us from Aristotle,
viz. that it is not even being, indicates precisely its elevation
above being, making it strictly comparable to the One of Plotinus
and other Neoplatonists. The particular originality of Speusippus
seems to consist in his having described the second principle
as above non-being. Certainly he described it as morally neutral
(neither good nor evil), just as its opposite principle was supposed
to be neither evil nor good.

Due to the discovery of the Speusippus fragment, Speusippus
emerges as an original thinker. His system is profound and
highly significant.

In this connection a reinterpretation of the meaning of the
subject matter of Aristotle's metaphysics becomes possible.
Such a new interpretation seems necessary, because the usual interpretation of Aristotle's definition of metaphysics as knowledge
of being-as-such *and* the supreme sphere of being seems to
contain a fundamental contradiction. Being-as-such designates
according to the usual interpretation, the most general and
emptiest concept. "Being" is what is common to all that exists.
But the supreme sphere of being, the divine, as it is also called
by Aristotle, is something specific rather than general. It is the
first being, not universal being. The interpretation here suggested
removes the contradiction. If we study the texts in which
Aristotle expounds his definition of metaphysics in and by
themselves, we discover that being-as-such is meant by Aristotle
to be the fullest, not the emptiest being, and fullest by being
fully indeterminate, i.e. not-limited. Just by being indeterminate
it can give being to all existents and therefore deserves the
predicate of divinity. Thus Aristotle can say without being

inconsistent that metaphysics deals with what is unrestricted and omnipresent (this is the meaning of καθόλου) *and* with what is first, viz. above all beings and source of their being, and for both reasons the most divine. Aristotle's metaphysics is strictly comparable to other Academic metaphysical systems; and indeed it is in the same context that we find the definition of metaphysics as the knowledge of being-as-such and the tripartition of being and with it the tripartition of theoretical knowledge into theology, mathematics, and physics. The latter is just as Academic as the former.

True to his doctrine that any knowledge deals with its subject matter and its opposite (this doctrine being a corollary to the doctrine that all being consists of opposites), Aristotle stresses that his metaphysics deals not only with being-as-such but also with non-being-as-such. Just as we should not interpret the concept of being-as-such as an abstract notion, we should not interpret the concept of non-being-as-such as a merely logical term. It is strictly ontic. But undoubtedly the tendency in Aristotle is to deny the complete coordination of being-as-such with non-being-as-such.

In the same context in which we find the definition of metaphysics as the knowledge of being-as-such we also find professed — not criticized! — the doctrine that ultimately all things (in our language: real and ideal alike) are derived from two opposite principles, viz. being-as-such and non-being-as-such. In other words, the words ὄν ᾗ ὄν should best be translated by "indeterminate being" and accordingly we should say: the subject matter of Aristotle's metaphysics is indeterminate being (and indeterminate non-being), which, because it is indeterminate, is unrestricted and therefore first and fully being.

It seems obvious that the introduction of concepts such as being-as-such and non-being-as-such creates specific gnoseologic problems. What kind of knowledge is adequate for entities differing so greatly from other existents? How can what is fully indeterminate be known? It seems that Plato, Speusippus, Aristotle, and Theophrastus were fully aware of this difficulty; in all of them we find theories trying to cope with it. Particularly characteristic is Aristotle's theory of noetic knowledge by θιγεῖν — above discursive knowledge and differing from it mainly in that it is not subject to the alternative of true and false but to another: knowledge or ignorance.

All this adds up to the assertion that some of the most characteristic features of Neoplatonism originated in the Academy and in Aristotle. It is perfectly legitimate to speak of an *Aristoteles Neoplatonicus*.

If we now ask one more question, viz. whether Neoplatonism originated in Plato himself, it seems cautious to answer: it may have originated in Plato, but it may have originated only in the first generation of his disciples as the result of either a legitimate or an illegitimate interpretation of Plato by his first generation disciples.

Appendix

Jaeger's evolutionary interpretation of Aristotle's philosophy is with particular succinctness rejected in: F. Dirlmeier, "Aristoteles", *Jahrbuch fuer das Bistum Mainz 5* (1950) 161–171. This non-evolutionary approach to Aristotle underlies Dirlmeier's commentaries of the *Nicomachean Ethics* (1956) and of the *Magna Moralia* (1958). The way in which the former is criticized in R. A. Gauthier and J. Y. Jolif, *Aristote, l'Ethique à Nicomaque* I (1958) does not seem to be fair. Dirlmeier is charged with lack of historic interest as if it were not just Dirlmeier's point that this interest distorts the true meaning of Aristotle's philosophy and leads to misinterpretations.

That Aristotle has ever meant to establish a system of philosophy has been denied by I. Duering in "Aristotle, The Founder of Scientific Method", *Lychnos* 1943, p. 43–46 (Swedish with English summary) and in "Von Aristoteles bis Leibniz", *Antike und Abendland* 4 (1954) 118–154, esp. 123.

INDEX OF NAMES

INDEX OF PASSAGES IN GREEK AND LATIN AUTHORS

(Some authors represented by one passage only have been omitted, as such a passage can easily be found with the help of the Index of names)

Editions referred to:

ALBINUS: ALBINOS, *Épitomé*, ed. P. Louis (Paris, 1945)

ALEXANDER APHRODISIAS, *In Aristotelis Metaphysica*, ed. M. Hayduck, Commentaria in Aristotelem Graeca v. I (Berlin, 1891).

AMMONIUS, *In Porphyrii Isagogen*, ed. A. Busse, Commentaria in Aristotelem Graeca v. IV/3 (Berlin, 1891).

ANATOLIUS: J. L. Heiberg, "Anatolius sur les dix premiers nombres", *Annales internationales d'histoire*. Congrès de Paris 1900. 5e section. Histoire des sciences (Paris, 1901), p. 27–55.

APULEIUS, *De philosophia libri* ed. P. Thomas (Leipzig, 1980).

ARCHYTAS: H. Diels, *Die Fragmente der Vorsokratiker⁹*, 3 vv. (Berlin, 1959–1960).

ARISTOTLE, *Opera*, ed. Academia Regia Borussica, 5 vv. (Berlin, 1831–1870).
—— *Aristotelis . . . fragmenta*, ed. V. Rose (Leipzig, 1886).
—— *Dialogorum fragmenta*, ed. R. Walzer (Rome, 1934).
—— *The Works of Aristotle* tr. into English, v. XII: *Select Fragments* [tr. by W. D. Ross] (Oxford, 1952).
—— *Aristotelis fragmenta selecta*, ed. W. D. Ross (Oxford, 1955).

BOETHIUS, *The Theological Tractates* . . . by H. F. Stewart . . . and E.K. Rand, The Loeb Classical Library (London and New York, 1918).
—— *In Isagogen Porphyrii*, ed. K. Brandt, Corpus Scriptorum Ecclesiasticorum Latinorum v. XLVIII/1 (Vienna, 1906).
—— *De institutione arithmetica libri duo*, ed. G. Friedlein (Leipzig, 1867).

CASSIODORUS, *Institutiones*, ed. R.A.B. Mynors (Oxford, 1937).

CLARENBALDUS: W. Jansen, *Der Kommentar des Mag. Clarenbaldus von Arras zu Boethius De Trinitate* (Breslau, 1926).

DAVID, *Prolegomena*, ed. A. Busse, Commentaria in Aristotelem Graeca v. XVIII/2 (Berlin, 1903).

DIOGENES LAERTIUS: *Lives* ed. R. Hicks, The Loeb Classical Library (London and New York, 1925).

DOMINICUS GUNDISSALINUS, *De divisione philosophiae*, ed. L. Baur, Beitraege zur Geschichte der Philosophie des Mittelalters v. IV/2–3 (Muenster, 1904).

DUNS SCOTUS: Joannis Duns Scoti *Opera omnia*, 26 vv. (Paris: Vivés, 1891–1895).

EUDEMUS: *Die Schule des Aristoteles. 8. Eudemos von Rhodos*, ed. F. Wehrli (Basel,1955).

GALENUS, PSEUDO: *Galeni qui fertur de partibus philosophiae libellus*, ed. E. Wellmann (Berlin, 1882).

GILBERTUS PORRETA, *Commentaria in librum De Trinitate*: Patrologiae Cursus Completus acc. J.-P. Migne, Patrologia Latina v. LXIV, p. 1255–1310 (Paris, 1891); J. R. O'Donnell (ed.), *Nine Medieval Thinkers* (Toronto, 1955).

HERMEIAS: *Hermiae Alexandrini In Platonis Phaedrum scholia*, ed. P. Couvreur (Paris, 1901).

HERO ALEXANDRINUS, *Opera* v. 4, ed. J. L. Heiberg (Leipzig 1912).

IAMBLICHUS, *Theologoumena arithmeticae*, ed. V. de Falco (Leipzig, 1922).

—— *In Nicomachi arithmeticam introductionem*, ed. H. Pistelli (Leipzig, 1894).
—— *De communi mathematica scientia*, ed. N. Festa (Leipzig, 1891).
—— *Protrepticus*, ed. H. Pistelli (Leipzig, 1888).
—— *De mysteriis liber*, ed. G. Parthey (Berlin, 1857).
ISOCRATES: ed. G. Norlin and L. V. Hook, 3 vv., The Loeb Classical Library (London-Cambridge and New York, 1929–1945).
LYDUS, IOANNES, *De mensibus* ed. R. Wuensch (Leipzig, 1898).
NICOMACHUS, *Introductio arithmetica*, ed. R. Hoche (Leipzig, 1866).
PARMENIDES: see Archytas.
PHILOPONUS, IOANNES, *In Aristotelis De anima*, ed. M. Hayduck, Comentaria in Aristotelem Graeca v. XV (Berlin, 1897).
PLATO: see Timaeus Locrus.
PLOTINUS: *Ennéades*, ed., tr. E. Bréhier, 6 vv. in 7 (Paris, 1924–1938).
—— *Opera*, ed. P. Henry and H.-R. Schwyzer, vol. I (Paris-Brussels 1951), vol. II (*ibid.*, 1959).
PLUTARCH, *Moralia*, ed. G. N. Bernardakis, 7 vv. (Leipzig, 1888–1896).
—— *Moralia*, ed. C. Hubert *et. al.*, v. I/3 (Leipzig, 1935); v. VI/1 (*ibid.*, 1954).
—— *Moralia*, ed. F. C. Babitt *et. al.* (The Loeb Classical Library), v. V, ed. F. C. Babbitt (London-Cambridge and New York, 1936, repr. 1957).
PROCLUS, *In primum Euclidis elementorum librum commentarii*, ed. G. Friedlein (Leipzig, 1873).
—— *In Platonis Timaeum commentaria*, ed. E. Diehl, 3 vv., (Leipzig, 1903–1906).
—— *Institutio Theologica*, ed. E. R. Dodds (Oxford, 1933).
PTOLEMY: *Die Harmonielehre des Klaudios Ptolemaios*, hg. von I. Duering, Goeteborgs Hoegskolas Arsskrift 36 (Goeteborg, 1930).
SEXTUS EMPIRICUS: ed. R. G. Bury, 4 vv., The Loeb Classical Library (London-Cambridge and New York, 1933–1949).
—— *Opera*, ed. H. Mutschmann, J. Mau, K. Janaček, 3 vv. (Leipzig, 1958, 1914, 1954).
SIMPLICIUS, *In Aristotelis categorias*, ed. C. Kalbfleisch, Commentaria in Aristotelem Graecia v. VIII (Berlin, 1907).
—— *In libros De anima commentaria*, ed. M. Hayduck, Commentaria in Aristotelem Graeca v. XI (Berlin ,1882).
SOPHONIAS, *In libros De anima paraphrasis*, ed. M. Hayduck, Commentaria in Aristotelem Graeca v. XXVIII/1 (Berlin, 1883).
SPEUSIPPUS: P. Lang, *De Speusippi Academici scriptis* (Bonn, 1911).
—— *Letter to Philip*: E. Bickermann & J. Sykutris, *Brief an Koenig Philipp*, Berichte ueber die Verhandlungen der Saechsischen Akademie der Wissenschaften, Philos.-hist. Klasse 80 (1928).
STOBAEUS, IOANNES: *Anthologium*, ed. C. Wachsmuth et O. Hense, 6 vv. (Berlin, 1884–1923).
Stoicorum Veterum Fragmenta, 4 vv., v. 1–3 ed. H. v. Arnim (Leipzig, 1903–1905), v. 4 (Index) ed. M. Adler (Leipzig, 1924).
SYRIANUS, *In Metaphysica*, ed. W. Kroll, Commentaria in Aristotelem Graeca v. VI/1 (Berlin, 1902).
THEOPHRASTUS, *Metaphysics*, ed. W. D. Ross and F. H. Fobes (Oxford 1929).
—— *De causis plantarum* in: *Opera*, ed. F. Wimmer, 3 vv. (Leipzig, 1854–1862).